Heretical Hellenism

HERETICAL HELLENISM

Women Writers, Ancient Greece, and the Victorian Popular Imagination

Shanyn Fiske

Ohio University Press
Athens

Ohio University Press, Athens, Ohio 45701
www.ohioswallow.com

Printed in the United States of America
Ohio University Press books are printed on acid-free paper ∞ ™

15 14 13 12 11 10 09 08   5 4 3 2 1

Library of Congress Cataloging-in-Publication Data

Fiske, Shanyn, 1974–
Heretical Hellenism : women writers, ancient Greece, and the Victorian popular imagination / Shanyn Fiske.
p. cm.
Includes bibliographical references and index.
ISBN 978-0-8214-1817-8 (cloth : alk. paper)
1. English literature—Greek influences. 2. English literature—19th century—History and criticism. 3. English literature—Women authors—History and criticism. 4. Popular literature—Great Britain—History and criticism. 5. Great Britain—Civilization—Greek influences. 6. Greek literature—Appreciation—Great Britain. 7. Greece—In literature. 8. Hellenism in literature. 9. Classicism—Great Britain—History—19th century. I. Title.
PR127.F57 2008
820.9'9287—dc22

2008017867

To my grandfathers,

DuJian Weng (1906–1986)

and Ernest Francis Fiske (1917–2008)

Contents

Acknowledgments

This book owes much to the advice and assistance of many people. Thanks first to Erin O'Connor and Jean-Michel Rabaté, who helped guide this project from its conception. My heartfelt thanks goes also to Mary Beard, who took time out of her sabbatical to help me during my research at Cambridge University and encouraged me always to probe every side of the story. I am grateful to Simon Goldhill, whose lectures on the *Odyssey* and on Greek tragedy inspired many an afternoon of writing. Thanks to Anne Thomson, archivist at Newnham College, who for months carted out boxloads of Jane Harrison papers for me. My gratitude also goes to my friend and colleague Ana Laguna, who read every draft of every chapter and always offered thoughtful advice. Thanks, finally, to my readers at Ohio University Press for helping me write a better book and to David Sanders, who has guided me through the publishing of this work.

My thanks to the Rutgers University Research Council for helping to fund research for my first chapter. Thanks also to Sue Lonoff for kindly allowing me to use her translations of Charlotte Brontë's French essays.

A small section of chapter 2, entitled "Between Nowhere and Home: The Odyssey of Lucy Snowe," was first published in *Brontë Studies* 32 (March 2007): 11–20. A version of chapter 4 was published by Indiana University Press in the *Journal of Modern Literature* 28 (Winter 2005): 130–64.

Introduction

Hellenism and Heresy

On December 7, 1909, twelve university students convened the inaugural meeting of the Cambridge Society of Heretics.[1] The immediate cause of the society's formation was a paper entitled "Prove All Things," penned by the master of Emmanuel College, Dr. W. Chawner. Read before the first meeting of the Religious Discussion Society, the paper rejected traditional Christianity and forwarded agnostic theories that prompted dons to rebuke the author for irresponsibly endangering young men's religious foundations while inspiring students to question long-held university rules such as mandatory chapel attendance. For the founding Heretics, Chawner's paper indexed a growing frustration among scholars and students with the mandates and limitations posed by Cambridge's centuries-long tie to the Anglican church, whose structures and principles had presided over all intellectual gatherings in the past.[2] Creating a forum for the inquiry of spiritual, aesthetic, and philosophical issues and rejecting in its bylaws "all appeal to Authority in the discussion of religious questions,"[3] the Heretics established a firm challenge to the theological boundaries limiting intellectual progress, particularly in areas where scientific research was beginning to question Christian historiography and pose a threat to humanistic curricular tradition. As a protest against institutional policies, the Heretics' formation was not an isolated event but rather a reverberation of radical changes to scholarly tradition in preceding decades. Such changes included the opening of the first women's colleges at Cambridge in 1869 (Girton) and 1871 (Newnham);[4] the 1871 University Tests Act, allowing nonconformists to accept fellowships at Cambridge as well as Oxford; and the integration of archaeology into the Classical Tripos exams in the 1880s,[5] which registered the legitimation of scientific study within what had previously been an exclusively literary and linguistic field. These changes within the university reflected still larger movements in Victorian society as a whole toward greater diversity in categories of knowledge on the one hand (represented by developments such as the Darwinian revolution, the growth of anthropology as a scientific field, and the celebration of technological progress, spectacularly exemplified in the 1851 Crystal Palace exhibitions) and a more inclusive population of knowers on the other (prompted by improvements in education for women and working-class children, rapid increases in literacy rates, and a subsequent burgeoning of newspapers, periodicals, and other popular reading material).

Charged with revolutionary fervor, the Heretics sought to reflect these larger social movements both through their unconventional treatment of subject matter and in the openness of their membership. In contrast to the exclusivity of previous scholarly societies such as the Cambridge Apostles, there was no limitation to membership numbers in the Heretics Society, and for the first time in Cambridge history, women were encouraged to join a university-wide association of intellectual debate. To emphasize the unorthodox nature of their subject matter and participants, the members invited Jane Ellen Harrison to be one of their two keynote speakers.[6] The first woman ever to give university lectures at Cambridge (in 1898), Harrison had become, by 1909, one of the most controversial figures on campus. Her first major work as a university scholar, *Prolegomena to the Study of Greek Religion* (1903), had openly challenged the text-based approach to the ancient world that dominated classical studies throughout the preceding century. The challenge was particularly sacrilegious at Cambridge, which had historically distinguished itself from its rival Oxford by its more rigorous focus on the technical details of translation.[7] Since the *Prolegomena*'s publication and integration into the Cambridge classics curriculum, Harrison had not only continued her efforts to extend Greek studies beyond the textual world but had unrelentingly attacked works by some of the most well-respected scholars in her developing subfield of ancient Greek religion. Such unabashed contrariness, combined with her dogged advocacy of unconventional theories, made Harrison a pariah in some scholarly circles and an idol in others.

At the time of the first Heretic gathering, Harrison was preparing a new edition of the *Prolegomena* and just beginning to conceive what would become her most inflammatory work of all: *Themis,* not to be published until 1912. She was reaching the height of her insurgency, and her inaugural address, later published as a pamphlet entitled "Heresy and Humanity," did not disappoint her expectant audience. "The word 'heretic' has still about it an emotional thrill—a glow reflected, it may be, from the fires at Smithfield, the ardours of those who were burnt at the stake for love of an idea," she began, expounding on the word with which she had christened the society:

> Heresy, the Greek *hairesis,* was from the outset an eager, living word. The taking of a city, its *expugnatio,* is a *hairesis;* the choosing of a lot in life or an opinion, its *electio,* is a *hairesis;* always in the word *hairesis* there is this reaching out to grasp, this studious, zealous pursuit—always something personal, even passionate. . . . *[H]airesis,* what you choose for yourself, is opposed to *tyche*—the chance from without that befalls you by no will of your own. Only in an enemy's mouth did heresy become a negative thing. . . . The gist of heresy is free personal choice in act, and specially [*sic*] in thought—the rejection of traditional faiths and customs, *qua* traditional.[8]

Harrison's opening statement sought not only to ennoble the insurrectionary foundations of the society but also to further her ongoing campaign against the intellectual stagnation that she feared was settling on the university in general and in particular on the field of study to which she had devoted her life. One of the chief weapons in her private arsenal was the defamiliarization of ancient Greek, a study that had become a lightning rod for debate between tradition and progress in the Cambridge community by the end of the nineteenth century.[9] Her address to the Heretics offers a glimpse of her subversive technique. In a parody of linguistic analysis that had become her rhetorical trademark, she proceeded through a series of tenuous associations, generalizations, and emotional introjections to extend a single Greek word into a personal narrative and a spiritual mission. In her hands, *hairesis* became a manifestation of her ideological ardor even as her speech enacted the rebellion and release prompted by her formulation of the term *heretic* into a banner of free choice in thought, belief, and action. For Harrison, for the Heretics, and for a newly legitimized generation of scholars, *hairesis* celebrated the passionate pursuit of knowledge against a bulwark of tradition that insisted on its limitations. In the re-creation of a word, an old empire of thought begins to crumble and a new one emerges into being.

Heretical Hellenism shares the renascent energy that underlay the founding of the Heretics Society and the work of Jane Harrison, which I discuss in detail in chapter 4. It seeks to dismantle the prevalent notion that knowledge of and appreciation for Greek literature, history, and philosophy were restricted in the nineteenth century to upper-class men who were formally schooled in Greek and Latin, believed they were rightful inheritors of an ancient legacy, and regarded their classical knowledge as a basis of cultural authority. I suggest, on the contrary, that Greek literature and mythology were deeply entrenched in Victorian popular culture and played a significant—if frequently overlooked—role in shaping the lives and minds of a population that had little or no formal classical training but held diverse views of ancient Greece that had evolved from a sense of exclusion from traditional classical scholarship and had been shaped in opposition to mainstream perspectives on the ancient world. It would be disingenuous to imply, of course, that the most prominent nineteenth-century hellenophiles shared a monolithic view of ancient Greece or that orthodox Victorian Hellenism constituted a unified, dominant discourse. Rather, I suggest that the authors and works discussed here posited their interpretations and interactions with Greek material against what each perceived to be a limiting, hegemonic ideology. Orthodoxy, in other words, can be defined by the voices and ideas that it appears to exclude and subsequently can take on as many nuances as its heretical detractors. My larger intent, then, is not only to draw attention to neglected aspects of Victorian Hellenism but to extend the implications of its more familiar constructs.

Toward these ends, *Heretical Hellenism* focuses on the half century before the establishment of the Heretics Society and explores two interrelated aspects of nineteenth-century England's relationship to the ancient Greek world that have attracted limited critical attention: the circulation of Greek literature and history in popular culture and women's involvement in the expansion of Hellenism beyond the boundaries of traditional humanist study. These two discursive trajectories intersect at the juncture of popular culture's indispensable contribution to women's classical education. Barred from the formal schooling in Greek and Latin that was given by rote to middle- and upper-class boys, girls in the nineteenth century had to satisfy their desire for classical knowledge through self-education—an endeavor that, for many, bore the urgency and excitement of sexual awakening. The late-Victorian poet and social critic August Webster wrote of female autodidacts:

> [T]here have always been [women] . . . who have felt the restlessness of intellectual faculties unnaturally cramped, the weariness of unsatisfied hunger of mind, and who in their drawing-room life have envied their schoolboy brothers their teachers and tasks, their books and their hours set aside for using them, as a crippled invalid on a sofa may envy the healthy their fatigues. . . . The highest education offered women was no measure of the highest education they contrived to get, for women of the sort spoken of took a higher than was offered them—some of them, in fact, *stole* [*sic*] it, working surreptitiously over their brothers' discarded schoolbooks and hiding away treatises on metaphysics and astronomy as novelists make naughty heroines hide away French novels.[10]

The erotic appeal of forbidden knowledge suggested by Webster's comment clung heavily to the classics, which was seen as an exclusively male prerogative. While for boys, classical knowledge was a mandatory part of the curriculum, the attainment of the same knowledge for girls was heretical in the ways defined by Jane Harrison's speech, involving zealous, self-motivated, and independent pursuits of learning that transgressed into male territory. Victorian novels and biographies abound with stories of girls whose fascination with the classics evolves from envy of their male counterparts and of sisters who learn ancient languages on their own to help their brothers with their studies. But not every woman had access to—or interest in—a brother's schooling, as did the young Elizabeth Barrett and Augusta Webster, or a husband's manuscripts, as did Dorothea Brooke Casaubon, or even a classics primer, as did Florence Dombey and Maggie Tulliver. Quite often, as in the case of Charlotte Brontë, women's exposure to the classics came from articles, translations, and reviews in popular journals and periodicals; their quest for elusive classical knowledge led them to popular reference works such as Lemprière's *Classical Dictionary* (1788) and widely available translations by Dryden, Pope, Chapman, and later authors. Such texts, while still marking the classics as a distinctly masculine body of knowledge, nevertheless made ancient myth and history accessible to a more diverse audience. In a bibliographical survey of English translations of Greek works, Finley Foster notes that "[t]he nineteenth century, quantitatively at least, is the most important period in the history of Greek translation. . . . More than half of the total number of translations [from Greek texts] printed between 1484 and 1916 were published during these years."[11] Foster goes on to point out that introductions to classical works proliferated in the mid-nineteenth century with collections such as A. J. Valpy's Family Classical Library (1830–34), which placed an emphasis on Greek rather than Latin literature, and Bohn's Classical Library (1848–1912), which offered a more extensive selection than Valpy's and featured a large number of new translations.[12] Of the former, the *Gentleman's Magazine* commented, "Mr. Valpy has projected a *Family Classical Library*. The idea is excellent, and the work cannot fail to be acceptable to youth of both sexes, as well as to a large portion of the reading community, who have not had the benefit of a learned education."[13] The *Weekly Free Press* also remarked on the Family Classical Library's extension of classical knowledge to women: "We see no reason why this work should not find its way into the boudoir of the lady, as well as into the library of the learned. It is cheap, portable, and altogether a work which may safely be placed in the hands of persons of both sexes."[14] Together with these concerted efforts to extend classical education to the lay reader, the proliferation of periodicals throughout the nineteenth century, the rise in literacy rates, and the increased leisure time of the middle classes made the popular press a major source for the distribution of knowledge about the ancient world.

Periodical articles held a particular appeal for women and other lay readers because, unlike textbooks and classics primers, these articles were often immediately relevant to current events, many of which centered on Greece as a site of both past cultural achievement and present political concern. England's purchase of the Elgin Marbles in 1817, the Greek revolution of 1821, and new hypotheses concerning the historical reliability of Homer's epics inspired numerous articles about Greek literature, culture, and history, all of which were written to appeal to the interests of the common reader. For instance, a series of articles in 1834 defending the unity of the *Odyssey* in *Blackwood's Edinburgh Magazine* strives to make Odysseus's longing for Ithaca comparable to the Victorians' respect for sanctities of hearth and home.[15] Even articles that engage in erudite argumentation (for or against the authenticity of the Homeric works, for instance) include translated citations of Greek works and analogies to which any reader—but particularly a female reader—might relate. An 1869 article in the *Contemporary Review* entitled "The Antiquity of the Homeric Poems" denounces the idea that "the unity of a character in an Odysseus or an Achilles was something like that in a child's doll, where one artist fashions the waxen bust, another the sawdust carcass, a third the flaxen wig, and so on."[16] While the doll analogy reinforces this writer's point that the art of epic construction is neither juvenile nor mechanical, it nevertheless extends itself to common understanding. If, as George Eliot suggested in *Middlemarch*, the study of ancient mythologies can be a deeply isolating task that removes withered scholars from the nourishing vibrancy of living history, the periodical press and other facets of popular culture ensured that representations of the ancient world remained relevant to modern concerns and accessible to the popular imagination.

The piecemeal knowledge that women received from periodicals and other popular sources certainly left large gaps of knowledge that in turn fostered intellectual insecurities. Lucy Snowe in Charlotte Brontë's novel *Villette* (1853) famously describes the laborious process by which she pieces together the scraps of her classical knowledge to complete an assigned essay for her teacher: "[T]he knowledge was not there in my head, ready and mellow; it had not been sown in Spring, grown in Summer, harvested in Autumn, and garnered through Winter."[17] Lucy's self-consciousness about her lack of formal classical training gestures obliquely at the organic nature of men's classical knowledge—which was made integral to the development of the male mind through systematic education. Women's sense of their exclusion was particularly keen when it came to Greek knowledge, owing to the difference in the alphabet and the greater unavailability of the language in common discourse. Even Elizabeth Barrett, who knew enough Greek to translate famously difficult Aeschylean tragedy and to correspond with Robert Browning in ancient Greek, expressed insecurities about her mastery of the language. Undoubtedly reflecting the poet's sense of inadequacy and amateurism, Romney Leigh in *Aurora Leigh* sneeringly dismisses the eponymous heroine's attempts at the ancient language as "lady's Greek without the accents."[18] The insecurities of these female autodidacts were echoed in the sentiments of those women lucky enough to attend university, many of whom were learning Latin and Greek for the first time. Margaret Merrifield, one of the first Newnham students and a close friend of Jane Harrison, wrote to her father in 1876 about a friend who "gets very 'depressed' over her work [in Latin and Greek] and comes to me to be consoled. [Her] coach [said] that she was 'very sharp but hopelessly inaccurate.' She was in a most melancholy state at the news, especially as she knows it is true. She gets at the general sense of a passage at once, and goes on with a sublime disregard for gender, number and case."[19] Newly accepted within the perimeter of an academic world where technical accuracy in translation was a measure of intellectual worth, the first women classicists were often subjected to the undisguised contempt of male tutors who thought little of their innate linguistic capacities and forced them to question their fitness for higher education.

But the patchwork classical education that women acquired outside of institutions and their tendency to bypass grammatical technicalities for "the general sense" also engendered a way of knowing that differed productively from the classical inheritance of men, which was based on rigid grammatical training and extensive memorization, all aimed at preparing middle- and upper-class boys for enfranchisement into exclusive social and political discourses. Commenting on the result of a mandatory Greek education for Victorian men, Frank Turner writes that "discussions of Greek history, religion, literature, and philosophy provided ready vehicles for addressing the governing classes of the country. . . . Discussions of Greek antiquity provided a forum wherein Victorian writers could and did debate all manner of contemporary questions of taste, morality, politics, religion, and philosophy."[20] The situation that Turner describes for the Greek foundations of Victorian culture applied exclusively to men, for whom classical training was a basis for political and social leadership. Indeed, as Turner notes, examinations for the Home Civil Service, the Indian Civil Service, and the Royal Military Academy all included sections of Greek translation. For women, Greek knowledge held far-less-ambitious goals, if no less influence. Isobel Hurst states that women "had one advantage over [men] who found the excessive repetition and grammatical analysis in the classroom dull and sickening: they did not experience alienation from classical literature . . . but could 'feel,' 'relish,' and 'love' poetry" (12). My findings suggest that women did feel deeply alienated from classical literature because of their lack of formal training, but this sense of alienation is precisely what made the classics—Greek in particular—so alluring and such a powerful means of self-expression. For women whose talents, aspirations, and characters led them to question social convention, ancient Greek and the distinctly alien world and foreign literature it offered provided a means of telling very different stories about themselves than the narratives prescribed by their own society.

These stories allowed for the exercise of "passion, intellect, [and] moral activity" that Florence Nightingale, home-schooled in Greek, famously declared were suppressed in a society that disapproved of women's autonomy and serious intellectual pursuit.[21] The tantalizingly subversive potential of Greek knowledge is amply demonstrated by the three focal figures of this book. Jane Harrison's love of Greek arose from an early attraction to its forbidden allure, and she later used her renegade approach to the ancient world as an instrument for defining her powerfully liminal status in academia. The young Charlotte Brontë arranged her scattered knowledge of Greek myth into a literary mosaic that challenged the imposing mandate of a respected classics professor and established the foundations of her literary aspirations. Greek history and mythology offered George Eliot a way of thinking through and justifying women's intellectual legacy during a crucial moment in her ascent to the position of Victorian sage. For each of these women, the value of Greek stemmed from a highly individual passion—a heretical desire to push the boundaries of knowledge beyond what each perceived to be an alienating and exclusive classical authority. The pursuit of these personal passions resulted in texts and ideas that evolved alternative approaches to the ancient world and developed applications of ancient literature and ideas to Victorian culture that subverted the traditional status of the classics as an elite, exclusively masculine field of knowledge.

While women experienced a deeply conflicted yet productive relationship with both Latin and Greek through the nineteenth century, the latter generated the most frustration and held the greatest allure, thanks largely to its dominance in Victorian culture. As David Ferris and others have recognized, Greek literature and art began to exert a strong influence on British thought in the latter part of the eighteenth century, owing particularly to the influence of German writers and thinkers such as Johann Winckelmann, whose *History of Ancient Art* (1764) and *Reflections on the Imitation of Greek Works in Painting and Sculpture* (1755) helped to establish Greece, in Ferris's words, "as a reference point for all subsequent art and literature" and "generated a view of antiquity as the model of a general cultural context in which the aesthetic served as a mode of historical knowledge."[22] Frank Turner juxtaposes the influence of Greek antiquity and the dominance of Roman literature and ideas in the first half of the eighteenth century: "Greek antiquity began to absorb the interest of Europeans in the second half of the eighteenth century when the values, ideas, and institutions inherited from the Roman and Christian past became problematical. . . . [T]he turn to Greece on the part of scholars, critics, and literary figures constituted an attempt to discern prescriptive signposts for the present age in the European past that predated Rome and [Catholic] Christianity" (2). Christopher Stray adds to this analysis of England's turn from Latinity to Hellenism the argument that the latter reflected a new spirit of individualism, social instability, and return to nature that dominated the Romantic ideal. "If Rome claimed respect because of its universality," Stray writes, "in an age of romantic particularism Greece asserted a superior status because it symbolized the power of the individual as a unique source of original value" (*Classics Transformed,* 15). The hellenophilia adopted by art critics and poets of the late eighteenth and early nineteenth centuries continued to develop in the Victorian age, acquiring more practical applications for England's educational, social, and political structures. Greek learning became a main point of both emphasis and contention in the country's evolving education system; revisionary histories of ancient Greece posited contending views of antiquity's relation to modernity, and these in turn yielded debates about the significance of Athenian democracy to Victorian political ideals.[23]

Although Victorian Hellenism as defined by its more prominent representatives does not constitute a monolithic body, previous studies have established the predominance of humanism within it as a foundation and guiding philosophy. As Turner points out, "the critical moral tradition of humanism provided the primary channel through which the civilization of ancient Greece became transformed into a useful past for a large portion of the educated British public" in the nineteenth century (*Greek,* 15). To enable a better understanding of the nature and scope of Victorian humanistic Hellenism—as well as the limitations of this tradition—a brief review of the roots of the term will be useful. Humanism, as Paul Oskar Kristeller points out, has a complex history involving various transmogrifications through the ages. The term *humanista* referred, in the fifteenth and sixteenth centuries, to a literary scholar trained in grammar, rhetoric, history, poetry, and moral philosophy and conversant with the classical origins of these disciplines. In 1808, F. J. Niethammer coined the term *Humanismus* to emphasize the importance of Greek and Latin in the secondary education curriculum, in opposition to the encroachment of scientific knowledge.[24] The application of humanism to Victorian Hellenism stems from an integration of these Renaissance and Romantic roots to describe, in Turner's words, an "ethical enterprise" involving "the moral or normative use of the past as a guide to the human condition in the present" (*Greek,* 15). This concept of the relationship between the Hellenic past and Victorian present is most famously expressed by John Henry Newman's idea of a liberal education. For Newman, Greek learning was fundamental to the conservative educational model that he sought to preserve against the increasingly utilitarian concerns of an expanding empire. In his *Idea of a University,* a collection of lectures delivered in 1852 at the Catholic University of Dublin, Newman expressed his nostalgia for the "time that Athens was the University of the world," and at the beginning of his discourse "Knowledge Viewed in Relation to Learning," he lamented, "It were well if the English, like the Greek language, possessed some definite word to express, simply and generally, intellectual proficiency or perfection, such as 'health,' as used with reference to the animal frame, and 'virtue' with reference to our moral nature. I am not able to find such a term. . . . The consequence is that, on an occasion like this, many words are necessary, in order, first, to bring out and convey what surely is no difficult idea in itself,—that of the cultivation of the intellect as an end."[25] Newman thus envisioned ancient Greece as presenting the spiritual intensity, moral purity, and intellectual focus that the Oxford Movement attempted to recapture for the modern world. His educational agenda took for granted the availability of ancient Greece as a reduplicable ideal of perfect culture. Not only did Greek serve as an instrument for disciplining the mind to intellectual proficiency, but ancient Athens stood for a time before science (defined by Newman as a category of knowledge rather than a specific discipline) was retrenched from its reference to mental perfectibility to a focus on external phenomena. This shift of focus was accompanied by a corresponding superfluity of language that evaded the concept of knowledge for its own end. By expressing his vision of the modern university in terms of an Athenian ideal, Newman attempted to claim the school of Hellas as a lost British legacy. If the superior Greek linguistic system represented a larger cultural heritage, then the study of Greek language, with its streamlined precision of thought and expression, ought to have broader cultural repercussions in restoring the value of purely intellectual ideas to a modern world overly concerned with external subject matter.

The assignment of cultural value to liberal knowledge that has no practical application or significance tended to elevate Greek above Latin, which still functioned as a living language in the church and in law. In 1877, W. Y. Sellar observed that "[f]amiliarity with Latin literature is probably not less common relatively to familiarity with the older [Greek] literature. The attraction of the latter has been greater from its novelty, its originality, its higher intrinsic excellence, its profounder relation to the heart and mind of man."[26] The claim for Greek's interiority gestures at the important fact that while Latin was the language of the Catholic mass, Greek was the language of the New Testament. This distinction was not to be missed by a Protestant nation recently recovering from the turmoil of the 1850 Papal Aggression and the midcentury Oxford Movement.[27] In 1855, Henry Alford, dean of Canterbury, wrote, "No other language will ever express the meaning of God's Spirit as it may be seen to be expressed and known by those who read the New Testament in the original Greek. . . . Is it worthy of our Protestant position . . . that while we cry 'Give the Bible to all,' we should suffer it, in its depth and glory and beauty, to remain a dead letter to ourselves?"[28] Richard Jenkyns notes that there was necessarily a tension between Victorians' Christianity and their hellenophilia, but he also acknowledges that writers' attempts to use the former to justify the latter contributed to Greece's centrality in Victorian thought. It is perhaps ironic, given the importance of Greece in Newman's educational and cultural agendas, that his conversion to Catholicism should coincide with the valorization of Greek as a reaffirmation of Protestant national identity. Nevertheless, the irony reminds us that Newman's conversion was in the first place prompted by what David Delaura has called Newman's attempt to install "an ideal of totality, comprehensiveness, inclusiveness, at a time when the image of the distinctively human was being either fragmented or radically reduced."[29] The centrality of Greek both in what Delaura calls Newman's "theological humanism" and in the Protestant backlash against Catholic influences emphasizes the malleability of Greece's symbolic signification and thus its adaptability to various educational and moral agendas. In the area of religion, the more that Greek—as a language, as a body of literature, and as a symbolic structure—was removed from the daily concerns of modern life, the stronger became its claim to an individual's private spiritual intercourse. Indeed, the same fluidity of meaning that made Greek a ready vehicle for Newman's educational program and for Protestant nationalism also suited it for the diverse personal and social aspirations of the woman writers examined in this book.

The malleability of Greek as a symbolic structure is perhaps even more forcefully demonstrated in the writings of Newman's disciple Matthew Arnold, whose definition of Hellenism creates a transhistorical phenomenon that both evokes and attempts to resolve the implicit tension between

Christian and ancient Greek historiographies. Arguing against the paralyzing effects of an overly stringent Protestant conscience on intellectual development and culture, Arnold stated in his preface to *Culture and Anarchy* (1869), "Now, and for us, it is a time to Hellenise, and to praise knowing; for we have Hebraised too much, and have over-valued doing."[30] *Culture and Anarchy* neatly reconciles the religious tensions posed by hellenophilia by seeing Hellenism as representative of an interior, intellectual development forming a necessary dialectical relation to Christian morality. Suffering from an overemphasis on Puritanical moral stringency, the country needed, in Arnold's estimation, a Hellenic ideological expansion that could only be realized through the formation of an elite establishment that would determine standards of behavior and guide the judgments of the nation at a moment when the human mind was becoming overwhelmed with an accumulating mass of facts: "[T]he literature of ancient Greece is, even for modern times, a mighty agent of intellectual deliverance; even for modern times, therefore, an object of indestructible interest," Arnold wrote in "On the Modern Element in Literature."[31] Arnold's consideration of Hellenism as a salvational force emphasizes the importance of the ancient Greek world not only to the general notion of culture but also as the basis for a set of spiritual assumptions rhetorically manipulated into a valorization of liberal education. In an 1882 response to T. H. Huxley's defense of the cultural value of a purely scientific education, Arnold asserted, "The instinct for beauty is set in human nature, as surely as the instinct for conduct. If the instinct for beauty is served by Greek literature and art as it is served by no other literature and art, we may trust to the instinct of self-preservation in humanity for keeping Greek as part of our culture. We may trust to it for even making the study of Greek more prevalent than it is now."[32] Arnold's words here not only offer a defense of Greek studies but also forward a claim for the intrinsicality of Greek culture to human existence, transforming the fragmentary reality of an antique civilization into a holistic ideal for the preservation of modern culture. The conditional "if" that aligns Greek literature and art with the "instinct for beauty" initiates an ideological substitution that the latter half of the statement takes as justification for a spiritually based political agenda. The tangible referent of "Greek literature and art" is made to stand for an intangible impulse not merely within the logic of the sentence but as a practical educational policy. The question of culture, Arnold asserted, must be referred to the life impulse itself, and since the Greek world is the physical embodiment of this impulse, its study in schools is a component of human vitality in general. The cultivation of a dead language is, in Arnold's theory, the restoration of an endangered aspect of the national and individual identity.

Newman's and Arnold's optimistic hopes for cultural regeneration through Greek revival were counterbalanced by darker visions in the latter part of the century as the Aesthetic movement grounded idealistic visions of Classical Greece in archaic sensuality and the Decadents sought in the Greeks a means both for celebrating the irrevocable fallenness of their own world and for challenging mid-Victorian religious and moral sensibilities. Walter Pater's essay on Johann Joachim Winckelmann, published first in the *Westminster Review* in 1867 and later collected in *The Renaissance* (1873), marked an important shift in the direction of Victorian humanistic Hellenism. Pater regarded Newman's formulation of Greece as "only a partial one. In it the eye is fixed on the sharp, bright edge of high Hellenic culture, but loses sight of the sombre world across which it strikes."[33] The Greek art that Pater viewed as an ideal model for his own time emerged, he argued, from a pagan sentiment that was "beset by notions of irresistible natural powers, for the most part ranged against man" (*Renaissance,* 160). While Arnold saw Classical Greece as the embodiment of "sweetness and light" and a cultural model, Pater, in David Delaura's words, provided a "rich prehistory" (209) for Arnold's serene Hellenic world by celebrating an archaic union of sensual and mental apprehension: "[The Greek] mind has not learned to boast its independence of the flesh," Pater wrote, "the spirit has not yet absorbed everything with its emotions, nor reflected its own colour everywhere" (*Renaissance,* 164). Although Greece remained a cultural ideal for Pater, his attitude was a product of late-Victorian disillusionment and as such was unencumbered by Arnold's struggles both to reconcile paganism with Christianity and to posit a larger vision of cultural renewal. Rather, Pater appreciated the pagan sensuality of the Greeks as a reduplicable experience for "a small band of elite 'Oxonian' souls" seeking "detachment from the vulgar actualities of Victorian life" (Delaura, 230). Although the move from Arnold's Hellenism to Pater's may seem to describe a withdrawal from culture at large, one must remember that Arnold's injunction to "Hellenise" was targeted at an exclusive, highly educated audience—in his view, the only site of real culture—and that their humanism had evolved, as Delaura has argued, from the "shared sense that the highest organization of the human powers was 'aristocratic,' a privileged mode of perception endangered in a rapidly democratizing society" (xi).

The vision of Greece as a response to Victorian vulgarity also directs, though toward a different end, the Hellenism of the Decadents, of whom Algernon Charles Swinburne has often been taken as representative. A self-described disciple of Aeschylus whose work abounds with Greek allusions, translations, and adaptations, Swinburne transformed Hellenism from a vehicle to a grave-marker of the mid-Victorian quest for a coherent set of cultural values. Rather than looking to Greece as a way of mending or escaping the ills of his time, Swinburne sought in Greek myth and poetry an affirmation for his contradictory and tumultuous age. His work draws on Greek sources to challenge Christian moral assumptions and to expose as well as celebrate the sensuous, violent, and alternately destructive and creative energies of nature and human nature.

> For the gods very subtly fashion
>   Madness with sadness upon earth:
> Not knowing in any wise compassion,
>   Nor holding pity of any worth[.]

Thus sings the Chorus in Swinburne's "Atalanta in Calydon" (1865).[34] Here and in his later Hellenic drama, "Erechtheus" (1876), Greek tragedy not only provides a structural model and narrative history for Swinburne but also, as Margot Louis and others have discussed, furnishes an ideology that comprehends both human suffering under the incomprehensible forces operating within and without the psyche and the spiritual strength that one must develop to endure such suffering. Although Swinburne's works raised debate in his own time and in ours about the accuracy of his Greek conceptions, such debate is less conclusive about the poet's authenticity than it is revealing of the malleability of Greece as a symbolic structure for later ages. The transcendent value that Newman and Arnold located in the rationality and clarity of Greek language and culture and Pater discovered in the unity of archaic sensibilities, Swinburne found in the Greek tragic outlook, which could provide for his own age a source of consolation if not of redemption.

Despite the discrepancies in their views of the Greeks, the Hellenisms of Newman, Arnold, Pater, and Swinburne—public school and Oxford men all—situate the Greeks firmly in elite, male domains of university, politics, and other venues of cultural authority. Arnold's references to Eton and "men of genius," as well as his numerous addresses to male contemporaries, clearly imply that if Greek art and literature are equated with the human (and humanistic) instinct for intellectual development and social improvement, these instincts are gendered; women are distinctly excluded from negotiations of Hellenism's place in Victorian culture. Pater likewise relegated access to the Greek world to an elite male population able to apprehend "the subtlest principles of the Hellenic manner" (*Renaissance,* 154). Indeed, perhaps even more firmly than Arnold, Pater drew distinct boundaries around Greek knowledge as a privileged, masculine body. As Linda Dowling notes, "Pater would throughout a long lifetime of writing demonstrate by his very neutrality and urbanity that he was writing from within the great tradition of humanist thought. Yet his writing would always consist of a daring texture of covert allusions working continuously and unmistakably to demonstrate that the reiterated liberal claims for liberty, individuality, self-development, and diversity as the qualities capable of rescuing England are unintelligible unless viewed within the context of a Socratic eros of men loving men in spiritual procreancy."[35] For Pater, as Dowling persuasively argues, Hellenism became a defining element of male intellectual culture and social regeneration that implicitly but absolutely excluded women and the female mind. Even Swinburne, whose work challenges so many Victorian orthodoxies, whose poetry often celebrates the female creative force and ventriloquizes Sappho, crafted his allusions to and adaptations of Greek sources with the consciousness of exhibiting his scholarly prowess to proclaim himself both an inheritor of the classical tradition and a formidable opponent of other prominent cultural authorities. Although his irreverent attitude toward Victorian values might seem the antithesis of Arnold's, Swinburne—like Arnold, Newman, and Pater—grounded his authority as poet, cultural critic, and self-styled prophet of his age on a privileged knowledge of Greek language and literature that situated him firmly within a male intellectual tradition and, paradoxically, legitimized his transgressive ideas. As David Riede points out, "Swinburne's reliance on a classical tradition that had become an exclusively male inheritance . . . cut his most ambitious verse off from the expression of what might be called a female point of view."[36] The contention between self-legitimation through appeal to tradition and a seditious impulse toward individual expression that Riede identifies in Swinburne witnesses the fact that the classical heritage claimed by male writers also posed fundamental limitations on the ways in which they were able to express their relationship to history and to their own age.

Studies of Victorian Hellenism have by and large followed the dominant, humanistic channels through which Newman, Arnold, Pater, Swinburne, and other influential Victorian men constructed their relationship to the Greeks. Delaura's work as well as those of Richard Jenkyns and Frank Turner in the early 1980s are landmark studies in the field of Victorian Hellenism and focus predominantly on the male, elite associations of ancient Greek studies. Linda Dowling took the field in a different direction with *Hellenism and Homosexuality in Victorian Oxford* (1994) by exploring the counterdiscursive possibilities of Hellenism in the construction of male sexuality, but her work further reinforces the notion of Greek knowledge as a male institutional and social discourse. Within the past twenty years, however, critics such as Yopie Prins and Lorna Hardwick have begun to explore women's involvement in the translation and adaptation of Greek poetry, and their studies have posited a distinct challenge to the gendered and institutionalized concept of Hellenism that dominated earlier works. Their writings reveal that women used Greek knowledge to assert authority in the male-dominated fields of scholarship and publishing, to express subjectivities and sexualities disallowed by conventional Victorian gender ideologies, and to challenge the authoritative structures of knowledge represented by Newman, Arnold, and other prominent male writers. Such studies have shown Greek knowledge to be a multifaceted intellectual arena for the negotiation of women's roles in Victorian society and in literary history and have paved the way for such books as Isobel Hurst's recent *Victorian Women Writers and the Classics* (2006), which offers one of the first full-length studies of the influence of classics on women writers in the nineteenth century. While Hurst's book takes into account the influence of both Latin and Greek on women's writing, her work and other recent studies have shown the idea of "knowing Greek" to be, in Simon Goldhill's words, "a bitterly contested area of social and intellectual activity,"[37] particularly in the fraught arena of Victorian gender politics.

Heretical Hellenism contributes to this widening sphere of understanding about nineteenth-century Greek knowledge by studying the diffusion of Greek myth, literature, and history throughout Victorian popular culture. Previous discussions of women's relations to the ancient Greek world have tended to concentrate on women with reading knowledge of the language and the ability to translate or otherwise work closely with original texts. Such a focus carries the implication, however inadvertent, that women can relate productively to Greek sources only if they achieve the literary-linguistic expertise of their male counterparts and cultivate the stringent technical expertise that, for educators such as Newman, testify to a superior quality of mind. In contrast, I focus on women who either did not know Greek or whose insecurities about their knowledge drove them to find means of interacting with Greek sources beyond close work with original texts. Their lives and works exemplify the intensely mediated nature of most women's interactions with Greek literature, history, and ideas in the nineteenth century and demonstrate the imaginative, counterdiscursive possibilities encouraged by such mediation. For these and other women with limited access to original texts, the translations, commentaries, and adaptations dispersed throughout popular culture offered a rich source of images and ideas from which to construct narratives of the Greek world that differed dramatically from the visions proffered by influential male critics. If, as I discuss above, Greek was an intensely malleable symbolic structure adaptable to the theories and agendas of various writers and scholars, it appeared even more so in the diffuse world of popular culture in which the heated debates, sensational re-creations, passionate commentary, and fragmentary translations of and about Greek sources revealed Greek knowledge to be a vexed discursive arena open to imaginative projection and creative interpretation.

For my exploration of the nature and origins of what I will call "popular Greek," each chapter of *Heretical Hellenism* uses one historical event or individual as a focal point for discussing broader questions about women's relationships to Greek in popular culture: How were the Greeks interpreted, adapted, and altered to appeal to the interests of a general audience? What were the cultural, ideological, and political contexts of these adaptations and alterations? How did women use the knowledge they acquired both as a means of self-reflection and as commentary on the world around them? Because of the often-piecemeal ways through which women acquired their Greek knowledge, generalizations about how women learned Greek risk inaccuracies; if they present histories of women's education, such as Rita McWilliams Tullberg's excellent study *Women at Cambridge* (1998), they often fail to consider the ways in which the vast majority of women acquired their knowledge. My own detailed study of individual writers' experiences of knowing Greek emphasizes the unique significance of Greek literature, mythology, and history for every woman who stitched them into the fabric of her imagination.

In addition, in this volume I explore more broadly the channels through which Greek was available to the lay Victorian readership. Studying venues of popular discourse such as the stage, periodicals, personal essays, and the novel, I argue that Greek studies, like many other regimes of knowledge in the nineteenth century, was not limited to upper-class political, social, and cultural institutions but, to borrow a Foucauldian paradigm, was located in multiple centers of discourse. Those centers with which I am chiefly concerned have not warranted extensive discussion, owing to the incohesion of the Greek knowledge they proffer. References to Greek myth are scattered through popular novels and periodical literature; reproductions of Greek tragedies are absorbed into melodrama and sensationalism. But this dispersal testifies to the endemic nature of Greek knowledge in Victorian culture. These fragments of an ancient corpus invite and evidence the imaginative projections of Victorians in general and women in particular who hungered for alternative narratives and means of self-expression beyond the confines imposed on their minds and lives by strict nineteenth-century gender codes. Yopie Prins cogently articulates this process of fulfillment through reanimation of the ancient past in describing Sappho's work: "Out of scattered texts, an idea of the original woman poet and the body of her song could be hypothesized in retrospect: an imaginary totalization, imagined in the present and projected into the past."[38] For Prins, Sappho's extant work and her ineffable being trigger in her nineteenth-century readers and poetic inheritors a desire for completion that constitutes a process of self-realization. *Heretical Hellenism* argues that ancient Greece in general, as it was presented to the Victorian popular imagination, was a fragmented entity, fabricated from archaeological artifacts, contesting hypotheses and interpretations, and imaginative reconstructions. But its fragmentarity is precisely what constituted Greece's appeal; by filling in the lacunae of their knowledge with their ways of imagining the Greek world, the women in this book used their unconventional knowledge to challenge the foundations of a humanist regime and its assumptions about the uniformity of knowledge.

The circumstances and consequences of Medea's rise to popularity on the mid-Victorian stage exemplify the power of ancient Greek myth and literature both to appeal to the Victorian imagination at large and to destabilize fundamental gender assumptions. As a study of Medea's evolution on and beyond the London stage in the mid to late nineteenth century, chapter 1 argues that the rising culture of sensationalism helped to launch Medea's career and that various adaptations of Euripides' tragedy throughout the 1850s, '60s, and '70s both challenged the Victorian objection to presenting women in a public, criminal context and heightened awareness of the social pressures driving women to commit violent acts. A focus of this chapter is Ernest Legouvé's 1856 adaptation of Euripides' *Medea,* the first serious attempt to re-create the Greek tragedy for a nineteenth-century audience. While riding the tidal wave of sensationalism prompted by such events as the Maria Manning murder trial, Legouvé's play also drew attention to pressing issues of abandonment and infanticide while prompting debates about women's maternal instincts. Scripts, theater reviews, and newspaper articles reveal Medea's role in inspiring and recording a greater sensitivity to the complexity of women's psyches, a resistance to labeling female offenders as aberrant or monstrous, and the public's growing acceptance of a heroine who challenges social mandates. Late-century adaptations of the Medea story by poets Augusta Webster and Amy Levy culminated in Medea's evolution from sensational stage object to a voice for expressing previously censored subjectivities.

Chapter 2 is an examination of how the presentation of Greek epic and tragedy in Victorian periodicals shaped the subjectivity of one particular author: Charlotte Brontë. I begin by examining the popular treatment of two important discussions about ancient Greece in the first half of the nineteenth century—the Homeric Question, surrounding the identity and genius of Homer, and the relation of ancient Greek tragedy to the developing aesthetic of realism. Both of these issues preoccupied Victorian critics and had a profound influence on Brontë's developing concept of her creative genius and of the realist narrative to whose development she would contribute. My discussion focuses on two essays from Brontë's juvenilia: "The Fall of Leaves" and "Athens Saved by Poetry," both of which borrow images, phrases, and ideas directly from articles about Homer and Greek tragedy in Brontë's favorite journals. These essays reveal that Brontë used her piecemeal Greek knowledge to argue for her creative genius, to craft persuasive arguments against the strict Aristotelian principles of her Belgian mentor M. Constantin Heger, and to develop a distinct aesthetic of female interiority. The chapter concludes by examining Brontë's incorporation of Odyssean references in her last novel, *Villette,* which uses a Homeric framework of homesickness to express the author's increasing sense of abandonment and loneliness in the final years of her life. A study of the popular journals read by Brontë emphasizes Victorians' passionate interest in ancient Greece in the first half of the nineteenth century, while Brontë's creative adaptation of popular debates reveals the importance of Greek issues in shaping her imagination and ideological convictions.

Chapter 3 is an assessment of George Eliot's novel *Romola* (1862) as a direct challenge to the humanist legacy that the Victorians inherited from the Renaissance and identified with the reanimation of ancient Greek culture and ideas. I argue that Eliot challenges the formalized and masculine ideas of knowledge resulting from the Renaissance's institutionalization of Greek knowledge, a legacy inherited by her culture. In *Romola*'s incorporation of Greek mythology, Eliot identifies another strand of Greece's legacy consistent with what she called "moral sympathy"—an innate desire for intellectual and emotional connectedness to which women are particularly sensitive because of their traditional exclusion from formal, institutionalized discourse. Studying such influences on Eliot as George Grote's theory of the "mythopoeic imagination" in his *History of Greece* (1846–56), the evolving field of mythography, and England's purchase of the Elgin Marbles, I suggest that Eliot presents in *Romola* not only a justification for women's right to the Greek intellectual legacy but also an argument for the importance of recognizing this legacy to rescue her own age from materialism, personal ambition, and the sequestration of knowledge.

Chapter 4 is a consideration of Jane Harrison and the crucial moments of the late nineteenth and early twentieth centuries when institutionalized knowledge of classics was radically changing under pressure from new fields of study such as archaeology and archaic religion. Harrison argued throughout her career that the only way to save classics from obsolescence was to harness it to the engine of individual passion and creativity. Leaving a lasting impression on both Cambridge classicists and twentieth-century writers, scholars, and artists including Gilbert Murray, Virginia Woolf, and Roger Fry, Harrison's life epitomizes the impact that one individual can have on scholarship through the force of her controversial ideas and powerful imagination. Tracing Harrison's development from a young girl longing to learn Greek to her first years at Newnham College and finally to her position as a prominent lecturer in Greek art and archaic religion, I argue that the unorthodox approach that Harrison took to ancient Greece and her incendiary influence at Cambridge are what preserved her longevity and the vibrancy of the field to which she devoted almost the whole of her adult life.

Heretical Hellenism is not aimed at being a comprehensive history of women's interactions with Greek in the nineteenth century. Rather, through representative case studies, it offers a narrative of how and why Greece held such appeal for Victorian women writers. Contrary to traditional humanist views, it did so not because Greece offered a parallel to the Victorian world but because Greek study provided a means of questioning assumptions about gender, religion, and the boundaries of legitimate knowledge. The women discussed in this volume created a form of Hellenism that contributed to the increasing autonomy and intellectual authority of their sex in the late nineteenth century, but perhaps even more important is that they demonstrate, for our own age, the malleability of the ancient world. This malleability, as Jane Harrison believed, is the key to the survival of the classics into modernity. Indeed, it was precisely because classics in Britain was firmly tied to conservative, primarily androcentric, cultural ideals that the discipline was in danger of becoming obsolete toward the end of the nineteenth century as critics such as T. H. Huxley, who endorsed a more practical, scientific education, openly criticized the elitism fostered by a "liberal education" grounded on the literary-linguistic study of Greek and Latin. Huxley's doubts about educational tradition were confirmed, as I discuss in the afterword, during the course of the First World War, when German tactical victories were credited to their superior technological and scientific training. Although the value of Greek learning suffered a setback in the first part of the twentieth century, Greek did not become entirely obsolete, because it was expanded to accommodate scientific approaches to the ancient world, being opened up to new fields such as archaeology, anthropology, and sociology and extended to a new range of writers and scholars. What is striking about the salvation of Greek and of classics in general at the turn of the twentieth century is that it did not depend on a detachment from personal, revolutionary agendas and on a disinterested concern to get at the truth of an ancient civilization. Rather, the modern discipline of classics was preserved and shaped throughout the nineteenth century and beyond by methodological and ideological conflicts between individuals with intensely personal investments in their limited and often biased perceptions of the ancient world.[39] The rich, passionate heterodoxy of Victorian Hellenism is precisely what I endeavor to reveal in this book. Drawn from sources scattered throughout popular culture, *Heretical Hellenism* emphasizes the unstable, malleable nature of nineteenth-century Greek knowledge and reveals it to be a more diverse phenomenon in Victorian England than has been previously supposed. This same diversity and capacity for reconceptualization is what is preserving classics from what some see as an impending obsolescence.[40] Now, in an age when Greek and Latin texts are increasingly read and taught in translation and students are more often exposed to classical sources through popular culture than through formal schooling, it is my hope that *Heretical Hellenism* can provide a historical rationale for a more expansive definition of classical knowledge and offer an interdisciplinary heuristic for understanding the place of classics both in the nineteenth century and in our own time.

Victorian Medea

From Sensationalism to Subjectivity

CHAPTER ONE

On the night of June 4, 1856, the auditorium of the Lyceum Theater hummed with anticipation of a sensational event: the British debut of Euripides' *Medea,* which had not merited a serious performance on the London stage for almost a century, because the heroine was considered too offensive for British audiences.[1] Marking a turning point in theater history, the present version, adapted by the French playwright Ernest Legouvé, invited particular curiosity. For the production starred the Italian actress Adelaide Ristori, who had broken onto the international scene only the year before in Paris and, almost immediately, had been lauded as a rival to Rachel Felix, the premier tragedienne throughout Europe for the previous decade. The intriguing antagonism between the two actresses was intensified by the fact that the part of Medea had originally been intended for Rachel, who turned it down at the last moment, claiming that she could not win sympathy for a character who murdered both her rival and her own children "in cold blood, treacherously and foully."[2] Having followed exaggerated reports of the actresses' rivalry and of Ristori's success in France, the British audience was, as the *Times* reported, "'gaping' with expectation long before the curtain rose."[3]

Of the Greek tragedies performed on the London stage in the latter half of the nineteenth century, Euripides' *Medea* was one of the most frequently enacted, with ten versions staged between 1845 and 1907.[4] The play's popularity is remarkable considering that Medea radically challenges deeply rooted Victorian values of female fidelity, passivity, and moral exemplarity.

Her myth involves such offenses as the betrayal of her father, King Aeetes; her flight from Colchis with the Argonaut Jason; responsibility for the murders of her brother Apsyrtus and of King Pelias of Iolkos; and the murders of her own children as vengeance against Jason's treacherous marriage to the Corinthian princess, Glauce (sometimes known as Creusa). Euripides' play is particularly subversive in vindicating her for this final crime through the deus ex machina of a golden chariot, which descends to rescue Medea from retribution and transport her to Athens, where she finds asylum with King Aegeus. A foreigner, murderer, and infanticide, passionately speaking out against women's suffering as wives and mothers, Medea demonstrates an intellectual strength and emotional impassivity antithetical to the images of faithful daughter, nurturing mother, and devoted wife that formed the bedrock of Victorian domestic ideology. Why, then, did Medea become so popular in the mid- and late nineteenth centuries? What does her popularity reveal about the relevance and relationship of ancient Greek tragedy to Victorian culture?

One answer is that Medea's rise to popularity on the Victorian stage both responded and contributed to the destabilization of gender assumptions and domestic values. Although sexual double standards were firmly in place throughout the nineteenth century, events such as the 1839 Infant Custody Act and petitions for divorce legislation between 1845 and 1857 increasingly recognized women's rights to autonomy and protested the injustice of their social and political inequality. As Edith Hall has pointed out, the questions of parental responsibility and spousal desertion that are central to Medea's plot found thematic resonance with women's rights issues raised by midcentury changes to Victorian marriage legislation.[5] Expanding on Hall's argument, I suggest that Medea's rise to prominence and her role in the reconfiguration of Victorian gender values were also tied to the play's interaction with a sensationalist culture that began to coalesce in the late 1830s and 1840s, bringing to spectacular prominence the image of the violent, manipulative, and socially deviant woman. While such representations spectacularized female aberrance, they also began to highlight the inadequacy of Victorian gender ideologies such that by the 1880s, the aberrant or criminal woman functioned less as a sensation than as a witness to the social inequities that caused her maladjustment.[6]

Medea's evolution in Victorian popular culture underscores the transformation of the aberrant woman from a sensational object to a dynamic representative of marginalized subjectivities. Medea's unique place in the transformation of attitudes toward female aberrance is witnessed by the fact that the years of her popularity correspond strikingly with widely reported trials of women murderers and with the rise of Victorian sensation novels and plays, most of which feature aberrant or abandoned women.[7] These coincidences suggest that the sensationalization of murderesses helped dismantle the Victorian taboo against presenting women in a highly public, criminal, or compromised position and thus not only guided Medea past moral censorship but also accumulated around her an aura of mystery, fear, pity, and respect that heightened her sensational appeal. But Victorian Medeas also challenged sensationalism's tendency to legitimate male, institutional authority by heightening awareness of the social causes behind women's violent acts and by agitating rather than resolving debates over women's social roles.[8] The gradual alterations in Medea's presentation throughout the century suggest that while making necessary concessions to a public unable to excuse her infanticide on the grounds of vengeance alone, playwrights also transformed the rationale for Medea's actions into an indictment of the sexual binaries that, as Mary Poovey has argued, were a "characteristic feature of the mid-Victorian symbolic economy"[9] but proved increasingly inadequate for explaining women's behavior as the century progressed. With her questionable motives and ambivalent occupation of conventional female roles, Medea bridged a historical and ideological divide between sensationalism's objectification of female aberrance and feminism's indictment of women's social victimization. Coevolving with a sensation press that eventually abandoned the spectacle of aberrant women to allow for multiple and more-complex forms of female subjectivity, Medeas on the London stage ultimately helped to transform prurient curiosity into critical self-consciousness.

The evolving tradition of women's closet drama united with late-century Hellenism in Augusta Webster's dramatic monologue "Medea in Athens" (1870) and Amy Levy's *Medea: A Play in Fragments* (1884). Composed by women with prominent voices in academic as well as popular circles, these two works culminate Medea's transformation from sensational object to a voice for the nascent feminist movement of the century's second half. Rejecting the patinas of spectacle and pity that cling to their earlier Victorian predecessors, the Medeas of Webster and Levy exhibit a self-consciousness and psychological complexity that recover the rich ambiguity of Euripides' tragedy while demonstrating its congruence with the sexual and racial politics of the late nineteenth century. Offering a stark contrast to the staid calmness of fifth-century Greece posited by traditional humanistic Hellenism, the evolution of Medea in

Victorian popular culture reflects a growing discontent with conventional views of female passivity and offers a way to imagine women empowered, rather than undone, by passionate natures capable of subverting restrictive social conventions.

Sensationalism and Legouvé's Medea

To better understand Adelaide Ristori's impact on her British audience in 1856, one should be aware of an event that occurred seven years previously and helped set the stage for Medea's success in London theaters: the widely reported trial of Maria Manning and her husband, Frederick Manning, who were jointly accused of murdering Maria's lover, Patrick O'Connor, and burying his body under their kitchen floor beneath a mantle of quicklime. Newspapers and broadsheets gave particular attention to the Swiss-born Maria, the crime's mastermind, whose volatile personality would make her trial one of the century's most sensational. Maria's last day in court offers a glimpse into her character. She twice interrupted the judge as he was pronouncing her death sentence and accused the jury, in accented English, of treating her "like a wild beast of the forest." She then turned her fury on her husband, whose counsel had attempted to lay blame for the murder on her head alone. "If I had wished to commit murder, how much more likely is it that I should have murdered that man (pointing to her husband), who has made my life a hell upon earth ever since I have known him,"[10] she reportedly cried, protesting her innocence to the last and demanding another hearing before a mixed jury of Englishmen and foreigners. Her final words as she was being led from the courtroom were "Shameful England!" according to the *Illustrated London News* and "Damnation seize you all!" according to the *Times*.[11] Reporting on the Mannings' public execution some three weeks later, the *Times* called Maria a "Lady Macbeth" who "could not have played her part with truer feeling of its character."[12]

Maria Manning's transformation from criminal to tragic heroine in the pages of the daily news exemplifies the media's amalgamation of courtroom and dramatic stage beginning in the early nineteenth century—a potent aggregation of space that precipitated the sensation culture of the 1860s,[13] when a flood of novels and plays would similarly exploit felony for its entertainment and shock value. Although crime had certainly existed in England before the nineteenth century, a series of industrial and legal developments enabled its unprecedented publication during this age, transforming murder into a "spectator sport."[14] The steam-press, invented in 1814 and generally adopted by 1840, allowed a tenfold increase in newspaper production over the handpress. The 1836 reduction of the newspaper tax to one penny, the cutting of paper duties and the invention of the electric telegraph in 1837, the rapid growth of the railway system after 1842, and the 1855 repeal of newspaper stamp duties all facilitated news collection and distribution, even as improving literacy rates and mass migrations into major cities expanded the reading audience.[15] In addition to these developments, the midcentury growth of the sensation press owed to increasing public fascination with women murderers.[16] Judith Knelman observes that "by mid-century the press had become adept at exploiting public interest in the criminal *because* she was a woman" (229). Henry Mayhew's 1850s interview with a street-orator (or patterer) confirms this claim. "'I patters hard on the women . . . as I points them out on my board in murders or any crimes,'" the patterer tells Mayhew. "I says: 'When there's mischief, a woman's always the first.' . . . It answers best, sir, in my opinion, going on that patter. The men likes it, and the women doesn't object, for they'll say: 'Well, when a woman is bad, she *is* bad, and is a disgrace to her sex.'"[17] Anathema on the one hand to a culture that exalted women's nurturing instincts and confinement to the home, the passionate woman capable of murder, manipulation, and violent emotional displays stimulated, on the other hand, a national interest in the destabilization of these same domestic ideals.

Maria Manning offers a case in point. Given the emblematic status of the "Angel of the House" in Victorian England's domestic ideology, the general reaction to her trial and execution is striking. Here was a woman who had cheated on her husband and involved him in a murder conspiracy, shot her lover, stolen his railway shares and attempted to sell them for her own profit, and then damned her adopted country for bringing her to justice. Yet newspapers, while supporting the jury's decision, were curiously ambivalent and even haltingly deferential toward her. While condemning her "insatiable cupidity and ambition," her "atrocious conceptions," and her "treachery," the *Times* also acknowledged Maria's "undaunted soul and her unflinching nerve," her "dominion over a sottish and a cowardly husband," and "the steadiness with which she could encounter her doom."[18] Maria's conduct at her execution, which was attended by anywhere from 10,000 to 30,000 people, according to various reports,[19] led the *Times* to comment on the "diabolical energy of character displayed by her throughout, which has attracted to her conduct a still larger share of public attention than that of Manning. Her handsome figure, foreign origin, and various other considerations contributed to this effect, and it is due to her to say that no man bore could have borne himself more firmly than she did in the terrible part which she had to perform."[20] In describing the interest that Maria held for the public, the *Times* identified several factors that would collectively constitute women's sensational appeal throughout the century—criminality, sexuality, and masculine temerity. These characteristics threatened Victorian social order by undermining notions of womanly propriety,[21] but for this very reason, they also held a lurid attraction for the public that the press did not hesitate to exploit, making of the woman criminal a prototype for the aberrant heroines of later Victorian sensation dramas and novels. Indeed, Maria Manning became the model for Madame Hortense, the insolent French housemaid and murderess in Charles Dickens's *Bleak House* (1853), and both Wilkie Collins and Mary Elizabeth Braddon evoke her name in the two novels that helped to kick off the sensation craze of the 1860s: *The Woman in White* (1860) and *Lady Audley's Secret* (1861).

The periodical industry, however, anticipated many of the techniques that novels and plays would later evolve to heighten sensational effect. In a rhetorical move characteristic of Manning reports, the *Times* article both provokes its readers' anxieties of cultural subversion and contains these anxieties within a fictive space that insulates them from social consequences. That is, by portraying Maria as an actress and thus relegating the horror of her crime and her death to the realm of spectacle and performance, the article can depict her as an erotic object while leaving womanly ideals intact. "Murder by a woman was so unthinkable in the patriarchal ideology of Victorian England that it had to be explained away as the action of a whore, witch, monster, or madwoman" (Knelman, 230). This characterization as fictive archetype not only defused the threat of the murderess but also made her an object of desire: "Maria Manning showed the public that a murderess could be a glamorous figure, and even that the pursuit of murderesses could be a sexual turn-on" (Knelman, 229). The *Morning Chronicle* exemplifies the conflation of fear and fantasy when it envisioned Maria as "the ideal murderess of our childish imaginations—a character darker than any novelist would venture to portray—a Clytemnestra of the Newgate Calendar, with all the masculine fierceness of her prototype."[22] Here, Maria's threat to social order is counterbalanced by her simultaneous portrayal as a character from myth and a figure of nursery-room fantasy. As in the *Times*, this article contains provocative images within fictional boundaries that allow its audience an illusion of intimacy with a social offender while keeping her at a safe distance. So effectively was Maria's image disseminated through popular culture that *Punch* ran a satirical article called "The Mannings at Home," commenting on the rosy reproduction of Maria in Madame Tussaud's Chamber of Horrors—the ultimate testimonial to Maria's reification in popular culture: "There she stands in silk attire, a beauteous thing, to be daily rained upon by a shower of sixpences. . . . [N]ever did assassination look so amiable—so like a quality to be introduced to the bosom of families."[23] As *Punch* apprehensively suggests, the domestication of Maria Manning through her transformation into fictive spectacle set a dangerous precedent of moral relativism that would underlie the sensation craze of the following decades.

The destabilization of established moral values was a primary characteristic of sensation culture, which may be distinguished from its gothic and melodramatic forebears by its dispensation with a polarized moral aesthetic. Melodrama, as Ellen Bayuk Rosenman argues, "pits absolute innocence against absolute evil and resolves this conflict by vindicating the persecuted heroine in a 'remarkable, public, spectacular homage to virtue.'"[24] Sensationalism, in contrast, complicates such values by housing virtue and vice within the same individual, thereby transforming melodrama's external struggles between villain and victim into psychological conflicts between dueling elements of a single character's personality. Maria Manning established herself as a model for the 1860s sensation heroine by cultivating a schizophrenic personality that, with the dramatizing aid of the press, strategically played on her audience's shock and sympathy. At one moment presenting herself as a composed, perfectly coifed, respectably dressed, and well-spoken young woman, at the next raging in broken English against her captors, Maria played to the hilt the roles of both beset heroine and treacherous virago. The former ingratiated her to her middle-class audience while the latter whetted its appetite for the spectacle of female aberrance.

Though written and performed four years before sensationalism hit London theaters and bookstands, Ernest Legouvé's 1856 adaptation of Euripides' *Medea* possessed precisely the duality of character, moral ambiguity, and spectacular effects that were features of the Manning trial. The accomplishment of these effects rested on two primary factors: Adelaide Ristori's acting and Legouvé's emphasis on Medea's fractured personality. I wish to explore each of these factors independently and in depth to show the play's correspondence with the politics and aesthetics of sensationalism. In the first place, Ristori seemed the perfect realization of Euripides' heroine: an ostracized stranger, unfamiliar with the conventions of a civilized Greek world, battling inexpressible internal demons. "The performance of Madame Ristori . . . has even surpassed expectation," wrote the *Spectator* of the opening performance. "She was no sooner seen, we may almost say, than her supremacy was acknowledged by a sort of instinct. The face, the deportment, the attitude, had the stamp of authority upon them."[25] The emphasis on Ristori's visual impact is important here, for the audience was unable to comprehend the actors' Italian and were thus left to focus on the visual and aural elements that heightened the actress's—and subsequently her character's—exoticism: her imposing physical appearance, her grandiloquent gestures, her expressive voice. "Even when she had uttered the first few lines . . . there was such a tenderness in her tone that a gasp of sympathy might be heard in every direction," the *Times* gushed. "The charm of the voice, the power of modulating it were so manifest that none could resist its fascination."[26] The *Illustrated London News* added to the accolades, remarking, "The effect of the first act was altogether terribly grand. When the curtain fell, it left a sensation of unparalleled majesty."[27] The term *sensation* here is used quite literally: Ristori provided a strong stimulus to the audience's bodily senses, evoking responses unprocessed by reason and, as Ann Cvetkovich has noted, "closely akin to sexual excitement" (22). These effects underlay the term *sensationalism* when it was recognized as a cultural phenomenon in the 1860s.

Observations about the contrast between Rachel and Ristori and the latter's predisposition toward passionate display further explain the Italian actress's sensational appeal. "Rachel and Ristori present the most vivid contrast," notes Henry Knepler. "The one was small, spare, almost thin, the other, more in tune with the ideal of beauty of the time, was tall and well, even amply proportioned."[28] Knepler goes on to explain that Ristori took full advantage of her powerful physical presence, excelling in roles that demanded much movement and energy and featured characters in the throes of agony or excessive emotion. "Here lay her great contrast to Rachel. Rachel had rejected Legouve's *Medee* [*sic*] largely because of the amount of physical action it would have involved: 'I see,' she wrote, 'that the part is full of rapid and violent movements; I have to rush to my children, I have to lift them up, to carry them off the stage, to contend for them with the people. This external vivacity is not my style. Whatever may be expressed by physiognomy, by attitude, by sober and measured gesture—that I can command; but where broad and energetic pantomime begins, there my talent of execution ends'" (85). Ristori, in contrast, was supremely fitted to the "broad" and "energetic" requirements of the performance. The nineteenth-century American critic William Winter explained that Ristori's forte lay in the violent nature of her acting: "The moods and conditions of human nature and experience that Ristori best portrayed are—with little exception—those that result from conflicts in the impassioned heart and amidst the amorous physical passions. . . . [H]er Medea . . . was chiefly victorious as a type of luxuriant animal vitality, exhibiting—under the shaping pressure of experience—rage, scorn, the tenderness of the female leopard, the delirium of outraged love and wounded pride, and the pathos of abject misery."[29] After witnessing Ristori's performance during her 1875 American tour, for which Medea was a fixed part of her repertoire, Henry James noted the shocking effect that such vitality might have on an audience unfamiliar with the demonstrative style that James attributes to Ristori's Italian origins:

> No one . . . can interpret tragedy in the superbly large way of Madame Ristori—can distribute effects into such powerful masses. . . . Coming thus of a pre-eminently expressive and demonstrative race, and watched by a peculiarly undemonstrative and impassive public . . . it is natural that Madame Ristori should seem very often to exaggerate, to grimace, to tear a passion into tatters. . . . Between herself and her audience there is a gulf—a gulf which she certainly bravely does her best to overleap, and which is kept open by no ill-will on the spectators' part, but by the inexorable difference of race, of language, of national temperament. She is judged altogether from the outside—from a distance; and as she sweeps to and fro through all the variations of her art, she seems hardly more than a sort of magnificent curiosity. The "nature" that she represents is not the nature of the house.[30]

Though commenting on the reactions of an American audience, James's remark on the distancing effect of Ristori's acting style might very well have applied to the British public, whose experience of foreigners in tragedy gravitated around French actors such as Rachel. The chasm that Ristori created by her exaggerated motions and her foreign appearance and language not only suited her to the role of Medea (likewise a foreigner) but also made her spectacular—a "magnificent curiosity"—in the same way that Maria Manning's foreignness transformed her into an object of both revulsion and fascination.

Ristori's *Memoirs* reveal an acting philosophy that fully embraces sensational affect. Ristori recalled the climactic moment in the second act, when Medea raises a poniard to slaughter Creusa and then recoils in shock at her own intentions: "It is needless to mention the good effect produced upon the audience by all these dramatic situations."[31] For Ristori, the definition of "dramatic" lay in the simultaneous repulsion and attraction that an actress can provoke in the audience—visceral emotions that transcend reason and are considered prototypical reactions to the heroine of a sensation novel (Cvetkovich, 50). To evoke these emotions in her audience, Ristori focused on the portrayal of outward expressions—a technique that Michael Booth identifies as "situational" rather than "holistic" acting. The actor "could play his part from situation to situation, playing each significant dramatic moment for what it was and extracting the maximum passion and effect from it, plotting his course through the play from emotional climax to emotional climax . . . [or he could] view the character as dramatically unified and attempt to show this unity, the governing 'idea' of the character, on stage."[32] Although, as Booth notes, the holistic approach was becoming dominant in the nineteenth century, Ristori was decidedly of the situational persuasion. When Ristori "speaks about realism and truth, what she means is that it is the task of the actor to study a part . . . and to re-create an impression of the emotional life of the character externally, rather than by searching within one's own subconscious," explains Susan Bassnett.[33] For Ristori, the insistence on identifying emotionally and essentially with a character one plays falsified the very art of acting. To assert an internal correspondence between one's emotions and those of the character would constitute not acting but rather being oneself.

This situational philosophy contributed to Ristori's sensationalism through its emphasis on visual effect and on the schizophrenic persona resulting from discrete portrayals of specific moments in a character's experience. Susan Bassnett confirms this idea, stating that the Italian actress was "concerned to create powerful stage effects, strong visual images that would have an almost photographic impact on the spectators. . . . [One of her key concepts] was the idea of the pose, the stage picture, the image that would be retained in the imagination after the performance had ended" (146). Elaine Aston similarly notes, "It is as a series of images that the mid-nineteenth century productions of Ristori's Medea are recalled."[34] In a play such as *Medea,* in which almost every occasion for a "stage effect" captures the central figure in a different state of intense emotion—from maternal tenderness to violent jealousy, from murderous rage to regretful anguish—the impact of Ristori's picture acting would have counteracted and overwhelmed Legouvé's efforts to emphasize a gradual transformation of character and to show Medea "arriving by degrees at such an excess of despair that she captivates us, transports us, so that from this same transport and at the moment that she kills we are able to say: This is horrifying, but I understand!"[35] Legouvé's intentions here suggest a vision of audience identification more in keeping with the ideal of "natural acting," which, as Lynn Voskuil observes, "equipped audiences as well as players with a powerful form of self-consciousness: the capacity not only to experience but also to understand their own feelings in epistemological terms, to recognize instinctively but also intellectually how their own emotions could function as important building blocks of character and community."[36] Ristori's acting undermined this social cohesion born of moral sympathy. As G. H. Lewes commented, Ristori "does not deeply move us, because [she is] not herself deeply moved."[37] Instead of sharing Ristori's feelings, the audience is instead set at a distance by the paratactic collage created through the actress's highly visual portrayal, with its climactic expressions of contrasting emotions.

Henry Knepler has remarked that the expressiveness of Ristori's gestures and expressions helped the actress to "transcend the boundaries of language" (125). The comment suggests a tension between Legouvé's script and Ristori's acting that corresponds with the transformation of textual meaning resulting from the transition between a verbal sign system and a gestural/kinetic sign system (that is, the mise-en-scène). "In performance," as Barbara Godard points out, "semiotic systems of movement, gesture, music, costume, space, architecture, come together with language to create something much more than a verbal text to be translated."[38] Patrice Pavis goes even further in privileging the mise-en-scène by describing it as "not the reduction or the transformation of text into performance, but rather their confrontation."[39] According to Pavis, the mise-en-scène is not the completion of a text but rather its denial because the mise-en-scène "speaks without words, talks about the text thanks to a completely different semiotic system which is not verbal but 'iconic.' . . . *Mise en scène,* even at its simplest and most explicit, 'displaces' the text and makes it say what a critical commentary, spoken or written, could not say:

it expresses, one could almost say, the inexpressible" (31–32). While the notion of a performance as criticism of a written text might seem to contradict the idea of fulfillment, both these theories can be seen as diminishing the authority of a logocentric authority, as language gives way to the interpretive powers and bodily presence of the actor, whose visual and auditory representations expose the polysemic potential of the enacted narrative. Although both Pavis and Godard are discussing the dynamics of the stage, the same conflict between verbal and visual representation could be applied to Victorian murder trials, at which, by law, criminals could not speak in their own defense. Instead, the murderess had to construct a visual narrative to counter incriminating evidence spoken against her. Maria expertly managed the manipulation of her image such that it endured long after her execution. As suggested by contemporary reviews of Ristori's performance, the audience's enthrallment with the actress precluded their judgment upon her character's crimes in much the same way that Maria Manning's courtroom personality obscured the atrocity of her murder. The courtroom had set a precedent for the stage, such that a criminal could be dissociated from her crime and could vindicate herself through sheer force of personality. Following in the footsteps of her real-life predecessor, Ristori as Medea replicated the performative dynamics of the murderess's relationship to her public—a public that, by midcentury, had become practiced at sacrificing moral scruples for sensational thrill.

One aspect of Legouvé's script that enabled Ristori's sensational mise-en-scène was the playwright's emphasis on Medea's barbarian origins. "I have made her . . . not a Greek or a wild woman, but a true barbarian," Legouvé wrote in his preface. "The hardships and curiosities of the Germans through the blood-thirsty religions of the races of the North Sea have permitted me to illuminate this tragic figure in a new and sinister light, by rendering her at once more terrible and less atrocious, by explaining finally her crime as connected with the culture where she was raised, with the country that she left: I have given her her gods as accomplices."[40] Legouvé had intended to use Medea's foreignness to suspend the audience's moral judgment and evoke further sympathy for her suffering. But his portrayal ultimately enabled Ristori's realization of a spectacularly fragmented character. The potential for sensationalism inherent in Legouvé's construction can be seen from the moment Medea's name is mentioned at the play's outset, when Orpheus—Legouvé's primary addition to Euripides' tragedy—scolds Jason for abandoning his wife, against whom all Greece has turned for the murders of Apsyrtus and King Pelias.

"[B]y what fell enchantments the barbarian woman e'er gained my heart," Jason states in self-defense; "I can no longer, at Medea's side, brave the hatred—the *horror* of the world!"[41] In this early scene, Legouvé prepares Medea's appearance on the stage by simultaneously provoking the audience's terror of a serial murderess and their compassion for her exile and abandonment. Medea's appearance in act 1, scene 3, escalates this Aristotelian evocation of pity and fear. Abandoned by Jason, whose cowardice before a jury of his countrymen may have recalled the puling Frederick Manning in the minds of a British audience, Medea is first seen seeking her lost husband and trying to provide for her children while battling the savage impulses that possess her soul. "Alas! compare not my deities with thine!" Medea says to Creusa's nurse, upon encountering her at Diana's altar. "The gods of my nation would despise such offerings [as Apollo's veil]—their dreadful worship is an endless series of slaughter—e'en our Venus thirsts for human blood" (8). By displacing the problem of Medea's criminality onto a question of racial difference, Legouvé separates character from crime: Medea's murders and violent impulses can be attributed to inborn forces beyond her rational control and therefore outside the realm of moral judgment. Her attempts to suppress these impulses and her self-condemnation release her audience from obligations of moral censorship while emphasizing the severity of her crimes. Although Legouvé may have intended to make Medea a more sympathetic character by giving her uncontrollable barbaric impulses, he also facilitated her transformation into a sensational object. As in the case of Maria Manning, the figure of the aberrant woman is divided in two: a spectacular, alien object and a rational consciousness that models the ideal spectator of her own monstrosity. Victorian anxieties about infanticide heightened the tension between these two aspects of Medea's character.

Medea and the Infanticide Epidemic

In British scholarly circles, Euripides has been a consistent presence from the mid-eighteenth century, when, owing largely to the influential theories of the Schlegel brothers, Greek drama began to be studied seriously by critics and appreciated by Hellenists. Euripides' works in general and *Medea* in particular became standard texts in public schools such as Eton, and according to M. L. Clarke, Euripides was the most popular of the three Greek tragedians among eighteenth-century scholars. At that time, however, scholarly attention to Euripides—and all other classical texts—

focused almost exclusively on niceties of translation, philological and metrical concerns, and manuscript collation and emendation, with the primary goals being to furnish secondary schools with textbooks from which to study the Attic language, to dispute earlier translations of specific lines or texts, and to enable "the educated man to read the tragedians with greater ease and a finer appreciation of their language and style."[42] Outside of scholarly circles, Euripides received much less consistent attention and was the least favorite among a general readership of "educated men" throughout much of the nineteenth century. As F. L. Lucas and others have noted, the Romantic poets tended to focus their attentions on other Greek models; even influential Victorian hellenophiles such as Arnold and Swinburne explicitly stated their preferences for Sophocles (Arnold) and Aeschylus (Swinburne), though Arnold's *Merope* (1858) attempted to restore a lost Euripidean tragedy and Swinburne's *Atalanta in Calydon* was seen by some as a translation of Euripides. Although Robert Browning and Walter Pater did appreciate this youngest and least conventional of the Greek tragedians, Euripides' plays were generally looked upon with disfavor because they neither presented the serene repose of Arnold's Hellenic ideal nor fulfilled the technical criteria laid out by Aristotle and respected by Victorian readers. Commenting on the Schlegels' influence over nineteenth-century views of Euripides, Ann Michelini notes that for these critics, "the art of Sophokles exemplified the Classical standard, since it was 'harmonious,' observant of proper generic boundaries (*Gränze*), and had the desired quality of completion (*Vollkommenheit*). Opposed to this figure was a strongly contrasting one that had more in common with the restless and individualistic modern poet. Between Sophokles and Euripides the step down from perfection was indeed an abrupt one, into progressive degeneration, at once moral, social, and aesthetic."[43] Besides his technical imperfections, philosophical inconsistencies, and sensational contrivances, Euripides, Michelini argues, was too modern to find favor with critics who were looking to Greece as the model of a more exalted culture. Compounding Euripides' failure in offering consolation to a modern world riddled with inconsistencies was his perceived threat to modernity's precarious hold on religious and moral principles. As H. D. F. Kitto states in his 1965 introduction to Gilbert Murray's influential *Euripides and His Age* (1918), "Aeschylus and Sophocles were splendid: they believed in the gods, they wrote beautiful poetry, they respected the immutable principles of dramatic art. . . . But, Euripides could not, or would not, obey the rules: he was careless or incompetent in making his plots; his poetry had none of Aeschylus's splendour or of Sophocles's dignity; and in what are after all more serious matters, namely religion and morality, he was a dangerous sceptic."[44]

In such an atmosphere of moral and religious censorship, *Medea* in particular lost ground. But the general neglect of Euripides' work and the disfavor into which *Medea* had fallen in the mainstream Hellenism of the early and mid-nineteenth century made this a particularly useful vehicle for the conveyance of controversial ideas in the latter half of the nineteenth century, when the illusion of a Golden Age revival became more difficult to sustain. Edith Hall has thoroughly discussed the continuity between midcentury debates about divorce legislation and the appearance of the first two nineteenth-century Medea adaptations: James Robinson Planche's *The Golden Fleece; or, Jason in Colchis, and Medea in Corinth* (at the Haymarket in 1845) and Jack Wooler's *Jason and Medea* (at the Grecian Saloon in 1851). These two burlesques, argues Hall, helped to familiarize a lay audience with Greek tragedy and the Medea figure while simultaneously acting out problems introduced by the proposed legalization of divorce, such as the plight of women abandoned by their ex-husbands with no means of providing for themselves or their children. Silenced because of her nonconformity to dominant nineteenth-century ideologies, Medea arose in the British popular imagination as a figure intimately associated with controversies surrounding women's shifting social status.

Besides the divorce debates, Medea's appearance in nineteenth-century popular culture was also entangled with heightened concerns about and legislation regarding infanticide. Fiona Macintosh has noted that Legouvé's *Medea* made a significant departure from Planche's and Wooler's versions of the play, both of which drew heavily from Franz Grillparzer's trilogy *The Golden Fleece,* first performed in Vienna in 1821.[45] Besides the shift from comedy to tragedy, one of the primary differences in Legouvé's play was his treatment of Medea's murder of her two children. Whereas in both Planche's and Wooler's works the murders are completely written out of the script, Legouvé's tragedy and the two 1856 burlesques that rapidly followed it carry out the murder.[46] The shift in the portrayal of Medea's infanticide marks an important transitional moment not only in Victorian assumptions about women's "motherly instincts" but also in attitudes toward aberrant women who demonstrated an "unnatural" lack of maternal impulses. Mary Poovey has pointed out that these instincts were "considered woman's definitive characteristic. . . . This instinct, theoretically, accounted for the remarkable fact that women were not self-interested and aggressive like men, but self-sacrificing and tender" (7). Poovey argues that while such characteristics as passivity and compassion were attributed to natural differences between men and women, they were in fact cultural constructs that justified women's separation from a competitive and often immoral social and political reality. Victorian Medeas, I suggest, helped to deconstruct what Poovey calls the "binary logic that governed Victorian symbolic economy" (12). Tapping into an intensely controversial issue at midcentury, Legouvé's portrayal of Medea's infanticide engaged in a dialogue with the sensation press that highlighted the inadequacies and contradictions in existing models of womanhood and exposed the concept of "maternal instincts" as a function of cultural negotiation.

Legouvé's influential decision to include Medea's infanticide was based on a view of the relationship between ancient and modern theater that differed considerably from those of previous British playwrights. A master of farce and melodrama, Planche, for instance, had written his burlesque partly as a satire of the 1845 Covent Garden performance of Sophocles' *Antigone*—an elaborate production that attempted to imitate the conditions of a Greek theater with its sixty-member chorus and Mendelssohn score. Planche's reaction to this production is revealing. *The Golden Fleece,* he states in his preface, was written to burlesque "not the sublime poetry of the Greek dramatist . . . but the *modus operandi* of that classical period, which really illustrates the old proverbial observation that there is but one step from the sublime to the ridiculous."[47] The comment indicates Planche's skepticism toward the authentic reproduction of Greek tragedy, whose genius he sees as tied to the performative context of the ancient Greek stage. In contrast, Legouvé regarded Medea first and foremost as a mythological figure. The purpose of his production was neither to re-create the script and physical details of Greek tragedy, as was attempted at the Covent Garden performance of *Antigone,* nor to explore the transmission of literary text to theatrical production. Rather, his intent was to explore Medea's relevance to contemporary concerns. His preface to the play states, "There are certain grand, legendary figures who resemble the sphinx: they never speak their last word. Such is Medea:—Medea is to maternal love what Othello is to love, the image of a passion that kills. But if one can understand without difficulty a lover who murders a beloved, the crime of maternal infanticide always appears to be a horrible mystery, a chasm of knowledge! . . . This is what has drawn me to this subject."[48] Two important ideas emerge from Legouvé's justification of his topic. First, although he states in a subsequent paragraph that his primary source is Euripides' tragedy, he clearly sees Medea's immortality as existing independently of her textual incarnations. By disengaging heroine from textual source, Legouvé disposes of concerns for authenticity and the problematic transferal of a classical text to a contemporary stage: for him, Medea holds unquestionable and irrefutable relevance for his own time. Second, Legouvé sees this relevance as based on the questionable idea of maternal love: for Legouvé, the myth of Medea unites two historical moments both struggling to reconcile the theory of maternal instincts and the fact of child murder.

This dilemma had particular resonance in England, where infanticide had begun to emerge as a focus of the sensation press ever since the imposition of the 1834 New Poor Laws, which denied mothers the right to demand their lovers' financial support for the care of illegitimate children and, in addition, withdrew free government support ("outdoor relief") for the care of such offspring.[49] In the 1840s, crop failures precipitated the popularity of "burial clubs" (or "murder clubs," as they came to be called). These were organizations that allowed individuals to take out insurance on family members and collect a considerable sum upon the death of the insured, who were often sickly children with parents all too eager to cash in on their child's death.[50] So many poor and desperate mothers reportedly killed or abandoned their children that by 1844, one minister of Parliament declared that "child murder was going on to a frightful, to an enormous, a perfectly incredible extent."[51] By midcentury, 12,000 mothers were reported to have killed their children with impunity.[52] George Behlmer, among others, has noted that the perceived infanticide epidemic in England in the 1850s and '60s may have been attributable not to an actual rise in such crimes but to exaggerations and general panic prompted by alarmists and the sensation press: "What differentiates concern over child-murder in this era from previous periods in English history is the intensity of the public reaction" (404). Behlmer goes on to observe that the press "titillated" its audience with reports of infanticide as a "national institution" (405). Whether exaggerated or not, the infanticide epidemic stirred debate about the culpability of murderous mothers, with one side championing the women victimized by government, society, and irresponsible men and the other accusing promiscuous women of seducing men into illegitimate unions.[53] The 1839 Infant Custody Act further muddied the moral waters by granting women separated from their husbands the right to petition Chancery for the right to see their children and for temporary custody if the children were under seven. The question of motherly instincts was thus caught between fear of an infanticide epidemic on the one hand and the increasing legal acknowledgement of women's right to their children on the other.

While Legouvé's opinion on the issue seems clear from his preface, the play itself and British responses reflect the highly contested nature of Medea's relationship to the maternity debate. In his preface, Legouvé states his intention to inspire sympathy for girls who have been "seduced like [Medea], abandoned like her, and, like her, are murderers out of despair." To this end, he takes pains to emphasize Medea's maternal instincts. At the outset, for example, Medea, distraught at her children's hunger, laments, "Why can I not exhaust my veins to their last drop, and bid them feed?" (9). This self-sacrificial, maternal concern is counterbalanced, however, by anxieties over a barbaric tendency to violence over which she has no control. She laments to Creusa that "the very transports of my passionate affection alarm my little ones! While kissing them, I often feel I *frighten them!*" (12). Not only does Legouvé's continuing emphasis on Medea's maternal affection depart significantly from the Euripidean original, but his simultaneous desire to portray her innate barbarity disrupts his ideal of motherhood. Legouvé's at once exaggerated and ambiguous portrayal of maternal instincts makes Medea's contemplation of her children's murder at the play's end seem specious, as does the play's climax, in which Medea kills her children to protect them from being snatched away by the Corinthian mob. Rather than putting forward a strong defense of maternal instincts, Legouvé's attempt to reconcile this ideal with Euripides' Medea ultimately reveals the contested nature of maternity in Victorian society.

The British media's response to the play highlights both the disharmony of Legouvé's conception and the debate that underscored it. While reviews praised Legouvé's initial presentation of Medea and her barely restrained violence, they universally condemned his exaggeration of her motherly compassion in the latter part of the play. The Frenchman's attempt to preserve Medea's maternal feelings rang false for a British press that was proving the inefficacy of such an argument with its daily articles on abandoned babies, baby-farmers, and murder clubs.[54] "The unity of the enchantress's character really lies in her idolatrous love for Jason, not in her love for her children [as Legouvé depicts it],"[55] noted the *Manchester Guardian,* pointing out the disruptiveness of Medea's maternal profusions. The *Spectator* noted,

> If ever there was a story in which the interest naturally works up, it is the old story of Medea: but M. Legouve is so anxious to vindicate the feeling of maternity, and so prudent in weighing the actuating wrong and the restraining sentiment against each other, that in the play the interest works down; and the last two acts, in which the child-murder is conceived and perpetrated, are not nearly so efficient as the first, in which the feeling of jealousy is first aroused. We strongly suspect that Madame Ristori, magnificent as she is in the part, would have felt easier in a play constructed more after the Euripidean model than in this truly modern work.[56]

The press's criticism of Legouvé's script is, I suggest, motivated not only by its perception of an inherent aesthetic flaw but also by its effort to keep its own story straight, as it were. That is, Legouvé's depiction of Medea's maternal love challenged the narrative of maternal infanticide that the press was cultivating, a narrative much more consistent with Euripides' original, in which maternal compassion is completely absent at the play's outset and emerges later only as a by-product of Medea's egotistical concerns. The criticism of Legouvé's conception thus not only indicates a growing disenchantment with the myth of maternal instincts but also witnesses the press's attempt to co-opt the narrative of infanticide for sensational purposes. Entering into a scene in which infanticide and murder trials had begun to destabilize assumptions about women's passivity and nurturance, Legouvé's script ultimately collided with the agenda of the sensation press. The fallout resulted in further exposure of the inadequacy of conventional notions of motherhood.

Pavis has argued that in "certain productions . . . *mise en scène* can show how the dramatic text is itself an imaginary solution to real ideological contradictions that existed at the time the fiction was invented. *Mise en scène* then has the task of making it possible to imagine and stage the textual contradiction" (36). The play's performance and media reactions exposed the contradiction not only in Legouvé's conception but also within Victorian society. In turn, these debates about women's nature ultimately foreground a problem of sexual binaries that lies at the crux of Euripides' tragedy. Helene Foley and Rush Rehm have argued, for instance, that in Medea's famous monologue about whether or not to kill her children,[57] Euripides stages a debate between the masculine, public self and the feminine, private self. Although according to Rehm the play ultimately struggles to establish a feminized poetics,[58] Medea can find no positive basis for action in her maternity and, in her admittedly self-devastating act of infanticide, is ultimately as trapped in her obedience to a male heroic code as she has been trapped in the female code of obedience, passivity, and inaction. "By dividing Medea's self along sexual lines," Foley argues, "Euripides creates, not a private psychological drama and/or an abstract struggle between reason and passion, but an ambiguous inquiry into the relation between human ethics and social structure."[59] Foley's argument for Medea's actions serves as commentary on the sexual binaries and social values that force individuals into personally and socially destructive acts. Her observations hold important implications for Medea's role in Victorian society as well. Legouvé's attempt to mold Medea's character in conformity to binary gender codes exposes the inadequacy of such binaries in explaining human action and their role in promoting unethical acts.

Medea's Evolution and Sensationalism's Demise

Despite criticism of Legouvé's conception of Medea's maternity, his play was a popular success and spearheaded a number of adaptations in following years that trace a revealing evolution in Medea's portrayal. Rather than depicting Medea as a woman divided between rational, nurturing subject and spectacular, vengeful object, later playwrights attempted to reconcile her dueling impulses into a complex but unified subjectivity that served as a critical lens for viewing not only contradictory gender binarisms but also the distortive operations of a sensation culture that promoted these binarisms. One way of approaching Medea's evolution in the later 1850s and 1860s is through examining the increasing self-awareness of the sensation press, which evolved from staging to exposing the theatricality of high-profile, criminal cases. The trial of Madeleine Smith in Scotland during the spring and summer of 1857 exemplifies the shift in the relation of press and courtroom. Smith's case, which came to be known as "the trial of the century," exposed to the British public in greater detail than ever before a woman's capacities for violence, passion, and manipulation. Simultaneously, the case made it harder than ever to classify women offenders into moral and archetypal categories.

Several factors contributed to the sensational appeal of Madeleine Smith, who, at the age of twenty-one, was accused of poisoning and killing her working-class lover, Emile L'Angelier, to prevent his exposing their sexual union to her family and fiancé. First, Madeleine was born of an upper-middle-class family, an unusual social standing for a murderess, which suggested that her crime was one of passion rather than abject desperation and increased her allure for an upper-class audience. Second, and more important, Madeleine's trial featured an unusual event in criminal courts—the reading aloud and subsequent publication of passionate love letters written by Madeleine to Emile, documenting their affair and its demise. Finally, Madeleine's tranquil, dispassionate appearance in court posed a striking contrast to the testimony of her heated love letters and lent the murderess a fascination that, like the performances of Maria Manning and Ristori, offset the horror of her crime and provided an ideal narrative baseline for the press. "Madeleine Smith . . . the prisoner, a very young lady of short stature and slight form, with features sharp and prominent, and restless and sparkling eye, stepped up the stair into the dock with all the buoyancy with which she might have entered the box of a theater," reported the *Times* on the third day of the trial. "Her perfect self-possession, indeed, could only be accounted for either by a proud consciousness of innocence, or by her possessing an almost unparalleled amount of self-control. She even sometimes smiled with all the air and grace of a young lady in the drawing-room."[60] As with reports of Maria Manning's trial, the descriptions here locate Madeleine firmly in scenes of polite society—the theater box, the ballroom—that rhetorically remove her from the sordid contexts of extramarital sex, social transgression, and capital offense. However, while Maria was typically presented as a spectacle—an object of fear, fascination, or pity—articles about Madeleine frequently portrayed her as a spectator, granting her a degree of subjectivity with which to reciprocate the voyeuristic and judgmental gazes of her audience. The *Ayreshire Express* noted that Madeleine "never ceases surveying all that goes on around her, watching every word of every witness, returning every stare with compound interest, glancing every second minute at the down-turned eyes in the side-galleries, and even turning right round upon the reporters immediately behind her, to see how they get along with the note-taking which is carrying her name and deeds into every British home."[61] These observations of Madeleine reverse the rhetoric of performance used to describe Maria Manning. Instead of envisioning the criminal soliciting the audience's shock and approval, Madeleine is herself an audience—indeed, a judge—of the onlookers supposedly sitting in judgment upon her. This role reversal creates a metadiscourse that self-consciously registers the theatricality of press and courtroom, whose narratives have little relation to reality and thus might be enjoyed with detached bemusement by the defendant.

The sensationalism that, in the Manning trial and in Legouvé's play, had been rooted in the visible spectacle of Maria's antics and Ristori's exoticism thus shifted in the case of Madeleine's trial to an interest in the unseen experiences and acts that remain impervious to the court's scrutiny. Madeleine, unlike Maria, could not be cast as a fictional stereotype, because her character remained an unsolvable mystery. The lure of the unknown and the wide gap separating courtroom drama from reality became strikingly obvious when Madeleine's letters were read aloud in court. "Letters written in the silence of the night, when no eye save one beheld the hand that traced the words, were read in a crowded hall of judgment, with a multitude of strangers listening eagerly to what was intended for the eye and ear of one alone," lamented *Reynold's Newspaper*, protectively taking Madeleine's side and pronouncing its judgment upon the prurient interests of the spectators. "[W]ild appeals, in which the mind appeared to be verging on distraction, were read coldly and unsympathizingly by the aged clerk of the court, for the purpose of being used as evidence against the writer."[62] Emphasizing the discrepancy between private experience and public spectacle, this article overwrites Madeleine's visible impassivity by implying unseen depths of vulnerability and suffering. Criticizing the courtroom for falsifying reality and victimizing defendants, such articles transformed the most incriminating pieces of evidence into the most compelling witnesses to Madeleine's innocence. Reflecting on the impact of the letters, the *North British Mail* made the following observation: "[She] has become quite a heroine with the majority of the opposite sex, who view her as a thoughtless but most interesting and warm-hearted young girl—one who, in the simplicity of her heart, in her first love affair, abandoned herself to the man of her choice, with an amount of confiding love and outspoken artlessness of purpose, which, censure and regret as they may, they cannot regard without sympathy and admiration."[63] As far as the press and the public were concerned, Madeleine was the model of Everygirl: her case may have served as living testimony to the chorus's reflection in Euripides' *Medea*: "Loves that come to us in excess bring no good name or goodness to men."[64] But in the tragedy, these words serve less as an indictment of Medea's actions than as sympathetic advice, and in Madeleine Smith's case, vast numbers of the British public, prompted by the press to consider the importunity of unseen evidence, were reluctant to condemn Madeleine. Indeed, if Madeleine's trial exemplified the consequences of disobeying social codes, the public's sympathy demonstrated the instability of such codes.

In his study of the rhetoric and social effects of popular trials, John Hariman argues that such cases can shape and symptomize historical change.[65] The contrast between the media's treatment of Maria Manning and of Madeleine Smith suggests a shift from the sensational thrill of spectacle, which tended to objectify aberrant women, to an interest in the murderess's subjectivity. While the latter may have been no less sensational in prompting emotive reactions from the public, it did so partly in the interests of turning the audience's gaze from criminal to context. Reflecting this rhetorical shift from spectacle to subjectivity is John Heraud's English adaptation of Legouvé's *Medea,* which opened at Sadler's Wells on August 8, 1857, a month after a verdict of "not proven" had concluded the Madeleine Smith trial. As theatrical editor of the *Illustrated London News,* which had a year earlier criticized Legouvé for the sentimentality of his *Medea,* Heraud was quick to exploit the effects of the Smith trial on public interest and values. The changes he made to Legouvé's script, though subtle, show his sensitivity to the public's readiness for an assertive, even transgressive, heroine. His Medea is a much more self-confident and emotionally resilient individual than Legouvé's, showing little regret for her barbarian roots, taking pride in her immortal inheritance, and maintaining her composure and self-possession throughout the play. For example, in act 2, scene 3, directly preceding Medea's first encounter with Jason, Heraud leaves out the nurse's report of Medea's distracted rantings. "Vainly did we seek to restrain her—she sprang forth like a lioness in her den," announces Legouvé's nurse. "Pale, distracted, sobbing, she ran towards us, exclaiming 'Jason! I must see him!' At first her face is bathed in bitter tears; anon she breaks forth into shrieks of rage and malediction!" (18). While these lines increase the volatility of Legouvé's Medea, they also dehumanize her and emphasize her lack of self-control. By choosing to proceed directly to Medea's indictment of Jason's infidelity, Heraud refuses to compromise Medea's sanity, thus diminishing her dependence on him and lending her argument more credibility. To her argument, Heraud also adds a protest against the injustice of the divorce laws to which Jason appeals. "Laws—laws—laws—" Medea retorts sarcastically. "But justice so regards it, who would not woman should suffer more than man the wrongs of love's inconstancy."[66] Medea's words no doubt comment on the recently passed 1857 Divorce Act, which granted divorce without an act of Parliament but also instituted a double standard that allowed men to sue for divorce solely on the grounds of adultery but demanded that women provide a secondary cause such as abuse or abandonment. Here, sensationalism gives way to social critique. In contrast to Legouvé, who had attempted to solicit such self-examination through pity, Heraud invites his audience to share Medea's anger and scorn while tempering the grief and lamentation displayed emphatically in Legouvé's version. The audience's support of Medea's argument thus stems from the strength of conviction rather than the exigency of despair.

Heraud's emphasis on Medea's strength is felt most strongly at the play's end, which differs significantly from Legouvé's, more closely following Euripides' original by offering an implicit sanction of Medea's infanticide. While Legouvé's version had concluded with Medea killing her children to protect them from the anger of the Corinthian mob and angrily accusing Jason of causing their deaths, Heraud restores Euripides' deus ex machina of the golden chariot, which confirms Medea's divine birthright. "In vain ye sage, insensate populace against a charmed life," cries Medea to the approaching mob. "Now, magic! aid me—Arise, my Car; and bear me from this fury" (45). Medea's magical rescue from the consequences of her actions no doubt brought to its audience's mind Madeleine Smith's vindication despite the conclusiveness of the incriminating evidence. The aptness of an ending that confirms Medea's strength of will was reinforced in 1861, when Matilda Heron staged her version of the play. Though Heron's must be considered more a translation than an adaptation of Legouvé's script, she nevertheless altered Legouvé's ending. Rather than killing her children to prevent their seizure by the mob, Heron's Medea kills them to prove her ultimate strength: "The gods are just—let one blow strike all!" she cries,[67] before plunging the knife into her children. This ending, like Heraud's, reinstates the determination of Euripides' Medea and reorients her final act from one of maternal instinct to one of willful vengeance: an immoral act in response to unethical actions done against her.

The media's treatment of women murderers followed a similar path of vindication, wherein these women were increasingly seen less as shocking monsters than as individuals with motivations not so different from those of average people. This subordination of spectacle to subjectivity extended the boundaries of normality and eventually led to the death of a sensation culture that depended on the detection, objectification, and elimination of abnormality. As Judith Knelman has observed, when sensationalism began to lose its hold on the public in the 1880s, there was a considerable shift in responses toward sensational women criminals as well.[68] Whereas earlier in the century, attitudes toward murderesses had been almost exclusively controlled by men, by the end of the century, women had begun to influence public opinion as well as the court system, insisting on examining the social factors causing criminality. Women, Knelman points out, "followed trials and commented on verdicts. They applied pressure when they felt that social justice had not been done. Some were bold enough to mock rather than attack the establishment" (235). The trial and execution of Florence Maybrick in 1889 for the fatal poisoning of her husband, James, offer testimony to radical alterations in the social reception of women murderers. In her book *Medea's Daughters*, Jennifer Jones writes that Florence's counsel had almost succeeded in convincing the jury of her innocence (James Maybrick was an addict of the arsenic that killed him), when it was revealed that Florence had carried on an affair with another man. "Florence's admission of adultery turned judge and jury against her, though no one seemed disturbed by James Maybrick's longtime extramarital affair. . . . Within half an hour Florence was found guilty and sentenced to death."[69] While Florence Maybrick's fate certainly testifies to the persistence of sexual binaries in the late nineteenth century, the overwhelming response to the verdict by irate women shows the transformation of the woman criminal from object of spectacle to focal point of protest for women's rights. "When Florence was convicted women cried out in fury, and almost half a million people, mostly women, signed petitions to the Home Office demanding a reprieve [and raising protest] against a legal system that continued to equate a woman's adultery with murder" (Jones, 38). In response to an overwhelming number of letters to the press in both Britain and the United States, the government commuted Florence's sentence to life in prison. Florence Maybrick's role as a catalyst in the growing women's movement anticipates Medea's position in the last decade of the nineteenth and first decade of the twentieth century. In 1898, Sarah Bernhardt's portrayal of the tragic heroine warned against the horrific potentials of the New Woman, but she was answered nine years later when Gilbert Murray's translation was staged at the Savoy. First starring Edyth Olive, then Sybil Thorndike, Murray's version was expressly written in support of the women's movement and was shown with a series of suffragist plays. Murray's translation survived well into the twentieth century, being performed throughout Britain and the United States as an inspiration for feminist causes. The entangled trajectories of Medea and the nineteenth-century sensationalist press thus eventually led to an expansion of perspectives on women criminals—perspectives that tended to emphasize women's strength despite their victimization by social forces, replaced the sensation of female aberrance with the possibility of multiple female subjectivities, and urged social changes to accommodate these diverse perspectives.

Medea Off-Staged

Webster's "Medea in Athens" and Levy's *Medea: A Play in Fragments* demonstrate Medea's late-century appeal to a generation of women whose education enabled their access to classical material and whose writing breached the divide between scholarship and popular culture. These two works offer a glimpse of how women writers in the latter part of the century appropriated Medea's powerful yet conflicted persona to articulate their experiences of a pivotal moment in women's history, when social changes were granting women greater opportunities for independence and self-assertion but also provoking intense frustration at the traditions and institutions that still limited their minds and lives. Webster and Levy were active during a time of landmark events such as the first Married Women's Property Act (1870) and the opening of women's colleges in Cambridge and Oxford. Women's autonomy, outspokenness, and deviation from social norms were becoming less exceptional, if no less threatening to traditionalists. As products of expanding views on women's subjectivity and social viability, Webster's and Levy's versions of Medea protest the midcentury sensationalization of female aberrance and its implicit reinscription of sexual binarisms while at the same time claiming her marginal status to represent their own positions vis-à-vis traditional views toward gender and race relations. Whereas Webster's coda to Euripides' story explores the elusiveness of women's freedom, despite advances in educational and employment opportunities, Levy finds in Medea's social ostracism a validation of individuality and racial difference.

Joining the general retreat of poets from the stage in the nineteenth century, both women rewrote Medea into dramas that resist performance, thus subverting the objectifying framework of the theater both through a formal withdrawal from sensual representation and by featuring a heroine whose complex, fragmented psyche defeats the criteria of unity by which midcentury performances were judged, almost exclusively by male critics.[70] Their removal of Medea from the public stage allies Webster's and Levy's works with an evolving nineteenth-century tradition of closet drama, a term that Catherine Burroughs notes served at this time "as a metaphor for privacy and intense intellectual engagement."[71] While the alliance with closet drama appears to reinscribe Victorian gender dichotomies that relegated women and women's work to the private sphere, it also claims for female subjectivity the same psychological complexity and intellectual seriousness that male poet-playwrights were attempting to establish as an antidote to the low-cultural reputation of popular theater. The adaptation of Greek figures to modern verse dramas and dramatic monologues—of which Shelley's Prometheus and Tennyson's Ulysses offer two diverse samples—was part of this movement to rehabilitate drama as a high-cultural practice. But whereas male poets' inhabitation of Greek personas tended to project a cultural authority based on a strong sense of literary tradition, women's adoption of Greek voices was often underscored with uncertainty about their relations both to the ancient past and to their changing social circumstances. For these women, closet drama provided a forum for intellectual and social experimentation. The closet, as Burroughs writes of early-nineteenth-century drama, offered a space for women "to rehearse roles and cultivate identities that conformed to and diverged from cultural expectation, to reflect upon their experiences of performing gender in public and private theaters, and to theorize about a variety of theatrical stages" (11). For women, then, closet drama—and the dramatic monologue that it comprehends—became a covert method of challenging the boundaries imposed by traditional gender roles while experimenting with alternatives beyond the prescriptions of conventional morality. Such a rehearsal space became even more imperative in the late nineteenth century as new social roles became available for women and changing cultural contexts demanded renegotiations of female subjectivity. Discussing the feminist politics of closet drama in the late nineteenth century, Susan Brown notes that writers such as Levy and Webster "could not afford the luxurious assumption of a unified self that transcends a largely irrelevant world. Victorian women had to establish identity and to deconstruct it at the same time, for establishing themselves as subjects equal to men meant coming to grips with the socially constructed, and therefore neither unified nor static, nature of identity."[72] Through their unstageable Medeas, Levy and Webster began to construct a vision of female subjectivity that both resisted the romantic illusion of a unified, transcendent self and explored alternative possibilities for self-conceptualization. Following a growing tradition of women's closet drama, both Webster's and Levy's Medeas discover, to borrow Angela Leighton's phrasing, that "the self is a thing of inner strata and differences, of overlaid repressions and deceptions."[73] In these verses, the spectacle of Medea's suffering, which had ushered her onto the mid-Victorian stage, resolves into the resilience of her multifaceted and ineffable mind.

Augusta Webster's recognition of Medea's potential as a bridge between ancient myth and Victorian reality is already evident in her 1868 translation of Euripides' *Medea,* which earned admiring commentary from reviewers who held her translation as equal if not superior to those of respected male scholars. The *Contemporary Review* commented that Webster has "enabled English readers to connect [the Greek] with the context and with the character and drift of the speaker. . . . In faithfulness and accurate interpretation she is second to none, and this in itself is saying a great deal for a lady-translator."[74] The *Westminster Review* was even more enthusiastic, seeing Webster's translation as a technically astute composite of scholarship and accessibility that spoke on behalf of women's increasing autonomy: "She has combined, what is the despair of the translator, accuracy with freedom. . . . We really do not know where to find another translation in which the spirit is rendered with such fidelity and beauty. And to us in these days, when the whole question of woman's position is being discussed, this passage [from the chorus, predicting women's increasing renown and freedom from male tyranny] has peculiar significance. We can only echo the wish so well rendered in Mrs. Webster's translation, and hope for a solution by the means expressed in the last lines."[75] The review shows Medea's potential in the hands of a woman translator to become a voice for the nascent feminist movement.[76] For the *Westminster* reviewer, Webster's translation of this passage appropriated a play that rightfully belonged in women's hands. Reading Webster's translation of the play's final chorus—in which "the gods work to many undreamed of ends" as a promise for the fulfillment of women's triumph over oppressive social forces, the reviewer concludes, "This must be the consolation for those who faint and despair of any better order of things than the present—a consolation which has supported so many noble spirits in all ages. Euripides's own fate, however, points a sad moral. He was misappreciated in his own day, and is still misunderstood in ours. Mrs. Webster has it in her power to do away with some at least of this injustice." The mention here of Euripides' fate alludes to the general disapproval of Euripidean drama throughout the first part of the nineteenth century but as the reviewer here suggests, Euripides' liminality may be precisely what makes him an appropriate representative for other marginalized subjectivities. Such critical reception of Webster's translation reinforced her conviction that intellectual labor, though often isolated from popular culture in academic fortresses, could—and must—have a direct impact on social reality.[77]

"Medea in Athens" might be counted as another step in Webster's attempt to make the classics relevant for the rising feminist movement of her time. A suffragist, journalist, translator, novelist, poet, and literary critic who built her career in academic and publishing fields dominated by men, Webster approached her second treatment of Medea with a poetic sensibility that resisted the "facile warm-heartedness" with which women poets were conventionally associated.[78] This resistance can be seen in Webster's preference for the dramatic monologue, which allowed her to access her speaker's interiority while maintaining the "critical awareness" that Robert Langbaum identifies as an essential element of the form. "[W]e understand the speaker of the dramatic monologue by sympathizing with him, and yet by remaining aware of the moral judgment we have suspended for the sake of understanding," writes Langbaum. "[S]ympathy frees us for the widest possible range of experience, while the critical reservation keeps us aware of how far we are departing."[79] The balance between imaginative projection and critical awareness was Webster's creative ideal, which she explicitly stated in an article she wrote for the *Examiner* called "Poets and Personal Pronouns," protesting the presumptive identification of poet and poetic subject. "We look to the poet for feelings, thoughts, actions if need be, represented in a way which shall affect us as the manifest expression of what our very selves must have felt and thought and done if we had been those he puts before us and in their cases," Webster asserted.[80] But this identification of reader and subject that the poet facilitates must be achieved, Webster continued, through the conscious distancing of the poet from his poetic subject: "[T]he rule of the poet's expression seems to be that it is not the revealing of him but of themselves to others" (*Housewife,* 155). For Webster, poetry was an instrument that both reveals the possibility of multiple subjectivities and negotiates the distance between a seemingly static self and the furthest reaches of experience.

In "Medea in Athens," this dual self operates on two levels: between a Medea of the past and the Medea speaking in the present, and between the poet and her subject. To understand the interaction between these two levels of duality, it is important to establish the poem's several departures from traditional versions of the Medea myth that specifically relate the Greek story to women's struggles for both social and psychological independence in Webster's own time. The monologue is set some years after Medea has left Corinth and relates her reflections after learning of Jason's death, an event that suggests at the outset the poem's interest in the issue of women's autonomy and in Medea's "afterlife" as myth. Whereas previous versions of the myth appendage Medea's actions to Jason's—she either assists him in his tasks or responds to his betrayal—Webster's poem focuses solely on Medea and her curiously ambivalent reaction to the sudden news of a death that she had foretold in Euripides' play:

> Dead is he? Yes, our stranger guest
> said dead . . .
> as if the tale ran that a while ago
> there died a man I talked with a chance hour
> when he by chance was near me. If I spoke
> "Good news for us but ill news for the dead
> when the gods sweep a villain down to them,"
> 'twas the prompt trick of words, like a pat phrase
> from some one other's song, found on the lips
> and used because 'tis there: for through all day
> the news seemed neither good nor ill to me.[81]

The speaker's sense of detachment from herself, a trope Webster often uses in her monologues, shows the two levels of duality in the poem. On one level, these lines are spoken by a woman who seems to have dissociated herself from distant events and must struggle to recall emotions long laid to rest. Words rejoicing over Jason's death are strange for Medea because the roles of tragic murderer, witch, and infanticide are so far removed from her present role as Aegeus's "envied wife." On another level, however, the speaker's hesitation in identifying herself with her past reflects the Victorian poet's struggle to understand Medea's relevance for her own time. Here, the dramatic monologue serves its unique function of putting the poet (and the reader) on the threshold of a position to which he "is not ready to commit himself intellectually" (Langbaum, 105). That is, at this early point, the poem anticipates the relevance of the Medea myth for the new, unheard story that is about to unfold, but the exact significance of past literature to present is still unclear. Webster's Medea, these first lines indicate, is not a woman we have previously encountered, yet her identity is inextricably tied to the mythic events with which we are familiar. An understanding of the new Medea of the present must depend on a comprehension of her relation to the past. The poem's consciousness that it is borrowing "from some one other's song" indicates this simultaneous sense of estrangement and attachment on the level of language. The implied connection between Euripides' "song" and Webster's poem establishes central questions for the rest of the work: What does Euripides' tragedy have to do with the work of a Victorian poet? What is the relation between this mythic Greek woman and the female subjectivity of this poem? In the cases of both speaker and poet, Jason's death initiates a search for unity in the recovery of the past: for the speaker, this constitutes a search for cohesion between the woman she was and the woman she is. For the poet, this is an interrogation into Medea's significance for literary and—implicitly for Webster—social history.

The Medea that first emerges from these searches is a powerful one that the speaker retrieves, significantly, by imagining Jason's dying thoughts:

> What god befooled my wits
> to dream my fancy for [Glauce's] yellow curls
> and milk-white softness subtle policy?
> Wealth and a royal bride: but what beyond?
> Medea, with her skills, her presciences,
> man's wisdom, woman's craft, her rage of love
> that gave her to serve me strength next divine,
> Medea would have made me what I would;
> Glauce but what she could.
>
> (4–5)

This appropriation of Jason's subjectivity seems, at first, a self-serving act of wish fulfillment: Medea dreams that in his dying moments, Jason regrets his treacherous second marriage, as he harbors an enduring love for his first wife. Christine Sutphin has read Medea's thoughts of Jason as an active and open expression of desire that challenges Victorian assumptions of women's sexual passivity.[82] But the emotional detachment from Jason with which the monologue begins does not justify this longing.

> Does [Jason's death] seem either good or ill to me?
> No; but mere strange.
> And this most strange of all,
> That I care nothing.
>
> (2)

Rather than becoming an object of desire, Jason serves as a conduit through which Medea recaptures the wisdom, passion, and energy of a past self that she no longer needs in her comfortable, domestic position. The impetus for her nostalgia is indicated by her disenchantment with her present condition, which, while peaceful, has begun to weary her "with all its useless talk / and useless smiles and idiots' prying eyes / that impotently peer into one's life" (2). The boredom and lassitude with which Medea views her present life indicates that she has engaged in a marriage of convenience that Webster perceived as all too common in her own age. As Webster describes, couples who marry for convenience "live together, not because they feel themselves companions by inclination and fitness, but because relationship or some other circumstance has thrown them together and kept them together, and they recognise the propriety of the arrangement" (*Housewife,* 202). Trapped in a dispassionate marriage of circumstance yet compelled to "go proud, / And treasure [Aegeus] for noblest of the world" (*Portraits,* 12), Medea has been forced to assume a mask of tranquil propriety at odds with her passionate nature. Her mounting desire to recapture Jason's significance to her life is also a yearning to recover the passionate being that she has abandoned with the assumption of domestic duties. The speaker's achievement of a momentary sense of unity with her past is reflected in the structure of the poem. In the midst of Medea's self-empowering memories, the poet makes reference to two lines from Euripides' tragedy—the lines in which Medea predicts her own escape to Athens and Jason's death: "For thee, as is most fit, thou, an ill man / Shalt die an ill death, thy head battered in / By the ruins of thine Argo."[83] Quoted in footnotes in Greek, these lines suggest, on a formal level, the monologue's unity with its literary ancestor. The Greek Medea's prophecy for the future and the Victorian one's reflection on the Greek past merge temporarily in a unitary vision of Medea's victory over Jason's oppression and over the emotional ties that bind her to him.

The speaker's sense of release from a traitorous husband and the conflicted feelings attendant upon it reflect Webster's ambiguous attitude toward women's position in England at the time of the poem's composition. Webster was writing at a moment of significant progress in women's rights, particularly in the realm of education. In 1863, Cambridge University made a modified version of its local examinations open to girls for the first time. These were qualifying exams for entry into the university, and although women were not allowed to attend university in 1863 no matter how well they performed, the exams helped to establish a standard toward which women could strive in their secondary schooling. In 1868, London University opened an unmodified version of its local exams to girls, prompting Webster to write the following celebratory piece in the *Examiner*: "[T]his change will bring another, even greater: a girl's time will be considered to have some value. . . . [T]hose who have noted the aimlessness and drifting and fussy futility of the days of most women in the classes where women have their maintenance provided for them and are understood never to be too busy over one thing to do another, as most of us must have noted, can easily see that this higher appreciation by others and by herself of the value of her time would in itself be an education to a girl" (*Housewife*, 96). This comment evidences Webster's disdain—shared by Florence Nightingale and others of her time—for the conventional idleness of the middle-class woman who was required to do nothing either to support herself or to exercise her mind. In 1869, when Girton College opened to women, Webster welcomed the new opportunities it created for women, but she also recognized the negative effects of such a development. She stated that "education has by no means yet come within the reach of the majority of women, and is most of all out of the reach of gentlewomen likely to be left penniless at their parents' deaths" (*Housewife*, 242). Those women excluded by family wealth from board schools (government-subsidized schooling for the poorer classes) had to learn to support themselves by becoming governesses. But Webster continued by observing that "the educational movement has succeeded in greatly raising the ideas of employers as to the qualifications indispensable for a governess and the proofs of fitness to be demanded of her" (*Housewife*, 242–43). The large population of middle-class women who were not privileged enough to attend university and for whom the possibility of employment had decreased would have to turn, with even greater avidity than in the past, to precisely the marriages of convenience of which Webster disapproved. These comments from her *Examiner* articles, written only a few years after the publication of *Portraits*, evidence Webster's insight into the implications of social improvements for women—on the one hand, women were certainly gaining valuable opportunities for education and autonomy; on the other, these same opportunities for the lucky few were driving the vast majority of women into a more desperate reliance on men.

This dual sense of freedom and constraint is expressed in "Medea in Athens" by the brief and illusory nature of Medea's victory over Jason. At the conclusion of her reflections, Medea's triumphant vision of revenge upon Jason resolves itself into an admission of her inescapable reliance on him as a basis for her own sense of cohesion:

> . . . Jason, Jason,
> come back to earth; live, live for my revenge.
> But lo the man is dead: I am forgotten.
> Forgotten; something goes from life in that–
> as if oneself had died, when the half self
> of one's true living time has slipped away
> from reach of memories, has ceased to know
> that such a woman is.
> . . . .
> I live what thou has made me.
> (8–9)

The crisis that the speaker reaches in these lines reflects the split subjectivity that Susan Brown identifies in Victorian women who long "to attain a measure of autonomy" even while they realize the external constraints that prohibit such freedom.[84] At the time of Webster's poem, such constraints included the fact that women could not earn university degrees and for the most part would continue (after a brief intellectual digression) on the path toward marriage or would seek positions as governesses or teachers. Medea's sudden desire for the man whom she had triumphantly left behind recognizes the illusory nature of women's autonomy. With Jason's death departs whatever sense of momentary triumph or hope for freedom that Medea had harbored; without this memory and hope, she must resign herself to the dull confines of domestic life. Driven not by love but by the desire to sustain her passionate spirit and hope, Medea's abrupt longing for Jason to live admits the irony of women's freedom: an event (that is, Jason's death) that had, for a Medea of the past, seemed the culmination of her triumphant freedom only emphasizes the elusiveness of such an ideal. Webster's monologue seems to suggest that women's visions of themselves have been so long framed by the actions and thoughts of men that they cannot achieve the very independence for which they seem to long. The life that Medea finds with Aegeus is a poor substitute for the passion and hopefulness of a younger Medea. In this context, Medea's last line, "I have forgotten thee," seems less a casting aside of her dependence on Jason than a farewell to the fantasies of her past self and a resignation to a half-life as a "happy wife."

 Webster's treatment of Medea as a woman fragmented by self-defeating desires recalls Adelaide Ristori's performance of the role, which was still in the actress's repertoire when "Medea in Athens" was published.[85] Despite the discrepancy in their motivations, the interpretive approaches of poet and actress are not far distant from one another. Just as Ristori believed that emotional identification with her characters compromised her artistry, so too did Webster's attempt to distance herself from female sentimentality cause her "to speak, not passionately and personally from the heart, but, detachedly, from the feelings and thoughts of others" (Leighton, 173). Both approaches result in a fragmented persona whose conflicting emotions and actions challenge the ideal of unity through which character was conventionally understood and evaluated by Victorian audiences. However, their distinct genres create very different effects through this fragmentation. Ristori's enactment presented visually striking images that emphasized Medea's social aberrance and thus enhanced her spectacular appeal. Webster's approach lacks such visual stimuli and, rather than reifying conflicting elements of Medea's character, traces her fragmentation to its external cause: a man who—through seduction, exploitation, and desertion—forces her to despise her own actions and being.

> Man, man,
> wilt thou accuse my guilt?
> Whose is my guilt?
> Mine or thine, Jason?
> Oh, soul of my crimes,
> how shall I pardon thee for what I am?"
> (11)

Medea's conflicted subjectivity is a result of her dependence on Jason; as the first object of her desire, he marks the boundary between potential and reality without which her sense of purpose and solidity dissolves. But as Webster emphasizes throughout the poem, the ineffability of Medea's fragmented persona constitutes her strength as a survivor, such that she is able to shed her past and conform to a new identity. "Shadows of me went misty through his sight," reflects Webster's speaker as she fantasizes herself haunting Jason's last thoughts and teasing him with the unfathomable nature of her identity. It is also, perhaps, the poet's intent that Medea continues to haunt later generations—not through the sensationalism of her emotional transports or through the unity of her character but through the possibilities of a fragmented persona that resists categorization.

Amy Levy's fragmentary drama similarly emphasizes Medea's resistance to categorization and the powerful potential of her fragmentarity. For Levy, however, the basis for this exploration of fragmentarity lies not merely in feminist but in racial motives. As previous criticism has made clear, Levy's work was underscored by her struggle with her Jewish identity, which complicated her attempt to fit into the male world of literature and scholarship. Her status as the first Jewish student to be admitted into Newnham College, Cambridge (in 1879), placed Levy at the forefront not only of women's rise into higher education but also of the Anglo-Jewish community's attempts to gain social respect. Her focus on classics, which she had studied through secondary school, and the publication of her first collection of poems in 1881 emphasized her precocity, while her title poem, "Xantippe," a dramatic monologue told from the point of view of Socrates' wife, established her feminist interests. "Were we not set apart," wonders her Xantippe,

> I and my high thoughts, and my golden dreams,
> My soul which yearned for knowledge.
>
> . . . .
>
> I grew
> To learn my woman-mind had gone astray,
> And I was sinning in those very thoughts—
> For maidens, mark, such are not woman's thoughts.[86]

Here, Xantippe's consciousness of being a woman is intimately linked with the theme of social ostracism, which preoccupied Levy throughout her life and, as Linda Hunt Beckman surmises, forced her to leave Newnham before taking her Tripos exams. Levy's early consciousness of being an outsider transpired, as her writing career developed, into a consciousness of her unique liminal perspective. As Cynthia Scheinberg has pointed out, Levy's "particular position as an Anglo-Jewish outsider who, through education and literary associations, became an insider in late-Victorian literary society" allowed her to critique those authorities such as Matthew Arnold who claimed a unitary perspective for all educated people.[87] For Levy, Scheinberg continues, "there is no common realm of experience to which we can all make recourse. . . . On the contrary, she works to valorize multiple or diverse subject positions" (180).

 For Levy, the fragmentarity of Medea's character becomes an expression both of the multiple subjectivities that an individual can occupy and of that individual's ability to manipulate these subjectivities to transform her liminality into a position of authority. The opening of the play finds Medea intensely self-conscious about her outsider status in Corinth and her desire to fit into Greek society. "Alas, alas, this people loves me not!" Medea laments in her opening monologue.

> . . . I am an alien here,
> That well can speak the language of their lips,
> The language of their souls may never learn.
> And in their hands, I, that did know myself
> Ere now, a creature in whose veins ran blood
> Redder, more rapid, than flows round most hearts,
> Do seem a creature reft of life and soul.[88]

Medea's social alienation has produced a sense of self-estrangement and a hyperconsciousness of racial difference. Her sense of racial difference is objectified when she is described by two Greek onlookers—Nikias and Aegeus, who serve as the chorus and comment on the actions of the play. "I like not your swart skins and purple hair; / Your black, fierce eyes where the brows meet across," remarks Nikias, looking upon Medea. As Linda Beckman and others have noted, this comment is overtly racist and reflects Levy's lifelong consciousness of the plain, dark looks that set her apart from the ideals of beauty in both England and Europe, where she wrote her Medea.[89]

But the objectifying effect of Nikias's gaze is counterbalanced by two important factors in the drama. The first is that Nikias's appeal to the audience's sensual apprehension is negated by the literary—rather than visual—medium of Levy's closet drama: the audience (reader) is never given a view of Medea. Medea's foreign appearance, therefore, and the monstrosity that Nikias implies remains confined to his own perception. The foreignness emphasized by Ristori's startling appearance is mentioned here only to be negated by the drama's negation of visuality. Indeed, without visual support for his commentary, it is Nikias's racist assessment rather than Medea's difference that is emphasized. This reverse objectification is confirmed by Nikias's awareness of Medea's countergaze: "[W]hen yonder Colchian / Fixes me with her strange and sudden gaze, / Each hair upon my body stands erect!" (38). The reversal of the objectifying gaze is further exemplified when Medea replies to Jason's admission of his engagement to Glauce,

> Behold me now, your work, a thing of fear–
> From natural human fellowship cut off,
> And yet a woman—sick and sore with pain;
> Hungry for love and music of men's praise,
> But walled about as with a mighty wall,
> Far from men's reach and sight, alone, alone.
>
> (43)

This passage marks an important moment of transition in Levy's Medea. On the one hand, she again laments her weakness and victimization as an exile. Her monstrosity—having become a "thing of fear"—is a result of what she has suffered at the hands of Jason and his unwelcoming country. On the other hand, her lament is an accusation against Jason and his countrymen. As Beckman and others have noted, Levy used Medea's persona not only to despair over her social ostracism but also to express her anger at such rejection. As Beckman observed of Levy's revisions to the play between 1882 and 1884, "Each time Levy reworked (or reread) the poem, she would have experienced a catharsis that came from speaking behind the mask of a female character, a stranger in a foreign land, whose rage has become archetypal in the literary tradition of the West."[90] The concept of using Medea as a mask to transform vulnerability into powerful anger is evident in the speaker's conclusion that she is "far from men's reach and sight," which carries a double sense of despair and triumph: while the Greeks and Jason have failed to see beyond the outward appearance of her foreignness to her humanity, their blindness offers Medea a strategy for self-defense. In the rest of the play, she turns the Greeks' and Jason's blindness to her true character and vindictive potential into a weapon against them.

The second part of Levy's play displays a very different Medea than the meek, despairing woman of the first scene. Revolting against Jason's rejection of her, Medea claims the power and ferocity that she has previously suppressed in her desire for social acceptance. Jason's mistreatment of her and her liminality compel a process of self-realization.

> Ah, Jason, pause.
> You never knew Medea. You forget,
> Because so long she bends the knee to you,

She was not born to serfdom.
    I have knelt
Too long before you. I have stood too long
Suppliant before this people. You forget
A redder stream flows in my Colchian veins
Than the slow flood which courses round your hearts,
O cold Corinthians, with whom I have long dwelt
And never ere this day have known myself,
Nor have ye known me.

(48)

Here, Medea's shift in character is not so much a transformation as self-discovery. Like Webster's Medea, Levy's heroine admits to being molded by circumstances and by her treatment by Jason. But for Levy's Medea, the identity that she ultimately claims as her own is one that has lain dormant and has at last found a proper means of expression in the circumstances of strife in which she has found herself. The power that Medea discovers in herself is thus based in rebellion and difference.

Medea's use of her alien status and the Greeks' ignorance of her motives as weapons against them is shown in the second act of the two-act play, which is dominated by Nikias's and Aegeus's commentary on Medea's murders of King Creon, Glauce, and her own children. These murders are not shown in the play, and Medea is absent throughout most of this final act. The elimination of the murder scene reduces the sensational potential of the play, and its absence places doubt on Nikias's and Aegeus's condemnations of her as a serpent, sorceress, and tigress—fierce images that dissipate given the reader's foreknowledge of how little these commentators know Medea. "O evil deed! O essence of all evil / Stealing the shape of woman!" cries Aegeus upon hearing of Medea's murder of her children; he then concludes, "This woman was dark and evil to her soul; / Black to her fiend-heart's root; a festering plague / In our fair city's midst" (55). These condemnatory judgments only emphasize Medea's palpable absence, bringing into relief her claim in the first act that she is beyond the reaches of the Greeks' understanding. The mistaken construction of Medea by Nikias and Aegeus as a heartless monster devoid of compassion is confirmed when Medea appears at the play's conclusion:

Here let me rest; beyond men's eyes, beyond
The city's hissing hate. . . .

I'm weary, weary; once I dream'd a dream
Of one that strove and wept and yearned for love
In a fair city. She was blind indeed.
They say the woman had a fiend at heart . . .
This is the end:
I have dash'd my heart against a rock; the blood
Is drain'd and flows no more; and all my breast
Is emptied of its tears.
    Thus I go forth
Into the deep, dense heart of night—alone.
(57)

It is tempting to read this concluding passage as one of defeat, in which Medea is not rescued by a golden chariot but is rather bereft and defeated by her actions. However, the context of vision and blindness that these final lines evoke and that have surrounded Medea since her first appearance on the Greek stage (as well as in the Victorian theater) suggest another reading. Medea may lament her loneliness and the futility of her efforts at conformity, but at the play's end, she has also become invisible to the eyes of the condemning crowd that view her as a monstrosity. Vision, as Medea has shown through the realization of her own naïveté, can be reclaimed; sleep is only a temporary state, and night inevitably gives way to day. Medea goes "into the deep, dense heart of the night," but sunrise also lies in the same direction. "There's sun on the earth, / And in the shades no sun;—thus much I know; / And sunlight's good" (56), as Medea states upon exiting the walls of the city. Levy's play is, as its title suggests, only a fragment, and the glimpses of Medea that we receive are but pieces of a larger whole. The darkness into which she disappears at the play's end holds the promise of rediscovery and revision.

Medea's multiple revisions on and off the Victorian stage demonstrate the intricately intertwined discourses of Hellenism and nineteenth-century popular culture. The view of the ancient world that this tragedy presents revealed a darker side to the "sweetness and light" with which Matthew Arnold was wont to associate Classical Greece, but it also highlighted and further destabilized fraught issues within Victorian society. In particular, the passionate, outspoken, resilient woman embodied in Medea and featured in so much Greek tragedy and myth provided a voice that both male and female writers could appropriate to comment on and influence the shifting status of women in the mid and late nineteenth centuries.

Fragments of Genius

Charlotte Brontë and the Discourse of Popular Greek

CHAPTER TWO

Charlotte Brontë did not know Greek. Although her lifetime (1816–55) witnessed one of the steepest surges of interest in the Hellenic world both in Britain and on the European continent, her gender excluded her from the formal classical training that middle-class boys could take for granted. Thus, while her brother Branwell could read Greek and Latin literature in their original languages and often quoted from classical works in his writing, Charlotte had to rely on translations.[1] Fortunately, the profusion of popular interest in Greece throughout the nineteenth century ensured her access both to independently published translations and to adaptations for popular journals, which were regularly read in the Brontë household. *Blackwood's Edinburgh Magazine,* the children's favorite, frequently contained translations from and glosses of Greek texts directed explicitly toward the lay reader as well as criticism and reviews of the latest scholarly debates.[2] In addition, the Reverend Patrick Brontë's classical texts from his Cambridge days were readily available to all of his children, as were books from circulating libraries in Haworth and Keighley.[3] With such resources at hand, the Brontë children were hardly isolated from the cultural and intellectual currents of their age—the scenario popularized by Brontë mythology. More anxious than her sisters to achieve a sophisticated intellectual repertoire, Charlotte in particular labored to acquire a patchwork knowledge of ancient history, literature, and mythology. Her learning and integration of this material into her works offer a view of the transmission and transformation of Victorian Hellenism from an exclusive, male discourse to a feature of popular culture.[4]

Essays from Charlotte's juvenilia and from her last completed novel index the popular treatment of two important discussions about the significance of ancient Greece to modernity in the first half of the nineteenth century; these discussions influenced the shape of popular Greek in general and Charlotte's personal aesthetics in particular. The first discussion revolved around the "Homeric Question," introduced by F. A. Wolf's *Prolegomena ad Homerum* (1795), which heretically questioned the genesis and unity of the *Iliad* and the *Odyssey*. Wolf's two central theories were, first, that these two great epics were composed of separate poems sung by rhapsodists and that there was never a single historic figure named Homer, and second, that these poems were not compiled and written down until the sixth century BC, centuries after their conception, by which time they had altered considerably from their original forms. Wolf's theories were crucial in the development of *Altertumswissen-schaften*, or the scientific study of antiquity in all its aspects—artistic, social, and religious as well as literary and linguistic—and laid the foundations for such fields as archaeology and anthropology in the late nineteenth century. However, in early Victorian England, the implications of Wolf's theories caused considerable anxiety. In the words of an 1850 essay in the *Quarterly Review*,[5] the doubts raised by Wolf shook "everything that had been for thousands of years accepted as the origin, construction, and authority of the literary monument which approached nearest in claim of antiquity to the Hebrew Scriptures, and had exerted an influence only inferior to theirs on the religious belief of nations, besides directing and governing, far more than any other writings whatever, the general sentiment and taste of the cultivated world."[6] To doubt Homer's singular genius was to topple the religious, political, and social ideals constructed upon it by that portion of the British population responsible for setting the course of the nation.

The second discussion, with somewhat less apocalyptic consequences if not equal investment on the part of its participants, involved the relationship of Greek tragedy to the developing nineteenth-century genre of realist fiction. From the century's outset, popular journals extolled Aeschylus, Sophocles, and Euripides for their extraordinary insight into the human psyche. However, as Hellenism expanded to include studies of social context as well as aesthetic artifacts, disengaging such insights from the cumbersome artifice of the ancient stage became increasingly difficult.

 Elements such as masks and the chorus, which became essential to an understanding of Greek drama, violated the ideal of transparency that was constitutive of Victorian realism. Given its formal constraints, to what extent should Greek tragedy serve as a model for Victorian literature? Competing perspectives on this question and on the Homeric controversy revealed an increasing uncertainty among scholars and the educated classes about Hellenism's modern legacy even as it helped launch the ancient world into the arena of popular discourse. For while the destabilization of Greece's exemplarity evoked anxiety in such defenders of traditional humanistic Hellenism as Matthew Arnold and William Gladstone, it also opened up interpretive entryways for individuals formerly marginalized from classical discourse.

One way in which journals such as *Blackwood's* precipitated the extension of classical discourse into a popular arena was by cultivating what I will call a discourse of fragmentation. This discourse depended on several key elements. First, as perhaps the most widely discussed classical topic in popular journals, the Homeric Question continually raised doubts about the unity of the most revered Greek works. Even articles that passionately defended the cohesiveness of Homer's epics nevertheless felt compelled to rehearse the opposing argument in such a way that lay readers' introduction to Greek antiquity was increasingly framed by anxiety over its value. Noticing the coincidence of Greece's popularization and destabilization, the *Quarterly Review* revealingly stated in 1840 that by virtue of the Homeric Question, those "who had never heard of Troy before, heard of it now; it whitened all library tables and darkened all schoolmasters' minds; it fluttered in pamphlets, and floundered in quartos, till Troy-weight was as familiar to collectors of books as to workers in gold."[7] The Homeric Question, while causing dissension in scholarly ranks, nevertheless had a democratizing effect on a general Victorian readership for whom interest in the *Iliad* and *Odyssey* became inseparable from debates about their suspect integrity.

The discourse of fragmentation that characterized Hellenism's treatment in popular journals also depended on the forms in which these journals presented classical material—namely, in selected excerpts distributed among multiple articles and volumes. *Blackwood's* series on the *Iliad,* for instance, spanned multiple volumes, as did "The Age of Homer" in *Macmillan's* and "Pastoral Greek Poems" in *Fraser's Magazine.* Such excerpting and serialization dramatized the fragmentary nature of a remnant antique corpus while placing the common reader in the role of an archaeologist-cum-artist whose imagination was crucial for the perfection of an incomplete body of work. In this sense, the Victorian journal's discourse of fragmentation promotes the refractional subjectivity of a Romantic aesthetic. In her study of the Romantic fragment poem, Marjorie Levinson has noted that such a work "contains a latent imagination of a reader, one who is capable of a particular response to the work's irresolution. . . . The work's irresolution is experienced as against [an] ideal integrity and extensiveness that it presumably could, would, or should have realized. The poem's irresolution is thus discovered by the reader as a determinate or shaped absence."[8] The snippets of Greek literature presented in popular journals—both in translation and in the original—constitute, like the Romantic fragment poem, an "inexhaustible semiotic event" (Levinson, 33) that appealed to the lay audience by suggesting the creative potential of the reader's own imagination. Unlike the vision of perfect Grecian unity projected by the nostalgia of Newman and Arnold, popular journals proffered an anti-Aristotelian ideal that recognized the fragment form as embodying the free play of the imagination, bound to the formal constraints of neither genre nor time.[9]

Charlotte's essay on Charles Hubert Millevoye's poem "The Fall of Leaves" and her composition "Athènes sauvée par la poësie," both written for her teacher, M. Constantin Heger, during her last months studying abroad in Belgium, exemplify the potential for imaginative free play extended by popular Greek's discourse of fragmentation. The latter essay in particular presents an astonishing mishmash of fragments from ancient Greek history, epic, and tragedy that not only draws from ancient Greek texts but also patterns itself both formally and philosophically on the fragmentary aesthetic of articles from popular journals, primarily *Blackwood's* but also others such as the *Quarterly Review*, *Fraser's*, and the *London Magazine*.[10] Written when Charlotte first began to envision herself as an author, both essays actively engage the Homeric Question and popular debates about Greek tragedy to launch a protest against Heger's rigid Aristotelian principles, which Charlotte felt were impeding her artistic growth. Moreover, in "Athènes," Charlotte ultimately evolved a theory of female interiority that would later become a trademark of her mature work. Her adaptation of the ideas generated by the Homeric Question and by discussions of Greek tragedy exemplifies the heretical possibilities inherent in these issues. In addressing the relationship between Charlotte's essays and popular Greek, I wish to challenge the view that her Belgian writing is valuable primarily because it is symptomatic of emotional trauma and that it operated solely within the closed circuit of her relationship with Heger. Instead, I suggest that the discussion between Charlotte and her teacher, carried out in the dialogue between her essay and his comments on it, acts out at a level of personal conflict broader cultural debates about Greece's modern legacy—a legacy whose fundamental cohesion and longevity are dependent on the tension between its opposing parts. My concluding examination of *Villette* demonstrates the continuing influence of Greek literature and its embodiment of a fragmentary aesthetic on Charlotte's work. Although by the early 1850s, her conflicted feelings for Heger had been eclipsed by grief over the loss of her sisters, she nevertheless returned to ideas first worked out through interaction with Greek sources in her Belgian *devoirs*. More specifically, the Odyssean references in the novel reach into the ancient past to articulate feelings that Charlotte was no longer able to address directly. The interlaced epic strands within the novel testify both to the lasting impact of Greek narratives in Charlotte's work and to the malleability of such narratives in the Victorian popular imagination.

The Homeric Question and "The Fall of Leaves"

Charlotte and her sister Emily set sail for Brussels, Belgium, in February 1842 with the intention of acquiring the continental education they felt was necessary to succeed in establishing their own school. Their experience at the Pensionnat Heger has been extensively documented both by Charlotte and by her biographers and requires only a brief summary of the most salient points. In her *Life of Charlotte Brontë* (1857), Elizabeth Gaskell was the first to detail the Brontës' relationship with their charismatic teacher, M. Constantin Heger, a classicist by training who set out to teach the Brontë sisters not only a fluid knowledge of French but also a system of literary analysis and techniques of composition in "sympathy with the intellectual, the refined, the polished, or the noble" styles of the best French Romantic writers.[11] More recently, Sue Lonoff, in an edited edition of the Brontës' Belgian essays, has emphasized the tremendous importance of Heger's instruction on Charlotte's maturation as a writer:

> For the first time, Charlotte was writing in a genre that forced her to be clear about abstractions. Heger's assignments made her think like a critic about an author's style, the effect of a

> passage, and the motives and perspective that prompted it. She also had to imitate style and substance, to write texts that echoed what she studied. In the juvenilia, she had attempted parodies and modeled her romances after Byron's. But her approach had not been reflective; character and action were paramount. For her *devoirs,* she could still compose episodes and portraits, but she also had to think about concepts. . . . Heger helped her define what she was doing. He guided and legitimated her impulse.[12]

According to all accounts, including her own, Charlotte worked diligently and happily under Heger's instruction during her first year abroad, despite misgivings about his method

Charlotte's essay on Millevoye's elegy "La chute des feuilles" ("The Fall of Leaves"), written two months after her return to Belgium, evidences her mounting skepticism toward Heger's aesthetic philosophy as well as the influence of popular Greek on her thoughts. Written with the express purpose of exploring the poem's effect, the essay digresses into a muted protest of Heger's analytical methods. "The mechanic, seeing an ingenious device, closely examines all its parts; he tries to delve into the principles that regulated its construction," she begins provocatively. "We too, when we behold a perfect work of the mind, can we not conduct the same examination and, in dissecting the details, attempt to discover the secret of their union? It is through study that the mechanic learns how to invent, and by employing similar means, can we not achieve a similar end? Yet, since this latter result is not quite certain, let us not flatter ourselves too much that we succeed, for fear of finding ourselves in the position of that German student who believed he was learning to create, in learning to dissect."[14] M. Heger had early on impressed his Aristotelian ideals of formal unity upon his students by asking them to pick apart pieces of literature and analyze them for style and synthesis.[15] Although the essay is cast as Charlotte's preparing to perform a similar analysis of Millevoye's poem, the narrator quickly comes to question the relevance of such an operation to a creative process that Charlotte regarded as mystical. Could the fusion of internal forces that constitutes the effect of a masterpiece differ essentially from the elements of formal unity represented by a work's structural components? More alarmingly, could the rational deconstruction of formal unity subvert the emotive act of artistic creation and undermine the power of the work?

 Charlotte's doubts about formal analysis and its relationship to artistic unity drew directly from discussions about the Homeric Question, which began to surface in British journals at the start of the century and were multiplying in the late 1830s and early 1840s as she was beginning to explore her creative talents, often modeling her style and ideas upon those of her favorite periodicals. Foremost among these was *Blackwood's Edinburgh Magazine,* which the Brontës' biographer Juliet Barker claims "formed the tastes and fed the interests of the Brontës for many years" (*Brontës,* 149). Founded in 1817 by William Blackwood to offset the Whig monopoly on Edinburgh's periodical press, *Blackwood's* (or "Maga," as the journal was familiarly called) was largely responsible for transforming "the miscellaneous periodical [into] a medium of critical writing."[16] Providing a forum for original criticism, *Blackwood's* attracted numerous prominent writers throughout the nineteenth century and into the next, including Walter Scott, Samuel Taylor Coleridge, Edward Bulwer-Lytton, and George Eliot, as well as helped many writers build their reputations. While certainly situating itself solidly in the echelons of "intellectual journalism" with its contributions to learned debates and literary affairs, *Blackwood's* also regularly included articles on issues of public concern (such as the Corn Laws and Free Trade) and stories with provocative titles such as "Buried Alive" and "The Murderers's [*sic*] Last Night."[17] Epitomizing what Grevel Lindop notes is the "very close interpenetration . . . between the academic, journalistic and literary worlds in Scotland,"[18] *Blackwood's* proved the ideal instrument for conveying the high-culture world of classics to the general audience and made its broad appeal "to the reader who wished not only to be informed of the latest developments but also to be diverted by lively criticism, entertaining fiction and poetry."[19] While, as Robert Morrison notes, *Blackwood's* strove to balance "the desire for unity" stemming from its Tory convictions with "the demand for variety" imposed by a broad readership, the resulting "inconsistencies" in treatment of diverse topics offered readers such as the Brontës a potpourri of opinions from which to construct their own ideas.[20] With sale numbers in the United Kingdom peaking at 100,837 in 1862,[21] the influence of *Blackwood's* extended far beyond Scottish borders, throughout England and into the United States, establishing a model for the modern literary periodical.

One of the most influential of *Blackwood's* contributors upon the Brontës was Thomas De Quincey, an erstwhile friend of the Lake poets and a frequent contributor on classical issues to *Blackwood's,* for which John Wilson, the journal's editor, had initially solicited his contribution. Although none of the Brontë children ever met De Quincey personally, they held such regard for his opinions that all sent him their work for evaluation at various times.[22] Their sense of familiarity with him was undoubtedly encouraged by his *Blackwood's* articles, which, in keeping with De Quincey's ambivalent attitude toward scholarship, were written with consideration for the non-Greek reader yet maintained an ideological sophistication that honored the intelligence of his lay audience.[23] The influence of De Quincey's Greek articles on Charlotte's early thoughts is evidenced by their incorporation into her devoirs. For example, the significance of her reference to the misguided "German student" in the above-quoted passage from her Millevoye essay becomes apparent when her full metaphor is read in dialogue with De Quincey's two-part article on "Homer and the Homeridae," published in *Blackwood's* one year before Charlotte first departed for Brussels. This article details the history of the Homeric controversy, beginning with F. A. Wolf and his German followers, whom De Quincey accused of harboring the "prevailing vices of German speculation; viz, 1st, vague, indeterminate conception; 2ndly, total want of power to methodize or combine the parts, and indeed generally a barbarian inaptitude for composition."[24] The criticism reflects the scorn of the British for the German tendency toward abstraction but also (and more significantly in its impact on Charlotte) directly pits the scholarly practice of analysis and ideologizing—epitomized by the Germans—against the creative skill of composition. If it is speculative to see De Quincey's criticism of Teutonic scholarship as the basis for Charlotte's skepticism toward the compatibility of deconstruction and composition, a later metaphor in De Quincey's article supports a more stable correspondence. Regarding the Germans' hypothesis that the *Iliad* was an oral-formulaic poem whose form and substance had continually evolved from the time of its conception, De Quincey's advice was, "Watch the fate of any intricate machine in any private family." The metaphor continued: "All the loose or detached parts of such a machine are sure to be lost. Ask for it at the end of a year, and the more elaborate was the machine, so much the more certain is the destruction which will have overtaken it. It is only when any compound whole, whether engine, poem, or tale, carries its several parts absolutely interlocked with its own substance, that it has a chance of maintaining its integrity."[25] Transposing the Greek word for skill or craft (*techne*) into a modern, industrial context of technology, De Quincey's metaphor directly addresses what Charlotte referred to in her Millevoye essay as "the master principle of Unity," but his concept of this ideal departs considerably from Heger's. Although De Quincey lent credibility to the Wolfian hypothesis that the *Iliad* was constructed of shorter, constituent poems, he argued that this aspect of its formal composition does not compromise the ultimate unity of the whole, which "would lie not in the mind conceiving, nor in the nexus of the several divisions, but in the community of the subject . . . the great crusade against Ilium" ("Homer II," 624). For De Quincey, unity is a function not of form and technique (corresponding to the Aristotelian concept of *techne*) but rather of meaning or output, which derives from utility. Like a machine, a poem acquires value from service; a technical knowledge of an engine's component parts, like a philologist's understanding of grammar and linguistics, differs essentially from an observer's emotional or physical appreciation of an engine's or poem's effect. Integrity consists in the service of form to function; indeed, insofar as a machine depends on the cooperation of diverse parts, De Quincey's metaphor seems to emphasize the superiority of composite structure. By evoking the metaphor of a machine, Charlotte's Millevoye essay creates a mosaic of disparate ideas whose juxtaposition subtly challenges both conceptually and structurally Heger's ideal of consistency.

De Quincey's article would have held particular appeal to Charlotte because his theory of unity does not merely achieve a compromise between opposing sides of the Homeric debate but does so by privileging the common reader's experience over that of the scholar, whose endless linguistic analyses and probings have, according to De Quincey, left in tatters a narrative corpus the very beauty of whose unity originally lay in the natural redistribution of its parts over time and usage. Speaking of the oral transmission of Homer's epic before its written preservation in the sixth century BC, De Quincey argued that "the integrity of that [epic] succession was guaranteed by its interwreathing itself with human pleasures, with religious ceremonies, with household and national festivals. . . . Sympathy in the audience must always have been a primary demand with the *Rhapsodoi*; and, to perfect sympathy, it is a previous condition to be perfectly understood" ("Homer I," 418). Consistent with his theory that poetry derives value from effect rather than form, De Quincey here credited the original merit of Homer's epics and their survival to their accessibility to a popular audience and to their plasticity in adapting to the changing needs of the people. It is when such works are taken out of their natural environment and dissociated from popular appreciation and sympathy that their unity is most threatened: "We moderns, from our vast superiority to the Greeks themselves in Greek metrical science, have had an extra resource laid open to us for detecting the spurious in Greek poetry; and many are the condemned passages in our modern editions of Greek books," he remarked facetiously. "[Critics have] contrived to riddle Homer through and through with desperate gashes. In fact, after being 'treated' and 'handled' by three generations of critics, Homer came forth . . . one vast wound, one huge system of confluent ulcers" ("Homer I," 421). By criticizing analytical scholarship for contributing to the disintegration of the Homeric corpus, De Quincey not only turned the tables on literary critics debating the unity of the *Iliad* and *Odyssey* but also suggested that the two works regarded by Victorians as staples of high-culture authority actually belong to a history of popular culture and in the minds and lives of a lay audience.

By using the Homeric debate to posit the redemptive force of popular reception against the destructive influence of philological analysis, De Quincey did not simply legitimate the interpretive resources of lay readers but specifically helped Charlotte Brontë to evolve a theory of creativity that would become a foundation for her literary aesthetic. Although what Charlotte's stance was on the Homeric Question (or, indeed, whether she even took a side in the debate) is unclear, her Millevoye essay draws strength from De Quincey's article to dissociate herself from Heger's academic ideals. Early in the essay, the efficacy of carefully planned composition, especially for "novices in literature . . . who want to imitate the great masters" is conceded, but the essay concludes with this startling assertion: "I believe that genius . . . has no need to seek the details, that it scarcely pauses to reflect, that it does not think about unity. . . . I believe there is no unity more perfect than that which arises from a heart filled with a single idea. It would be as impossible for the torrent, swollen with rain, driven by the tempest, to turn from its impetuous course, as for a man stirred by passion, shattered by grief, willingly to abandon his despair or his joy and speak of things alien to them" (*Belgian Essays*, 244, 246). This metaphor of genius as a great river fittingly describes Charlotte's method of composing in a trancelike state and echoes De Quincey's similar image of Homer's genius:

> Homer, the general patriarch of Occidental literature, reminds us oftentimes, and powerfully, of the river Nile. . . . [I]t is inevitable that your thoughts should wander upwards to the dark fountains of origination. . . . A great poet appearing in early ages, and a great river, bear something of the same relation to human

> civility and culture. In this view . . . the Hindoos consider a mighty fertilizing river, when bursting away from torrent rapture from its mountain cradle, and billowing onwards through two thousand miles of realms made rich by itself. . . . Hence arose the profound interest about the Nile: what cause could produce its annual swelling? Even as a phenomenon that was awful, but much more so as a creative agency. ("Homer I," 412)

Brontë critics have frequently remarked on Charlotte's obsession with the idea of genius. Certainly, this idea may have been inspired by the great writers of her own time—Byron, Wordsworth, and Coleridge, among others. But the genius of Homer—because the most controversial—was perhaps the most prominent focal point of this concept and could not have failed to interest Charlotte.[26] In her Millevoye essay, she transposed De Quincey's river metaphor from a literary-historical to an individual context to claim a place in a history of literary geniuses, the source of whose creative agency must remain, she implied, as mysterious as Homer's identity.

The concept of genius as a natural power resistant to rational analysis led both De Quincey and Charlotte to two important conclusions about the nature of literary composition. The first is that writing is not essential to composition. In pointed opposition to Heger's insistence on linguistic clarity, Charlotte asserted, "I believe that all true poetry is but the faithful imprint of something that happens or has happened in the poet's soul. . . . [Is not] language . . . but the wax in which [genius and an activating emotion] stamp their imprint?" (*Belgian Essays*, 244). Charlotte's idea that language is not essential to creation resembles a similar hypothesis about Homer's epics—that the absence of writing in fact constituted epic genius. In an 1837 translation of Johann Gottfried von Herder's essay "Schriften zur Griechischen Literature," *Blackwood's* had introduced this idea: "These poems [Homer's epics] were not composed to be *read*. They were *sung*. They were intended to be *heard*. The profession of the rhapsodists was too much opposed to the art of writing, for them to do any thing to facilitate its progress. . . . After the general introduction of writing, the minstrel craft gradually declined. Prose came into being. . . . Traditionary lore was intrusted [*sic*] to letters. The muses, who, as daughters of Mnemosyne, had hitherto preserved and promulgated the treasures of memory, were silenced. Books were the grave of the Epos."[27] Here, Herder seems to imply that writing not only marked the death of the epic but also threatened genius itself.[28] Four years later, De Quincey furthered this view when he discussed the early stages of Homer's transition from oral to written narrative: "When the text of Homer had once become frozen and settled, no man could take liberties with it at the risk of being tripped up himself on its glassy surface, and landed in a lugubrious sedentary posture, to the derision of all critics, compositors, pressmen, devils, and devillets. But whilst the text was yet piping hot, or lukewarm, or in the transitional state of cooling, every man who had a private purpose to serve might impress upon its plastic wax whatever alterations he pleased" ("Homer I," 414). By de-emphasizing the importance of writing—indeed, even pointing out its treachery—both Herder and De Quincey legitimated genius that is independent of the literary training elemental to high culture. By assuming a similar attitude toward language as the mere "wax" upon which an idea rests, Charlotte likewise established herself against Heger's high-culture principles.

The second conclusion that both De Quincey and Charlotte reached about literary composition constitutes an aesthetics of fragmentation. "To compose a great poem, an epic or a tragedy, undoubtedly, one needs a plan, erudition and reasoning," Charlotte conceded. "But to write a fugitive little poem like 'The Fall of Leaves,' does one need anything other than genius cooperating with a feeling, an affection, or a passion of some kind? If, for example, the feeling holding sway for the moment over the spirit is sorrow, could it not be that genius whets the sorrow and that sorrow purifies the genius?" (*Belgian Essays*, 244). As Sue Lonoff points out, Charlotte's assessment of Millevoye's poem was essentially misguided—the French poet actually spent a great deal of time planning and revising his work. Charlotte's appeal to great works of epic and tragedy suggests that rather than deriving her conclusions from a study of Millevoye's techniques, she was following a theory of composition similar to De Quincey's in his assessment of Homer: "But, you say, all poetry must have some connexion internally at least," De Quincey wrote in defense of his concept of the *Iliad's* unity. "True, but this circumstance is more noticeable and emphatic with regard to long narrative poems. . . . An ode, a song, a hymn, might contain a single ebullition of feeling. The connexion might lie in the very rapture and passion, without asking for any effort on the poet's part" ("Homer II," 630). It is almost impossible to overlook the similarity of Charlotte's theory to De Quincey's—a theory that directly opposes Heger's emphasis on structure and technical detail. "Genius, without study and without art, without the knowledge of what has been done, is *force* without the lever. . . . *Poet* or *not*, then, study form,"[29] Heger wrote in his final comments on Charlotte's Millevoye essay. But the argument between Charlotte and her teacher was not simply about form and content, inspiration and labor. Mediated by the Homeric Question, it also involved an argument about history—both the private history of Charlotte's convictions and the literary history she would choose to affirm.

"Athens Saved by Poetry" and the Problem of Unity

"Athènes sauvèe par la poësie," written a few months before Charlotte's final departure from Brussels, demonstrates more explicitly than any of her other works the influence of popular Greek on her maturing aesthetic principles. The essay derives from a passage in Plutarch's *Life of Lysander,* where the Spartan general is conferring with his allies about the fate of Athens after its defeat in the Peloponnesian Wars.[30] A suggestion is made to burn the city to the ground. However, after the discussion, "when the leaders were gathered at a banquet, and a certain Phocian sang the first chorus in the 'Electra' of Euripides,[31] which begins with 'O thou daughter of Agamemnon, I am come, Electra, to thy rustic court,' all were moved to compassion, and felt it to be a cruel deed to abolish and destroy a city which was so famous, and produced such poets."[32] The level of detail in Heger's instructions to Charlotte when he assigned her this essay remains unknown,[33] but the idea of poetry powerful enough to save a city must have enchanted her as an aspiring writer, while simultaneously offering her another opportunity to examine the issue of poetic effect that she had abruptly abandoned in her Millevoye essay almost a half year earlier. Meanwhile, the lack of detail devoted to the episode in Plutarch's predominantly militaristic biography left Charlotte much room for invention. Taking her cue perhaps from Plutarch's splicing of tragedy into his history, Charlotte constructed a mosaic of classical images and genres by incorporating sources unmentioned by Plutarch and substituting her own sources for those that he did mention.[34] By thus transforming a historical document into a fictive one, Charlotte demonstrated an Aristotelian preference for the "more philosophical and more elevated" nature of poetic probability (*to eikos*) over historical actuality (*to hekaston*).[35] However, her regard for the ancient Greek past as a malleable narrative space derived not from Aristotle but from her exposure to the discourse of fragmentation constitutive of her popular Greek sources, which "Athènes" ultimately appropriates for its argument against Heger's Aristotelian aesthetics.

Charlotte's reliance on popular Greek sources is apparent from her essay's opening description of Lysander's victory party, supplemented with explicit references to the *Iliad*: "Lysander himself, the cold, the crafty, the ambitious seemed to yield to the influence of the moment; he invited the chiefs of the army to a banquet in his tent; he ordered his helots to serve a rude but abundant repast, like the one that Achilles prepared for Ulysses and his companions, when he himself did the cooking with 'his inaccessible hands.' . . . Lysander carved up the meat with his dagger and distributed portions to his guests" (*Belgian Essays*, 334). This passage pieces together two disparate scenes from the *Iliad* whose integration into Charlotte's narrative states a definitive opposition against Heger on the vexed issue of narrative unity. The precise nature of Charlotte's opposition needs to be understood in the context, first, of the episodes she combined from the *Iliad* and, second, of the *Blackwood's* article from which she drew her rhetorical inspiration. The first reference in this passage is to *Iliad* 9, which finds the Greeks debating over the wisdom of pursuing a war that many of them, primarily Agamemnon, feel doomed to lose, since Achilles has withdrawn from battle over Agamemnon's stealing of Briseis. Upon the advice of a council of elders, Agamemnon resolves to return Briseis along with numerous other gifts if Achilles will fight again, and he sends Odysseus, along with Ajax and Phoenix, to persuade Achilles to accept the proposal. Achilles greets the envoys and prepares a meal for them, carving, roasting, and serving the meat for his guests,[36] before scorning Agamemnon's bribes and stubbornly refusing to fight on his behalf. Charlotte's second reference is a direct translation from George Chapman's 1611 rendering of Achilles' "*xeiras aaptous*" ("inaccessible hands") in *Iliad* 20, which finds the hero riding away in his chariot after a gruesome killing spree, enraged by Patroclus's death.[37] In this episode, Achilles is again resistant to persuasion, but this time to the pleas of Trojans: "[Achilles] was not to be persuaded [by pleas for mercy]; for not at all soft of heart or gentle of mind was the man, but exceeding fierce. . . . [T]he son of Peleus pressed on to win glory, and with gore were his invincible [inaccessible, per Chapman] hands bespattered."[38] Sue Lonoff surmises that Charlotte's possible sources for her Homeric allusions may have included the library at the Pensionnat Heger and an English bookstore in Brussels containing a copy of Chapman's translation. To these sources might also be added a series of five articles on the *Iliad* published in *Blackwood's* between April 1831 and February 1832. The articles were written by the Scottish poet and essayist John Wilson (a close friend of De Quincey's, Robert Southey's, Wordsworth's, and Coleridge's), who makes, in his article, precisely the same association of Chapman's "inaccessible hands" with the scene of Achilles' feast in book 9. Wilson's association of these scenes goes some way toward explaining why Charlotte might have chosen to fit together two seemingly contradictory images.

Prompted by the recent publication of William Sotheby's *Iliad* translation, Wilson's five articles for *Blackwood's* give a thorough summary of and commentary on the epic's most significant scenes while contrasting and evaluating selections from a wide variety of translations by Chapman, Pope, Dryden, Sotheby, and others. Directed explicitly at readers who "have no Greek," the articles aim to cultivate an appreciation for Homer, whom Wilson regarded as a singular genius. Given this stance on the Homeric Question, one of the central arguments running throughout the articles is the unity of the *Iliad*, which, Wilson argued, rests primarily on the construction of Achilles's character. "That man is not ignorant of Homer who has read, even in translation, the First Book of the Iliad. He knows the grandeur of Achilles. . . . Achilles is now out of sight—but not out of mind. Out of his wrath arises the Iliad; whether he be present or absent in the flesh, there he is in the spirit, from beginning to end."[39] Achilles, Wilson suggested, is not only the primary subject of one epic poem but literally *is* Homer. The strength of his character stands as proof of the *Iliad*'s singular genesis as well as the existence of one poet whose power rested in the perfect balance of opposing qualities: "Was Homer savage or civilized?" the first article asks at the outset. "BOTH. So was Achilles. . . . Paint him in two words—STORMY SUNSHINE."[40] Although Wilson may have disagreed with De Quincey on the issue of Homer's identity, he nevertheless shared De Quincey's view of unity as a counterbalance of opposing forces.[41] For De Quincey, these opposing forces reside in the different poems that make up the *Iliad*. Wilson traced them to the dissident elements within an individual character. The *Iliad*, Wilson argued (taking a distinctly anti-Aristotelian stance), may seem in its tonal variations to be constructed by different poets, but, just as Achilles' dynamic character is a composite of conflicting personality traits, so too does the poem's internal tension testify to Homer's versatility as a writer.

This quality of unity through opposition is demonstrated most remarkably, according to Wilson, by the scene of Achilles' feast for Agamemnon's ambassadors. Wilson found this scene so important that he spent close to ten pages of close print discussing it in the third article and revisited it again in another three pages of his fourth installment: "Achilles is a savage—a barbarian, forsooth—but half-civilized. . . . There he sits, the bravest and most beautiful of mortal men, a musician, perhaps a poet," as the ambassadors find him strumming on a lyre before his tent. "As the ambassadors entered . . . [Achilles] himself, harp in hand, [was] rising from his seat, and advancing towards them, stately as the beautiful Apollo. How courteous that princely greeting! . . . Take the entertainment in the Tent—from first to last—and it is a noble one. Where saw ye ever Three such Men-cooks as Achilles, Patroclus, and Automedon? Lo! the son of Thetis—the goddess-born—with the spit in his 'inaccessible hands!'"[42] Quoting from Chapman because he found Chapman's rendering the best in this scene ("Chapman is Homer"), Wilson transported the description of Achilles' "inaccessible hands" to book 9 to emphasize the contrasting sides of Achilles that constitute his character's unity: the gentlemanly musician who strums his lyre and entertains his guests with every civility; the savage warrior whose hands slay human enemies as mercilessly as they carve meat for a banquet. For Wilson, the existence of such extremes in Achilles' character constitutes the ultimate unity of the poem and testifies to the singular genius of its creator.

Charlotte's similar transplanting of Chapman's "inaccessible hands" to the banquet scene of book 9 is too idiosyncratic to be coincidental. By evoking this combination of imagery, she not only allied herself with Wilson's aesthetic of unity through opposition but also indicated her adoption of his anti-Aristotelian position. Heger's commentary on her essay exposes the philosophical underpinnings of Charlotte's narrative. "This beginning is perhaps a little lacking in nobility," he wrote in the margin next to her opening description of Lysander's banquet. The comment indicates the Aristotelian standard to which Heger was holding Charlotte's adaptation and derives from Aristotle's categorization of epic in that branch of "serious" poetry based on a "mimesis of noble actions and the actions of noble people."[43] Heger's comment suggests that Brontë's description of the Spartans' gluttonous repast violates the dignity of epic form and does not correspond to the nobility of character appropriate to the epic setting and to Lysander's portrayal as an epic hero.[44] But Charlotte's reference to the Spartans as eating "with the voracity and taciturnity of twelve wolves" drew directly from the fourth article in Wilson's *Iliad* series, where he commented on the effectiveness of Homer's wolf metaphor in describing the savagery of Achilles' Myrmidons, elaborating for three pages on the effectiveness of various translations in capturing Homer's description: "Homer says not a syllable about the Myrmidons, except that Achilles went about ordering them to arm—he lets loose upon us in a moment the wolves themselves—and seeing them, we see the Myrmidons. . . . There is not another such savage similar as this in all Homer. . . . Homer was feasting his poetic eyes on the feasting wolves of the mountain forest—on an image of rural active life" ("Sotheby's IV," 857–59). Wilson here acknowledged the savagery of Homer's metaphor only to praise the poet's ability to render the scene in all its horrific power. For Wilson, this ability proves the "sublimity" of Homer's writing, which is grounded in the evocation of fear: "As delight is the source of beauty, so pain and fear, and power, which subdues pain and fear, are the sources of sublimity." Just as Achilles' unity as a character is composed of contrasting elements, so too does the powerful, elevating, epic effect of the *Iliad* as a whole depend on moments of awesome and savage power juxtaposed against those moments of beauty with which nobility is more frequently associated. Epic effect, according to Wilson, is produced by the resonance of contrasting forces.

Wilson's idea that the unity of the *Iliad* is composed of contrasting effects not only anticipated De Quincey's similar interpretation a decade later but also echoed an argument in the *Quarterly Review,* published only a few months prior to Wilson's series on the *Iliad* and more directly overturning Aristotle's evaluation of epic unity. Entitled "Origin of the Homeric Poems," this article directly contrasts "technical unity" of the epic with what it calls a "unity of interest": "Much of the difficulty has arisen from seeking in the Iliad a kind of technical unity, foreign to the character and at variance with the object of the primitive epopee," states the article. "The question is not, whether the whole fable is strictly comprised within the brief proposition of the subject, in the simple exordium, but whether the hearer's mind is carried on with constant and unfailing excitement—whether, if the bard had stopped short of the termination of the poem, he would not have left a feeling of dissatisfaction on the mind. . . . [We cannot find room] for more than a brief and rapid outline of that unity of interest which appears to us to combine the several books of the Iliad, if not into one preconceived and predistributed whole, yet into one continuous story."[45] The "unity of interest" here described replaces the Aristotelian notion of formal unity with an aesthetics of fragmentation that identifies the value of the *Iliad* with the "most delicate allusions between the most remote parts" ("Origin," 150). This aesthetics of fragmentation is precisely what Charlotte adopted in her evocation of Homer's "savage" allusions—allusions that discard the imposed, artificial symmetry of Aristotelian nobility for the conflicting elements both in individuals and in events that defeat summary moral judgment but constitute the seductive value of narrative. Through its syntactic juxtaposition of incongruous images, Charlotte's essay suggests that the unity of a piece must be understood in the dynamic, even frictional, relationship of individual parts to one another.

Charlotte's aesthetics of fragmentation is further illuminated by another of Heger's criticisms in the opening lines of her essay. Under her word "inaccessibles," he drew a wavy line to indicate what he called a "barbarisme," which is a word borrowed from Aristotle's definition of *barbarismos*: "Impressive and above the ordinary is the diction that uses exotic language (by 'exotic' I mean loan words, metaphors, lengthenings, and all divergence from the standard)."[46] For Heger, barbarisms were Frenchified English words that Charlotte had noted in an early letter "nearly plucks the eyes out of [M. Heger's] head when he sees [them]."[47] Though she no doubt anticipated Heger's dislike of such words, Charlotte nevertheless inserted one into her essay, putting it in quotation marks (as did Wilson) as if to provoke Heger's reaction. She clearly wanted to make a point—namely, that there is not any living language capable of fully rendering the meaning of the Greek. Chapman had expressed this in his 1611 preface: "And much lesse I wey the frontlesse detractions of some stupide ignorants that . . . whisper behind me vilifyings of my translation—out of the French affirming them, when both in French and all other languages but his owne our with-all-skill-enriched Poet is so poore and unpleasing that no man can discerne from whence flowed his so generally given eminence and admiration."[48] Though Chapman does elsewhere proclaim the poetic superiority of English (above French and Italian), his defense of his improvisational treatment ("sleight comment and conversion") of the *Iliad* points to the gap between an understanding of the poem's meaning and the languages available to cast that understanding into appreciable form.[49] Wilson expressed a similar sentiment in *Blackwood's* by remarking in his first article, "All translation of the highest poetry, we hold, must be, such is the mysterious incarnation of thought and feeling in language, at best but a majestic mockery—something ghostlike; when supposed most substantial, suddenly seeming most a shadow—or change that image, why, then, like a broken rainbow, or say, rather, like a rainbow refracted, as well as reflected from the sky-gazing sea. Glorious pieces of colour are lying here and there, reminding us of what, a moment before, we beheld in a perfect arch of heaven" ("Sotheby's I," 668). This statement by Wilson emphasizes the inevitably fragmentary nature of any translation from Homer, who comes to represent the perfection of thought that language fractures in the process of recording. Having spent a good deal of 1843 doing her own translations, Charlotte would have been keenly sensitive to the difficulties that Wilson and Chapman indicated.[50] By using in her essay a French translation of an English rendition of the Greek, she was conveying to Heger not only that her own knowledge of Greek was fragmentary but also that by deconstructing the formal elements of her writing, Heger was failing to understand the more perfect mental conception of which writing is only the scattered reflection.

Charlotte's resistance to Heger's principles of composition and interpretation is played out in her depiction of the interaction between Lysander and the bard. The dialogue is nowhere to be found in Plutarch but mirrors Charlotte's increasing sense of creative suffocation. "'Yes!' cried Lysander: '[Athens] will perish, this old enemy of our Lacedaemon, and this very evening I will have her elegy sung [by] one of her sons.'"[51] The poet is led up from the dungeon.

> "Slave!" said Lysander, "Dost know why I have summoned thee? . . . It's to make thee sing, and since folk in the profession must always have a fine subject to inspire them, I will give thee one: 'The Sack of Athens.' <Suppose that>[52] tomorrow that insolent town will be destroyed from top to bottom. Invoke then the Muses, and like a second Homer, sing a second Troy. Go to it!"
>
> The poet played with his chains, which he wore as if they had been the most superb ornaments of gold and gems. "I don't know how to sing," he said nonchalantly.[52] (*Belgian Essays,* 336, 338)

In Plutarch's version of this story, the bard who sings the lines from Euripides' *Electra* is a Phocian and thus an ally of Lysander's camp.[53] Brontë's revision of the bard's nationality is significant for two reasons. First, the slave-master relationship between the Athenian singer and the Spartan Lysander adds an element of coercion that is nowhere implied in Plutarch's work but intimates Brontë's increasing sense of oppression by Heger, whom she called her "master." Second, the opposition between Athens and Sparta established in Charlotte's revision projects her personal disagreement with Heger onto the screen of a larger ideological conflict about the purpose of art.

This ideological conflict was sparked by the Homeric Question. De Quincey gave a clear outline of it in his 1841 article "Homer and the Homeridae" in *Blackwood's* when he noted that the preservation of Homeric epics was in large part attributable to the efforts of Lycurgus, a ninth century BC ruler of Sparta, and of Solon, the famed seventh-century lawgiver of Athens:

> For Christian Europe, the names France and England are by analogy what for Greece were the names Sparta and Athens; we mean, as respects the two great features of permanent rivalship and permanent leadership. From the moment when they were regularly organized by law and institutions, Athens and Sparta became the counterforces of Greece. About 800 B.C., Lycurgus draws up a system of laws for Sparta; more than two centuries later, Solon draws up a system of laws for Athens. And most unaccountably, each of these political leaders takes upon him, not passively as a private literary citizen to admire the Homeric poems—that might be natural in men of high birth enjoying the selectest advantages of education—but actually to privilege Homer, to place him on the matricula of denizens, to consecrate his name, and to set in motion the whole machinery of government on behalf of his poems. Wherefore, and for what purpose? On the part of Lycurgus, for a purpose well-known and appreciated, viz., to use the *Iliad* as the basis of public instruction, and thus mediately as the basis of a warlike morality—but on the part of Solon, for no purpose ever yet ascertained. . . . What Lycurgus did was rather for an interest of Greece than for any interest of Homer. The order of his thoughts was not, as has been supposed—"I love Homer; and I will show my love by making Sparta cooperate in extending his influence;" no, but this—"I love Sparta; and I will show my love by making Homer co-operate with the martial foundations of the land; I will introduce a martial poem like the *Iliad*, to operate through public education and through public festivals." For Solon, on the other hand, Homer must have been a final object; no means towards something else, but an end *per se*. ("Sotheby's II," 624)

 De Quincey's article suggests that the basis of the contrast between Athenian and Spartan government and society rests on their respective attitudes to poetry, with Athens promoting a philosophy of *ars gratia artis* and Sparta using art for political ends. To evoke the conflict between the two city-states is to suggest a basic contrast of artistic philosophies.

The contrast Brontë establishes between the Spartan commander and the Athenian bard similarly evokes a debate between the two attitudes toward art held by their respective city-states. Brontë's depiction of Lysander demanding the bard "like a second Homer" to sing of Athens's destruction illustrates a mindset that not only regards art as a means rather than its own end but also, by implication, constitutes the destruction of artistic value. The Athenian bard's refusal to supply Lysander with song retaliates against the notion of art as political machinery and represents Charlotte's argument for the independence of creative power from a nationalistic agenda. "He was a true Athenian, elegant, gracious; an Athenian who had been brought up in the groves of the Academy, who had fed on the philosophy of Plato and Socrates, on the poetry of Sophocles and Euripides. Despite his rather slight stature and his somewhat effeminate features, there was in his noble attitude and classic contours something indefinably superior that raised him far above those Spartans."[54] Despite the anachronistic references to the Academy, Charlotte's description of the bard emphasizes an intellectual superiority that is intrinsic and "indefinable" and shapes the bard's bearing, conduct, and thought. Embodied by the proud poet, Athens becomes abstracted from a particular geographical and political designation to a mystical interior component of individual creativity. The poet's later attempt to "save Athens" thus constitutes an attempt to preserve a concept of artistic creation that can remain independent of political or institutional constraints.

Charlotte's framing of the opposition between the bard and Lysander recognizes a central difference in her own and Heger's views on art, education, and nationality. Like Lycurgus, as he is described by De Quincey, Lemprière, and Plutarch, M. Heger was strongly nationalistic and believed that the primary goal of education was the cultivation of a common social good and body of values. In a speech he gave at an 1834 prize ceremony at the Athénée Royale of Brussels, where he taught, he had expounded his teaching philosophy:

> In order to understand the immense importance of education, remark, gentlemen, that the whole political organization exists

> only by the safeguard of two powers: Education and Legislation; we do not hesitate to state that the more potent of these powers is Education. . . . Power has the mandate of establishing and maintaining order: but what means is there more moral, more powerful, in assuring peace, maintaining order, the execution of laws, than enlightening the citizens of their duties, than suppressing the seeds of vice in the heart of the young . . . ? Do you want there to be order . . . then teach men the same principles; give them the same ideas of duty (*devoir*); inspire them with the same social beliefs. . . . [C]onformity of sentiment will engender community of effort, and the great problem of finding a solid social foundation will be resolved.[55]

Heger delivered this speech only four years after Belgium won its independence from France, and his emphasis on education as a foundation of social solidarity is understandable given his country's efforts to develop a national identity.[56] But the fact that he gave a copy of this speech to Charlotte upon her graduation from the pensionnat in 1843, ten years later, testifies to his continuing belief in the nationalistic aims of education. Although Heger's philosophy is sound in itself, its manifestation in practice must have exacerbated Charlotte's increasing ambivalence toward her position as his student, since she had no intention of submitting herself to Belgian social conformity and was feeling increasingly alienated in her foreign surroundings.[57] In contrast to her inquiries into the nature of genius and her interest in art per se, Heger's view of learning as an essentially political act might very well have made her question the seriousness of his investment in her education. Indeed, his opinion that a primary goal of learning is to acquire a sense of national "duty" must have made Charlotte's submission of her "devoirs" seem a pretense that betrayed her artistic philosophy. Meanwhile, if the "power" of education lies primarily in its enforcement of a national cause, then what exactly was the nature of Heger's authority over his foreign student? If, in her earlier essays, Charlotte sought to engage Heger in debate over the nature of art, her evocation of the ancient rivalry between Athens and Sparta seems resolutely to acknowledge fundamental differences between herself and her teacher. In the last section of her essay, Charlotte set out to define the exact components of her aesthetic philosophy, which constructed a mosaic of her readings in German philosophy and of fragments from popular debates about the significance of Greek tragedy to modern realism.

Poetry may have saved Athens from burning by Lysander's men, but ensuing history was not so kind. Not only did Sparta tear down its walls at the end of the Peloponnesian Wars, but the Romans, the Byzantines, the Turks, and a host of other nations invaded the city and severely damaged its buildings and monuments in the following centuries. When Thomas Bruce, seventh Earl of Elgin and British ambassador to Constantinople (1799–1803), reached Athens in 1800, the once-glorious capital of art and architecture had been reduced to ruins. Nevertheless, the British were beginning to regard these fragmentary Greek remains as aesthetic exemplars despite their shattered state.[58] Lord Elgin, with an entourage of artists, arrived in Athens (which was then under the rule of the Ottoman Empire) with the initial plan of making plaster casts and drawings of its artifacts for the improvement of English art, architecture, and artistic appreciation. Instead of reproductions, however, he sent back to England some of the actual remains of the Acropolis with the intention of rescuing them from further destruction. Including sculptures, friezes, and statues dating back to the Golden Age of Pericles,[59] the "Elgin Marbles" were put on temporary display from 1807 to 1816, when they were bought by the British government and moved to the British Museum.[60] Parliament's decision to purchase the marbles established a relationship between ancient Greek art and British realism that would resonate throughout the rest of the nineteenth century.

Assessing the artistic value of the Elgin Marbles was one of several tasks assigned to the select committee formed in 1816 to advise Parliament on their purchase. To this end, the committee called on numerous artists and art critics, all of whom had been educated in an academic tradition that sought in art ideal representations that "allegorically exemplified universal ethical codes."[61] Despite this fact, their testimonies before the committee demonstrated a decisive shift in aesthetic values and established a new precedent for the direction of nineteenth-century art. Though there were some who criticized the Greek statuary as being inferior to Roman works such as the Apollo Belvedere and the Laocoön, traditionally regarded as representations of ideal beauty,[62] the majority of the committee's consultants praised the realism and originality of the marbles, supporting a new artistic model based on the marbles' rough finish, anatomical correctness, and forceful grandiosity in stark contrast to the grace and gloss of the Roman sculptures, which were seen as mere copies of previous Greek works. When asked directly to contrast the Grecian Theseus with the Apollo Belvedere, the Royal Academy painter Richard Westmacott commented that "the Theseus has all the essence of style with all the truth of nature; the Apollo is more an ideal figure."[63] When asked the same question, Westmacott's colleague Sir Thomas Lawrence remarked that "there is in [the marbles] an union of fine composition, and very grand form, with a more true and natural expression of the effect of action upon the human frame, than there is in the Apollo, or in any of the other most celebrated statues. . . . There is . . . that variety that is produced in the human form, by the alternate action and repose of the muscles, that strikes one particularly."[64] These testimonies not only influenced the government's decision but also triggered a national debate, carried out in such prominent journals as the *Examiner* and the *Edinburgh Review* and *Quarterly Review,* about the marbles' historical value and national significance. William Hazlitt, seeing the marbles as an antidote to the "affectation" and "vanity" of British art, echoed the consultants' preference for realism over idealism in an article for the *Examiner,* stating, "Art is the imitation of nature; and the Elgin Marbles are in their essence and their perfection casts from nature—from fine nature, it is true, but from real, living, moving nature."[65] The celebration of realism here (as in the consultants' testimonials) bears the undeniable traces of Romantic idealism—the marbles are an imitation of nature, but only nature in its finest form. Nevertheless, these opinions indicate an important shift in aesthetic principles. Received in the Romantic spirit of naturalism, the purchase of the Elgin Marbles in 1816 helped to lay the foundations for discussions of realism in the second half of the century.[66]

The turn toward realism initiated by the Elgin Marbles extended, in the discourse of popular journals, from discussions of Greek sculpture to Greek tragedy, an artifact of ancient society that, like the marbles, lay in fragments but testified to an internal, psychological truth mirroring the external, physical verity of Greek statuary in originality, grandeur, and transhistorical value.[67] A year after the purchase of the Elgin Marbles, *Blackwood's* included in its inaugural volume a four-part series of "Remarks on Greek Tragedy" exemplifying the cross-genre extension of an emerging realist aesthetic. Greek tragedy, the first article states, "was drawn directly from nature, and the likeness was pleasing because it was the faithful copy of a fair original; not, as too frequently happens among the ancient Romans and the modern nations of Europe,—a servile imitation—a tame copy of a copy. . . . Its whole interest arises out of the simple expression of natural feeling in situations of suffering and sorrow."[68] The same preference for naturalism, originality, and intensity that had led to the purchase of the marbles is applied here in evaluating the raw emotionality of Greek tragedy. In both cases, Roman art and literature, previously seen as the epitome of aesthetic achievement, suffer in contrast to the faithfulness of Greek art to living models. The bias toward Greece extended, moreover, from art to artists. Not only was the content of Greek tragedy praised for its emotional truth but also Greek tragedians were regarded as privileged with unique psychological insight. The composition of Greek tragedy, according to the article, "requires a knowledge of the nature of man, and of those general laws by which he is governed in every stage of society, which is the portion only of a gifted few. . . . The dramatic writer must be endowed with the eye that can unveil the human heart, detect the passions in their source, and trace them in their intricate windings, and give to all the utterance" ("Remarks," 39). The tragedian's insight into the human heart is described with the same praise of anatomical precision as that lavished upon the marbles. Similarly, the stiff formality, cold correctness, and "stale morality" used to describe inferior dramatists evokes the critiques of Roman sculpture. In contrast, echoing the kinetic energy attributed to the marbles, the article praised the Greek tragedians for their ability to integrate emotional intensity with "a love of virtue" that had turned their tragic stage into "a temple for the purification of the national manners." The uneasy coexistence of idealism and realism here reflects, as do initial judgments of the Elgin Marbles, the nascent stages of the latter's formation. Anticipating J. H. Newman's, Matthew Arnold's, and Thomas Babington Macaulay's praise of Sophocles and Aeschylus as moral teachers, *Blackwood's* vision of Greek tragedy in 1817 seems blithely to bypass the incest, matricides, murders, and betrayals crowding the ancient plays to deliver a prescription for nineteenth-century literature, which, at the time, was welcoming the mixture of psychological realism and moral didacticism epitomized by Jane Austen's novels of manners, to which Virginia Woolf would later compare Sophocles' tragedies.

As Jeannette King has discussed extensively, comparisons of novels with Greek tragedy had become commonplace by midcentury, with Aristotelian ideas of the noble hero, poetic justice, and catharsis providing reviewers with criteria for judgment and novelists with structural and thematic models that exemplified, as many writers believed, elemental truths of the human condition. In reference to George Eliot's and Anthony Trollope's incorporation of tragic elements in their works, King asserts, "The traditionally ennobling effect of tragedy on humanity represented an ideal of the affective power of literature; it also represented, therefore, a model for the moral status and function of the novel. They believed that tragic drama had, in fact, been supplanted by the novel as the mirror of life and as a teaching form."[69] Nevertheless, King argues that "with its emphasis on the nobly heroic, undertaking great actions of high moral seriousness, the tragic ideal was . . . for many critics, totally incompatible with realism." (6). Such pervasive debates about the relevance of tragedy to novelistic realism reinforce the point that in the nineteenth century, questions about the nature and function of realism were inextricable from discussions about the nature and function of tragedy, for which the Greeks provided the original model. With archaeology and anthropology not yet securely established as fields of research, Greek tragedy became a screen upon which the nineteenth century could project its own, often contending, aesthetic ideals and became (like the Elgin Marbles) "ultimately less important than the narratives of identification [it] enable[d]."[70]

The narrative of identification based on Greek tragedy was, however, complicated by the performative elements of the Greek texts. The masks, choruses, music, and ceremonials that were known fixtures of Greek tragedy conflicted with the nineteenth-century objective of transparency. Promoting this form as a model for nineteenth-century literary realism required disengaging the valuable psychological insight of the plays from the context of the ancient Greek stage. This separation of literary and performative elements was dealt with in various ways. Regarding such elements as the chorus as an "unnatural restriction" on the action, the 1817 *Blackwood's* article redeems the literary quality of Greek tragedy by characterizing the tragedians as "eminent poet[s]," not dramatists, and by arguing that Greek dramatic convention "arose out of necessity not choice" ("Remarks," 352). The article implies that such elements as the chorus were burdensome even for the Greeks, preventing their tragedy from reaching its highest potential. Modern interpretations could and should dispense with the disruptive performative context and benefit from the dramas' superior literary merit. The *London Magazine* (1820–29), London's answer to *Blackwood's* and "Maga's" chief rival, used a similar tactic in its 1823 article "On the Tragic Drama of Greece" in defending the practical necessity of masks on the Greek stage: "[O]wing to the vastness of the theatric area, the spectators could not have discerned the play of the natural features [of the actors and] . . . as the performances took place in open daylight, the lines of the face were not brought out in such relief as they are by means of the false lights of the modern theater. . . . [T]he Greeks were ingenious in devising contrivances to obviate the fatal inconvenience of their enormous theater."[71] Despite its admission of the inferiority of the Greek stage, this article similarly defends the Greek tragedians as poets whose works should be studied for their evocation of sublime passion, dignity, grandeur, and pathos. By dissociating poetic value from dramatic context, these early articles facilitated the transformation of tragedy from a performative genre to a literary trope.

As the century progressed, however, the expansion of scientific interest into sociological arenas made it increasingly difficult to regard Greek antiquity as a collection of transhistorical artifacts isolated from their social context.[72] The idea of Greek tragedy's serving as a model for Victorian literary realism thus became more problematic in view of drama's vastly different social function in ancient culture. The revised view of Greek tragedy is apparent in an 1831 article in the *Quarterly Review*. Discussing *Popular Specimens of the Greek Dramatic Poets,* a recent compendium compiled expressly for those "whose occupation, and still more whose sex precludes them from studying those interesting remains of antiquity in the original languages," the article emphasizes that Greek tragedy needed to be seen not simply as the creation of a single genius but rather as shaped by and serving an important cultural function:

> [T]he noble repose [of Greek tragedy] . . . should lead to a calm mental review of the causes and consequences of those [daily] excitements, thus purifying the sources of action, and leading to a course of action nobler than itself, and more properly adapted to the high functions which the customs and institutions of their country had laid upon the spectators. . . . [Greek tragedy] was careful that in beings thus regarded with awe [as the figures in tragedy], and whose language and feelings were intended to keep up the highest moral tone in the public mind, no unguarded word or movement, no familiar household term or action should occur to break the spell, or tempt the spectators' minds to leap the eternal barriers which were meant to stand between themselves and those creatures of another and a nobler day.[73]

In marked contrast to the 1817 *Blackwood's* article that imagined Greek tragedy as modeled directly upon the reality of human feeling and behavior, this article sees it as the diametrical opposite of daily reality. As a social event, tragedy was a crucial element of common life, but the stories it depicted were meant to serve as a counterbalance to and corrective of the passions that ruled real human behavior. In emphasizing tragedy's social function, the article draws a distinction between the moral didacticism and emotional realism that the *Blackwood's* article had attempted to attribute simultaneously to the form. The two are in fact incompatible: the disorder and impulsiveness of everyday life cannot serve as models of dignity and restraint. To fulfill its moral function, Greek tragedy must instead portray the lives of beings above and beyond the abilities of the average human being.

Thomas De Quincey made an even more emphatic argument against the realism of Greek tragedy in an 1840 *Blackwood's* article entitled "Theory of Greek Tragedy." "The Greek tragedy is a great problem," states the first line, identifying an ongoing debate about the aesthetic value of the ancient genre. The difficulty in determining such value, according to the rest of the article, lies in the fact that modern and ancient drama, while sharing the common goal of mimesis, target vastly different objects. Modern tragedy, De Quincey argued, attempts to imitate the life of the spectator, in the reality both of his internal thoughts and feelings and of his external actions. Greek tragedy, in contrast, attempts to "aggrandize" and "idealize" the common life of the audience. There is no attempt in Greek tragedy, De Quincey contended, to imitate reality as is:

> [There is] a habit amongst the tragic poets of travelling back to regions of forgotten fable and dark legendary mythus. Antiquity availed powerfully for their purposes, because of necessity it abstracted all petty details of individuality and local notoriety; all that would have composed a *character*. . . [Antiquity] . . . reduced the historic person to [a] sublime state of monotonous gloom. . . . All this apocryphal gloom aids that sanctity and awe which belong to another and a higher mode of life; . . . a life sequestrated into some far off slumbering state, having the severe tranquillity of Hades—a life symbolized by the marble life of sculpture; but utterly out of all symmetry and proportion to the realities of that human life which we moderns take up as the basis of our tragic drama.[74]

Here De Quincey challenges the notion that there is anything natural or real about Greek tragedy, either for the Greeks or for a modern audience. Derived from rituals honoring superhuman deities and accommodating the giant apparatus of the theater, Greek tragedy evolved an art form altogether opposed to modern concepts of realism. The "tableux vivans [*sic*] which preside . . . through the several acts" of Greek tragedy are inherently opposed to an artistic ideal centered on "a development . . . of human character; or, . . . of human passion . . . on the common human standard."[75] What the Greeks wanted in their theater, De Quincey asserted, was the distillation of the eternal from the fleeting reality of the individual life. Tragedy was the form befitting such extrapolation because the Greeks "felt it possible to present this mode of being in states of *suffering,* for suffering is enduring and indefinite" ("Theory," 149). For De Quincey, the various narratives of the Greek tragic stage are not representations of the human condition so much as lenses of extrasensory perception through which the audience could escape the boundaries of daily consciousness. Certainly, Greek tragedy was comparable to statuary, but neither, in their frozen grandeur, could claim the quality of realism.

Discussions in periodicals about the nature and utility of Greek tragedy expressed important concerns about literary realism in general: How might literature balance a reflection of individual reality with a broader social function? Is the goal of realism to capture the fleeting, personal details of lived life or the transcendent elements of common human experience? The second half of Charlotte's essay "Athènes sauvée par la poësie" attempts to address these questions by finding a compromise between the various viewpoints on Greek tragedy expressed by periodical literature and ideas about tragedy that she found in her studies of German in 1843. The philosophy of narrative realism that resulted from this compromise establishes a rich dialogue between the scattered remnants of Greek tragedy and the fragmented state of the modern condition.

The Athenian bard in Charlotte's essay does sing, despite his initial refusal to do so, but he does it in a way that escapes Lysander's narrative framework. Midway through her essay, Charlotte leaves behind the Iliadic allusions, militaristic setting, and description of events moving forward in time and shifts to a series of images leading backward through the bard's memory, thereby counterposing an aesthetic of interiority against the Spartan general's tyrannical, utilitarian agenda. "Memories of his childhood came back to him, the dreams that had soothed him on his mother's knees. He recalled the ancient legends that constituted the mythology of Greece, legends terrible and sad: the royal race of Pelops, hounded always by a dark destiny; the fate of the king of kings returning victorious from ten years of war in a distant land to perish on his dishonored hearth; Clytemnestra stained by her husband's blood, Orestes exiled, and Electra slave and orphan. These memories served as his subject; he picked up his lyre—he sang" (*Belgian Essays,* 342). The shift from epic to tragedy is here paralleled by a process of internalization that dissociates the bard's creative inspiration from Lysander's external compulsion. The bard's retreat into his memory and away from his audience suggests that whatever effect his words may have on them will be accidental to what Charlotte called in her Millevoye essay "something that happens or has happened in the poet's soul" (244). Consistent with the popular view of tragedy as reflective of internal truth, the Homeric bard transforms himself, by his inward gaze, into a tragedian whose purview is the landscape of the human psyche.

The importance that Charlotte placed on interiority is evidenced by the amount of space she allots to her reinterpretation of tragedy. While Plutarch quotes only a single line from the first chorus of Euripides' *Electra,* Charlotte devotes the remaining half of her essay to Electra's story, primarily expressed by Electra in an extended lament. Set off by a hard break in the text, her Electra section marks a rhetorical shift that seems, at first, to borrow directly from De Quincey's *Blackwood's* article:

> The steeds of the Sun . . . plunge into the ocean; the waves engulf them. . . .
>
> Then comes Night, calm and grave. . . . She passes over the cities, leaving silence and slumber in her wake. . . . She passes over the barren desert. . . . She enters an ancient forest, dark and deep, and there she stops; it is her cherished abode.
>
> Night veils her brow and bows her head. . . . Obscurity surrounds her; silence accompanies her. . . . Neither man nor beast exists in that region of shadows; . . . this forest is peopled by rustic phantoms: amid the gnarled branches of the trees leer grotesque Satyrs . . . monstrous Fauns . . . Dryads . . . Oreads. . . .
>
> Who speaks? Whence comes that voice which suddenly breaks the silence? So far from any town, so far from human habitation, who wanders here? What mortal? what woman? for listen! it is a woman who speaks. [The voice belongs to Electra, crying out for her murdered father.]
>
> "Oh Agamemnon! Agamemnon!"
>
> Night trembles, frightened by that doleful cry; the forest resounds with it. (342, 344)

 Discarding the frame narrative altogether, this opening conveys the audience into a world of sensual negation signaled by words such as *silence, slumber, darkness, obscurity, shadows,* and *Night,* an embodied force that obliterates the bard's world of action and external conflict. Contrasting sharply with the vivid scene of Lysander's camp, with its "red hangings, dazzling lamps, purple wine, inflamed faces," Electra's story summons the "state of monotonous gloom" with which De Quincey associated Greek tragedy. Emerging from this unearthly abyss, Electra seems one with her timeless, immortal landscape, her character engulfed by the "enduring and indefinite" suffering that De Quincey identified as a primary element of Greek tragedy. Electra's removal from the world of action and interaction seems to ally Charlotte's concept of Greek tragedy with De Quincey's argument for its removal from the world of common humanity.

But Charlotte's fictional re-creation of the remote world described by De Quincey is actually an interpretation of it. Whereas De Quincey dismissed the mythical world of Greek tragedy as moribund and irreconcilable with the "composition of character" essential to modern realism, Charlotte used her mythical scene to designate a different level of understanding that is essential to all tragic effect. Her difference of perspective corresponds with a central element in the aesthetic philosophy of Friedrich Schiller, whose philosophy and writings Charlotte would have been exposed to in numerous journals, including *Blackwood's,* even before she began translating his works in 1843.[76] In an 1825 article entitled "The New School of German Drama," for example, *Blackwood's* identified Schiller as a primary influence in reconciling the statuesque dignity of Greek tragedy with modern experience. The basis for the compromise between the modern desire for intense emotional experience and the classical ideal of elevated compassion lies, for Schiller, in tragedy's appeal to two levels of understanding. "[W]e can receive the most vivid impressions of some suffering, without being brought to any noticeable degree of compassion, if these impressions lack truthfulness," wrote Schiller in *On the Art of Tragedy.* "We have to make ourselves a concept of the suffering we are supposed to be taking part in. That requires that the concept coincide with something already previously at hand in us."[77] There are two levels of tragic experience indicated here. First, tragedy appeals to the audience's identification of and with a particular situation represented on stage. Second, Schiller pointed to a "concept" of suffering that preexists our understanding of specific situations and represents the transhistorical element of humanity. Tragic effect, Schiller contended, is actually an extrapolation from concrete experience. "The ultimate purpose of art is to depict what transcends the realm of the senses,"[78] he asserted in "On the Pathetic." Schiller's theory mingles realism with Platonic idealism by suggesting that art serves as a catalyst for uniting the poet and audience in a sublime, supersensory realm that is even more real than sensual experience. While De Quincey might have regarded these feelings as detached from reality, for Schiller, the essence of man lies in his unique powers of moral reasoning, which lift him above the base, sensual elements of his nature and allow him to access an essential shared humanity. Tragic suffering should guide man from the reality of a specific experience to the level of intellectual understanding that is the essence of his humanity. The "universal phenomenon" of man's "pleasure in compassion," Schiller argued, draws man to tragedy and is rooted in his desire to access his better, moral self.[79]

Schiller's philosophy that tragic suffering appeals to man's moral reason and encourages his better self would seem an ideal explanation for why the story of Electra might have softened the "hyena hearts" of the Spartan soldiers, urging them to save Athens from destruction. Charlotte's depiction of Electra re-creates this rationale by existing in a realm between mortal suffering and asensual sublimity. Emerging first as a disembodied cry from a world of darkness and silence, Electra represents that meeting point between rational understanding and sensual negation that is the ideal state for experiencing moral compassion. Charlotte thus supplemented Plutarch's single line from Euripides' *Electra* with a theory of tragic effect. This theory, while borrowing Schiller's theory of compassion, dispenses with his emphasis on tragic form, which he defined as "the imitation of an action leading to suffering."[80] Charlotte may have agreed with Schiller that there is a deeper level of understanding than that which appeals to the concrete experience of the senses, but she denied that the specific emotional state of suffering can be expressed through action or even fully articulated through language or vision. Her view is apparent from Electra's opening lament to the dead Agamemnon, which, while corresponding to the long monodies that introduce Electra in all three of the Greek plays in which she features, excludes that specificities of time, place, and circumstance that would have been requisite for a theatrical script.[81] Charlotte's audience knows nothing of Electra's appearance, nothing of the movements that accompany her lament; indeed, she seems frozen in place. In contrast to the descriptions of the bard and

 Lysander, Electra's presence is entirely defined by her self-conscious withdrawal from sight and hearing.

> "Agamemnon—my father! They have driven me from thy grave; they have torn from my hands the urn that contains thy ashes. They revile me, they threaten me when I weep for thee! I have fled the precincts of my tyrants; I have sought these solitudes to weep alone. Alone, do I say? No, the Fury follows me. She is ever on Electra's traces."
>
> The voice stops; the rustling of the wind and leaves makes the refrain of her cry. But Electra knows not how to quell the agonies that torment her; again she invokes Agamemnon, she returns to her dark memories. (*Belgian Essays,* 344)

Electra's lament here departs radically from the detailed summaries that begin the Greek plays, as does the total absence of anger or desire for revenge—the driving motives of the Greek Electras.[82] This refusal of any moral appeal stems from Electra's inability either to understand or to articulate the vague agony inside her that seems to exceed any external cause or solution. Posing a stark contrast to her extremely articulate Greek counterparts, each of whom efficiently channels her emotional energy into a direct plan of action, Electra's suffering in Charlotte's re-creation is defined by its resistance to signification and its disconnect from external reality. By occupying a private space of silence, retreat, and negation, Charlotte's Electra affirms the experience of tragic suffering as a withdrawal into isolated interiority. Charlotte's writing of the bard's recitation thus transforms tragedy into a private act through which the stage becomes a metaphor for the written display of an interior reality that excludes the possibility of sensual expression.[83]

Charlotte's adoption of drama as a narrative trope seems to affirm the idea of nineteenth-century journals that Greek tragedy is an example of literary realism that needs to be dissociated from its performative context. But whereas journal articles dismissed stage apparatus as merely disruptive, Charlotte's emphasis on the incompatibility of suffering and spectacle is rooted in an argument against the viability of the socially centered catharsis crucial to the Greek tragic context. Wandering in a self-imposed exile, Charlotte's Electra embodies the physical and emotional isolation that, according to Schiller, defines the condition of the modern individual. Comparing the modern (or "sentimental") man to the ancient Greek (or "naïve") man, Schiller states: "We consider someone to have a naïve character if in making judgments about things he overlooks their artificial and affected relations and fixes only on the simple nature of them" (*Essays*, 186). The naïve man "operates as an undivided sensuous unity" (200). In contrast, the modern man "can only express himself as a moral unity, that is to say, as someone striving for unity. The agreement between his feeling and thinking, something that actually took place in the original condition, now exists only ideally" (201). Schiller goes on to state that art "separates and divides [the modern man]; by means of the ideal he returns to the unity. Yet because the ideal is an infinite one that he never reaches, the cultured human being in his way can never become complete as the natural human being can be in his way" (202). Schiller ultimately concludes that the ancient poet "wins the day insofar as it is a matter of the simplicity of the forms and what is *physical* and capable of being displayed sensuously. But the modern poet in turn has the better of the ancient when it comes to . . . what cannot be portrayed and uttered, in short, what in works of art people call *spirit*" (204). As with many of the German Romantic philosophers, Schiller used an ideal of Greek "wholeness" to define negatively the modern condition. The "moral unity" of the modern artist must posit the unachievable horizon of the ancient past to justify his own existence. A social exile, unable to understand or articulate the cause of her agony, Charlotte's Electra epitomizes the modern individual: mourning for the lost sense of intimacy (that is, with her father), attempting to unify thought and feeling, yet haunted by the knowledge of its impossibility. Drawn from Greek history and tragedy as well as nineteenth-century journals, Charlotte's Electra is a character constructed of fragments, but her very fragmentarity reflects the shattered condition of the modern spirit. Charlotte's rejection of the performative elements of tragedy as well as her departure from earlier accounts of the Electra myth acknowledge the loss of a time when the expiation of suffering in art could cathect into lived reality. In such a time, suffering might be regarded as a temporary experience, capable of opening outward toward resolution in a larger drama and through actual human relationships. But for those who can only achieve "moral unity," suffering becomes constitutive of being itself, and artistic reality must be contingent on an awareness of its own idealism.

Toward an Aesthetics of Fragmentation

Whereas the lines recited by the bard in Plutarch's history are taken directly from Euripides' *Electra*, Charlotte's retelling of the myth borrows not only from Euripides' *Electra* but also from Sophocles' version of the tragedy and from Aeschylus's *Agamemnon*.[84] In gathering together alternative and supplementary accounts of Electra's story, Charlotte creates a sense of literary continuity that compensates for the experience of isolation and fragmentation that defines Electra's character. The final part of her Electra narrative suggests that the power of the imagination that materializes in literary history can dissolve the need for external catharsis as well as compensate for the historical loss of social and individual integrity. This is evident when Electra's experience of absolute despair propels her to imagine a sympathy that she cannot find in reality. Retreating into her "dark memories," Electra may withdraw from any hope of social reintegration or self-expression, but the act of remembering also establishes an emotional alliance that leads her out of her cognitive vacuum and gives expression to a suffering that she cannot articulate:

> Who then sits at Agamemnon's side in the triumphal chariot? It is a woman wearing a veil. How mute and motionless she stays in the midst of the joyous tumult; she resembles the mysterious image of Sais, the goddess of truth. Agamemnon alights; he clasps his spouse to his loyal heart. In that moment a cry, a harrowing cry, is heard; there is the veiled statue, standing in the chariot; the veil is rent and all Argos recognizes Cassandra, princess, prophetess, and slave! Oh I see her still, her ghost appears before my eyes in the shadows of this forest! White, stiff, petrified, as if her veins were filled with ice in place of blood; all disheveled, her locks in disarray, streaming at the mercy of the wind; her white shoulders gleaming beneath her wild hair; . . . And her great dark eyes—what fire shone in them! what flash of inspiration! They were not a woman's eyes, they were a god's—or a demon's—I know not which; . . . Apollo showed himself in the orbs of his prophetess and fixed on the king his supernatural gaze. "Woe! Woe!" she cried. "Woe betide the lion who seeks the she-wolf's lair!" And she spewed forth curses whose horror made Argos quake, but none gave them either credence or attention. (*Belgian Essays*, 346, 348)

Charlotte adapted this final scene from Aeschylus's *Agamemnon*, where the Trojan princess arrives in Mycenae with the returning king: "Woe, woe, woe! O Apollo, O Apollo!" cries Cassandra, after a long period of silence.

"Oh, oh! What fire! It comes upon me! Woe, woe! Lycean Apollo! Ah me, ah me! This two-footed lioness, who couches with a wolf in the absence of the lion, will slay me, wretched that I am."[85] From Cassandra's cries of "woe" to Apollo's presence as a "fire" taking possession of his prophetess to the (slightly reversed) lion-wolf analogy, Charlotte's Cassandra directly evokes Aeschylus. The similarity between her version and the Greek play is displayed not only through Cassandra's language but also through the vividness of her presentation. Unlike the de-dramatized appearance of Electra, Cassandra's entry is marked with striking visual detail that directly corresponds with the descriptions offered by Aeschylus. "She bears herself like a wild creature," remarks Aeschylus's chorus upon seeing the captured princess. "Nay, mad she is and hearkens to her wild mood," agrees Clytemnestra.[86] Cassandra's entry here is not merely framed by scenes from Aeschylus's play: Charlotte's appeal to literary history is also propelled and determined by the generative and transforming force of Electra's imagination, which projects onto Cassandra an alternate version of herself. The parallels between the two women are striking: Cassandra is introduced into the story with the same question and answer ("qui? . . . c'est une femme") that prefaced Electra's entry; she also emerges, in Electra's creation of the scene, from the same shadowy forest that Electra had entered at the beginning of the essay. Finally, she embodies the sense of displacement and incoherency that Electra feels. For as Electra states, "[N]one gave [Cassandra's cries] either credence or attention." None, that is, except Electra, who, by evoking Cassandra's suffering, redeems the escaped meaning of the prophetess's cries while finding expression for her own impossible reality.

By identifying Electra's memory with her own intermingling of literary texts, Charlotte created a unique aesthetics of fragmentation that defines a cooperative relationship between past and present in which each restores a lost or escaped meaning to the other. Unable to find expression or sympathy for her suffering, Electra retreats into her memory and imagination and appeals to a figure whose lamentation provides the denouement and articulation of Electra's own inexpressible agony. Literature is thus given an organic memory—one that is able to adapt the past to its own needs. This transformative agency is demonstrated in Charlotte's (and Electra's) interpretation of Apollo, the god of poetry. In the homecoming scene from Aeschylus's *Agamemnon,* from which Charlotte adapted this final part of Electra's narrative, Apollo is Cassandra's persecutor, and she tears off his insignia in fury as "mockeries" of herself. In

 Charlotte's version, Apollo becomes a force of inspiration, allowing Cassandra a power of expression that Electra admires and desires for herself. Through her personal memory (which is also the textual memory of Charlotte's essay), Electra transforms Cassandra's victimization into an empowered subjectivity. Drawing from as well as revising accounts from Euripides, Sophocles, and Aeschylus, Charlotte thus constructed an archive of literary associations, each element of which recalls and revises others, conveying the idea that it is only through the reformulation of the past that the present can achieve a sense of its own reality. In the end, by bringing together two characters who never meet in any of the Greek plays, Charlotte created a modern narrative unity whose power lies in forging the missing links of a past forever suspended in the hope of future completion.

The sense of a story that awaits future completion is fully conveyed in the suspended conclusion of Charlotte's essay. With Cassandra's appearance, Electra disappears entirely into the role of observer and narrator, leaving the reader to wonder at her fate as the essay returns to the outer narrative of the bard. "Here the poet, breathless, paused to breathe," Brontë concluded:

> He glanced around the tent to gauge the effect his verses had produced. Oh horror! Lysander, his captains, and his helots, lying on their couches or on the ground, were all fast asleep. Here was the explanation for the respectful silence that, until now, had encouraged him to continue, and that he had thought to be the sign of fixed attention, of overwhelming emotion. Oh shame! Oh indignity! His Athenian soul rebelled against an insensitivity so brutal. Still, after the first effervescence of his rage, he told himself that it would be too absurd to get annoyed at the stupidity of a dozen barbarians, and laughing softly at them and at himself, he seized the opportunity to leave the tent and return to Athens, which he reached in perfect safety.[87]
>
> The next morning, on awakening, Lysander seemed to have entirely forgotten the poet and his project of vengeance. . . . [H]e set about framing a treaty with the Athenians, interrupting himself from time to time to remark that the names of Agamemnon, Electra, etc., were continually ringing in his ears, and that he knew not whence this came, since he had never in his life bothered about those persons. (*Belgian Essays,* 348, 350)

In his final comments on her essay, Heger attributed Charlotte's ironic conclusion to her "uncertainty about how to make a dignified descent." "The author, frightened toward the end of the heights to which he thought himself raised, began to laugh at himself" (350), noted Heger, indicating that Charlotte must have been stricken with self-consciousness of her inadequacy in handling the material of epic and tragedy. The remark implies that Charlotte failed to sustain a sense of literary and historical continuity with her ancient sources. It may, however, have been Charlotte who had the last laugh. For what Heger understood to be a failure of the author's obligation to her reader is also Charlotte's final statement about the nature of narrative effect. The fragmentary echoes that ring in Lysander's ears and exert a mysterious influence on his thoughts and actions reinforce Charlotte's belief that narratives derive their lasting power not from their formal unity but from an effect that operates below the conscious state of sensual apprehension. Heger's complaint about the absence of a dignified conclusion reflects his resistance to the fragmentary aesthetics that Charlotte proposes. His concluding remark to Charlotte that "one should not make fun of one's reader" may have been a recognition of his student's deliberate obstinacy, but the very fact that Charlotte may have played such a trick suggests that she, like the bard, ultimately escaped the authority of her master, unharmed and with the fragments of her genius intact.

The Odyssey of Lucy Snowe

Greek references appear throughout Charlotte's more mature work—in *The Professor* (completed in 1846, published in 1857), in which the Eton-educated hero makes passing references to Greek literature and mythology, and in *Shirley* (1849), in which the eponymous bluestocking heroine pens a French essay entitled "Le Première Femme Savante" that revisits the ideas of genius explored in Charlotte's devoirs. But it is in her last finished novel, *Villette* (1853), that Charlotte again fully engaged the Greek literature and mythology that had become fixed in her imagination through her reading of popular periodicals. Specifically, this last novel, a heavily autobiographical account of her experience in Brussels, draws on the central theme of homecoming in Homer's *Odyssey* as a means of understanding and narrating Charlotte's troubled experience of home life when she was conceiving and writing *Villette*. As clearly demonstrated in her letters from this last period of her life, the deaths of Branwell, Emily, and Anne within two years of each other destabilized Charlotte's once-secure sense of home. After these losses, the loneliness and anxiety that haunted a once-comforting place of retreat instilled in Charlotte a homesickness that lacked any possibility of earthly resolve. This same irresolvable longing equates Lucy Snowe with Homer's epic traveler, who spends the first twelve books of the *Odyssey* striving for a home that seems perpetually out of reach and venturing into a foreign land where the treacheries of an unfamiliar territory and the clandestine machinations of strangers threaten his mental and physical stability. For both characters, "homesickness" is defined by the desire not so much for a specific place as for an ideal of human intimacy and understanding that becomes ever more alluring in its inaccessibility. While it would be untenable, given the available evidence, to prove that Charlotte used the *Odyssey* as a template for her novel, the resonance of certain images and ideas in *Villette* with passages from Homer that would have been familiar to Charlotte goes some way toward illuminating the problematic definition of "home" both for Lucy Snowe and for Charlotte in the last half decade of her life. Furthermore, her return to Homeric ideas demonstrates the persistence of Greek images in Charlotte's mind as she sought to express emotions that, like Electra's inarticulable despair, escaped the compass of familiar language.

It is clear, from the images and ideas in *Villette,* that Charlotte revisited John Wilson's *Blackwood's* essays on Homer's epics, particularly his two lead articles on the *Odyssey,* published in January and February 1834. In these sequels to his *Iliad* essays, Wilson continued to defend the unity of the Homeric corpus by comparing translations from various writers and making the epic accessible both textually and thematically for a lay audience. Wilson's process of picking and choosing the best English representations of Homeric passages would have validated Charlotte's piecemeal approach to the classics. Indeed, Lucy Snowe's description of gathering bits and pieces of information for her classical essay (picking facts like fresh herbs and "shred[ding] them green into the pot")[88] gestures toward Charlotte's similar incorporation of classical material in the novel. Her approach would have been bolstered by Wilson's frequent argument that translators may be "most like Homer" for one scene and completely unlike Homer for another, thus suggesting that modern knowledge of ancient Greek is inescapably fragmentary, even in the case of those fluent in the language. Statements such as "at present, there really seems to be nothing in English so like the Greek as our own prose"[89] distinguishes understanding of Greek from linguistic training while validating the knowledge of readers such as Charlotte who gathered their classics from popular sources and works in translation. Wilson's pieces on the *Odyssey* would also have appealed to Charlotte because of his emphasis on the universality of the human experiences in the story, despite Homer's distance in time and space. In asking his readers to sympathize with Telemachus's postadolescent embarrassment of seeming too attached to his mother or Penelope's hopeful dreams of her husband's imminent return, Wilson presents the *Odyssey* as a model of the domestic experiences that the nineteenth century was so interested in exploring in its own narratives and that were central to Charlotte's novels. Perhaps the strongest of the transhistorical themes that Wilson set out to delineate are those of home and homesickness: "You would sympathize with Ulysses longing for rugged Ithaca, even in Ogygia's enchanted isle; for home-sickness is the malady of a noble heart, and conjugal affection its most endearing virtue," the first article concluded ("Sotheby's Odyssey I," 26). His second article began with the same theme: "A tender and profound interest has been breathed into our hearts in all that concerns Ithaca; it is invested with the hallowed charm of Home" ("Sotheby's Odyssey II," 153). As Karen Lawrence has pointed out, the *Odyssey* is and has been interpreted as a masculine text, largely concerned with Odysseus's adventures away from home, "encod[ing] the traveller as a male who crosses boundaries and penetrates spaces."[90] But the two opening segments of Wilson's series, intended to cultivate appreciation for Homer's epic in the lay reader, focus on domestic issues and emotional concerns that not only emphasize the transhistorical value of the *Odyssey* but also make the epic particularly appealing to a female readership.[91]

For many reasons, the themes of home and homesickness held a profound interest for Charlotte in the years leading up to and during the conception of *Villette.* In the first place, the deaths of Emily in December 1848 and Anne in May 1849 left her with a sense of desolation that would dissipate little in the remaining years of her life and that she felt forcefully in the sudden emptiness of her home. "I tried to be glad that I was come home," she wrote to her friend Ellen Nussey, upon returning to Haworth from the coast after Anne died. "I have always been glad before. . . . [B]ut this time joy was not to be the sensation. I felt that the house was silent—the rooms were all empty—I remembered where the three were laid—in what narrow dark dwellings—never were they to reappear on earth."[92] Ironically, though Branwell, Emily, and Anne were the ones who had been taken away from their home by death, it was Charlotte who was left to feel like an exile, unable, despite her physical capacity to return home, to reclaim the emotional catharsis of homecoming. "I am now again home," she wrote during the same period to William Smith Williams. "I call it home still—much as London would be called London if an earthquake should shake its streets to ruins" (*Letters,* 2:224). For Charlotte, the sudden disjunction between the sense of homecoming and the act of returning to Haworth would be a recurring phenomenon that prolonged her grief over the deaths of her sisters—the "two human beings who understood me and whom I understood" (*Letters,* 2:260). The impact of this disjunction was particularly heavy because during the late 1840s and early 1850s, Charlotte was traveling more than at any other time in her life. In addition to trips to London to meet with her publishers, she received numerous invitations from a growing list of acquaintances. The sense of homesickness plagued Charlotte before and after each of her trips: "[I] recalled the last time I went [to London] and with whom and to whom I came home, and in what dear companionship I again and again narrated all that had been seen, heard and uttered in that visit," she wrote to Williams in November 1849. "Emily would never go into any sort of society herself, and whenever I went, I could on my return, communicate to her a pleasure that suited her by giving the distinct, faithful impression of each scene I had witnessed" (*Letters,* 2:290). At least part of the joy of traveling had, for Charlotte, lain in her return to Emily and the narration of her adventures for her sister's behalf. Though Charlotte daily desired to go abroad and to escape the solitude and dreariness of the parsonage, the fear of amplified agony upon her return kept her rooted: "You will recommend me I daresay to go from home," she wrote to Ellen in a bout of depression, "but that does no good. . . . I cannot describe what a time of it I had after my return from London. . . . [T]here was a reaction that sunk me to the earth—the deadly silence, solitude, desolation were awful—the craving for companionship—the hopelessness of relief—were what I should dread to feel again" (*Letters,* 2:487). Depressed in her solitude, plagued by memories, yet afraid to leave Haworth, Charlotte was, in the years leading to *Villette,* haunted both by the desire for home and by the knowledge of its irrecoverability.

In one central respect, then, Charlotte's situation when she was writing *Villette* was drastically different from the period of her life upon which her novel was based. Though she had been physically absent from home while studying in Brussels and had felt desperately homesick during her last few months at the Pensionnat Heger, she could turn for consolation to writing long letters to Emily and to the knowledge that her sisters would be awaiting her return at Haworth. In the 1850s, in contrast, she was physically at home yet stricken with an aching and incurable homesickness. The discrepancy between these two experiences underlies what many critics have noted as the novel's ambivalence toward the idea of "home." Tony Tanner, for instance, in his introduction to the 1979 Penguin edition, writes that "Lucy is everywhere not-at-home," since she feels intensely isolated among both strangers and friends.[93] More recently, Eva Badowska has noted that Lucy remains "homesick while being at home,"[94] since M. Paul leaves for foreign shores shortly after he presents her with the gift of Faubourg Clotilde. The novel's ambiguous, even evasive, definition of home might be better understood in the context of Wilson's articles on the *Odyssey,* which not only identify home as the primary goal of Odysseus's journey but also suggest that homesickness is an essential element of Odysseus's heroic nature, testifying to his endurance, fidelity, and strength of character. Although *Villette* was written more than fifteen years after the publication of these articles, the novel's images of home and ideas of homesickness suggest that this *Blackwood's* source rose again in Charlotte's mind as she struggled to narrate a long-ago journey while recognizing the impossibility of return.

One of the central ideas in Wilson's treatment of the *Odyssey* that seems to have resonated with Charlotte is his argument that the significance of home lies not so much in the designation of a physical place as in a quality of relationship. More specifically, home is equated with a loved one who has intimate knowledge of the traveler and awaits his return. This point is apparent in Wilson's lengthy descriptions of Penelope's anxieties for Odysseus and her prophetic dream of his return. But he conveyed the idea most poignantly in describing the old nurse Eurycleia's concerns for Telemachus as the boy sets out at the epic's outset to search for news of his father: "His nurse loved him more than did even his own mother . . . and [had] no care—no love—nothing to live for—but that bright Boy climbing up to manhood. . . . She the slave belonged to him, Prince Telemachus; but he belonged to her, Nurse Eurycleia: and now that he is about to sail in search of his Father, it is to her he confides the secret—for in that still, simple, sworn heart of hers he knows it will lie buried beneath a weight of wishes for his return" ("Sotheby's Homer I," 8). Here, as in his descriptions of Penelope's thoughts of Odysseus, Wilson displaces the geographical point of return (Ithaca) with the sentient harbor of a specific human being in whom the traveler can place his deepest confidences. The sense of belonging that holds the nurse to the boy describes not only a relation of material ownership but also an exclusive intimacy of knowledge that binds one to the other despite physical separation. Wilson's explanation of their relationship suggests that even in the dire circumstances under which Ithaca is placed by the invading suitors, the island is still home for Telemachus because of his shared trust with Eurycleia, the concept of whose consuming thoughts for his safety serves as his point of return.

The idea of home as defined by return to a loved and trusted other certainly corresponds with Charlotte's feelings in the years after her sisters' deaths, and the idea emerges prominently in the relationships between Mrs. Bretton and Graham and between Polly and her father during *Villette*'s opening chapters, which are dominated by the theme of return. The Brettons' emotional connectedness is demonstrated as Mrs. Bretton awaits her son's return from a visit "expecting him through all [the] hours" of the evening (72). The domestic idyll of the Bretton household seems affirmed by the mother's anxiety for her son's safe return (like that of Eurycleia for Telemachus) and her expectation of his imminent arrival (like Penelope's dream of Odysseus's homecoming). The idea of home as defined by anxious expectation and exclusive knowledge is further reinforced by the reunion between Mr. Home and Polly, who recognizes her father's approaching the Bretton house before any sign of his identity appears to others. "She had sat listlessly, hardly looking [out the window] . . . when—my eyes fixed on hers—I witnessed in its irid [*sic*] and pupil a startling transfiguration," Lucy reports. "The fixed and heavy gaze swum, trembled, then glittered in fire; the small overcast brow cleared; the trivial and dejected features lit up; the sad countenance vanished, and in its place appeared a sudden eagerness, an intense expectancy. . . . Neither in mien nor features was this creature [Polly] like her sire, and yet she was of his strain: her mind had been filled from his, as the cup from the flagon" (70–71). The sense of belonging to one another that binds Eurycleia and Telemachus is echoed here in the relationship between Polly and her father, whose intimacy consists of a mental compatibility capable of enduring beyond any physical change of appearance or place. Their mutual affection compensates for the disintegration of the Home household as well as for the deficiencies of Mr. Home, who, Lucy notes, is indeed "homely-looking." The fact that the two Homes quickly reestablish their domestic routines in the Bretton house for the short duration of

Mr. Home's visit emphasizes the irrelevance of physical place to a sense of homecoming. Though Mr. Home must leave Polly again, the brief glimpse of their relationship ensures that each has and will provide the other with a point of return.

Perhaps more strikingly Odyssean than her definition of home as a point of return and shared intimacy is Charlotte's concept of what home is *not* and her sense of the elements of homesickness. In the *Odyssey,* the very opposite of home for Odysseus is the nymph Calypso's island, Ogygia, where the hero has been held prisoner for nearly ten years: "Ogygia! A glimpse of the spiritual world of old that still fluctuated waveringly between sense and soul, and was constructed by poetry of idealized realities, that may cease to be seen on troubling of the ether, but can never cease to be, if mind be immortal. Ogygia! it is felt to be 'self-withdrawn into a wondrous depth' of seclusion! Though 'light the soil and pure the air,' and the scenery composed of all familiar objects, yet is the region felt to be almost as preternatural as if it were submarine—and Calypso's cave as wondrous as a Mermaid's grotto" ("Sotheby's Odyssey II," 156). Wilson certainly described Ogygia as an idyllic place, but he also suggested that its very perfection prevents the nymph's island from ever being a home for a mortal whose vast experiences of suffering have made it impossible for him to resign himself to the careless life of a god: Odysseus "could not be charmed into oblivious sleep even if a lullaby were sung in a voice divine" ("Sotheby's Odyssey II," 165). For Odysseus—and Wilson's mortal readers—Ogygia is a place of deep estrangement where even nature loses its familiarity, owing to the sublimity of its surroundings. Though Ogygia may be a poetic ideal, it can never offer the sense of belonging and return for a mortal traveler.

The disturbing sense of alienation from the familiar similarly plagues Lucy in her relationship with the Brettons, who (as Calypso does for Odysseus) provide her with a place of physical safety but in whose presence Lucy continually feels a sense of unease. At the novel's outset, Lucy is removed from her family by her godmother, and although she appreciates the peace and material comforts of the Bretton household, she is also unsettled by her sense of its unreality. Suspended in a time and place "where Sundays and holidays seemed always to abide," Lucy's godmother leads an idyllic, static existence not unlike that of Calypso on her remote, timeless island: "My visits to [my godmother] resembled the sojourn of Christian and Hopeful beside a certain pleasant stream, with 'green trees on each bank, and meadows beautified with lilies all the year round'"

 (62). The reference to John Bunyan's allegory in *Pilgrim's Progress* and an eternal summer suggests that Lucy's visits to Bretton are departures from reality—disruptions, however poetic, to her life's continuity. Indeed, just as Ogygia's idyllic setting, while providing Odysseus a temporary haven after his devastation at sea, ultimately heightens his anxiety to return to his own home, Bretton offers Lucy a respite that simultaneously emphasizes her inescapable attachment to a home that is implicitly the opposite of the Bretton household. Harboring an "unsettled sadness" and "faint suspicion" (62) of unknown tragedies at home, Lucy remains spiritually tethered to the permanent claims of the unstable environment to which she belongs and with whom she shares a history.

This same sense of unease that haunts Lucy at the novel's opening returns at the beginning of volume 2, as Lucy recuperates from her fainting spell at the Brettons' home, La Terrasse. La Terrasse, as it appears to Lucy, bears a striking resemblance to Ogygia—an underwater world, removed from the troubles of known reality:

> My calm little room seemed somehow like a cave in the sea. There was no colour about it, except that white and pale green, suggestive of foam and deep water; the blanched cornice was adorned with shell-shaped ornaments, and there were white mouldings like dolphins in the ceiling-angles. Even that one touch of colour visible in the red satin pincushion bore affinity to coral; even that dark, shining glass might have mirrored a mermaid. When I closed my eyes, I heard a gale, subsiding at last, bearing upon the house-front like a settling swell upon a rock-base. I heard it drawn and withdrawn far, far off, like tide retiring from a shore of the upper world—a world so high above that the rush of its largest waves, the dash of its fiercest breakers could sound down in this submarine home, only like murmurs and a lullaby. (254–55)

The similarities between this passage and Wilson's descriptions of Calypso's island are evident—from the image of the submarine cave to the mermaid denizen to the obliviating influences of the oceanic lullaby. More important than the synchrony of imagery, however, is Charlotte's transformation of Homer's myth into a metaphor for Lucy's psychological disorientation. The aquatic cave in which Odysseus is physically trapped here conveys Lucy's disturbing confinement in a protected, yet surreal, space. Though Lucy returns to the Brettons (and they to her), their house can never be a point of homecoming for her after her emotional suffering. Lucy recognizes that "the details of what I had undergone belonged to a portion of my existence in which I never expected my godmother to take a share. Into what a new region would such a confidence have led that hale, serene nature!" (254). Even Dr. John, in whom Lucy begins to confide these darker sides of her experience, fails to give her the sympathy she seeks. Comparing the seal of Graham's letters to a "single Cyclops'-eye of vermilion red" (318), Lucy suggests the inhuman and dehumanizing nature of his scientific assessment of her feelings. Just as Odysseus's famous announcement of his name to Polyphemus nearly foils his escape and brings on the curse that will delay his homecoming, so too does Lucy's encouragement of Graham's attentions put her in danger of becoming forever the nobody in the Cyclops's cave.[95] Her eventual withdrawal from him acknowledges the danger of allowing her aching homesickness to jeopardize her very existence.

Lucy's and Odysseus's mutual homesickness draws them together in a way that transcends the dissimilar conclusions of their stories. For although Odysseus does eventually achieve the homecoming that Lucy (and Charlotte) seeks in vain, Wilson's article emphasizes that Odysseus's homesickness is a primary manifestation of his heroism. Wilson introduces Odysseus at the epic's opening with admiration for his heroic endurance, "There is mysterious mention of shipwreck on account of sin—and one guiltless and great Survivor is spoken of and then named—who is to take the place in our imaginations of all the other heroes living or dead—affectingly named—for he has been and is to be a Sufferer—'All but Ulysses!'" ("Sotheby's Odyssey II," 2). The shipwreck that robs Odysseus of his men is also, in Wilson's estimation, a force of fate, isolating Odysseus as the sole survivor and amplifying the heroism of his quest for home. Odysseus's homesickness thus serves as an internal testament to his heroic suffering and survival. This same association between survival and homesickness identifies Lucy as the hero of her story.[96] After settling back as an observer of Polly and the Brettons for the first three chapters of the novel, Lucy describes the tragedy that will make her a homeless wanderer at the opening of chapter 4:

> [I]t cannot be concealed that, in that case, I must have fallen overboard, or that there must have been wreck at last. I too well remember a time—a long time, of cold, of danger, of contention.

> To this hour, when I have the nightmare, it repeats the rush and saltness of briny waves in my throat, and their icy pressure on my lungs. I even know there was a storm, and that not of one hour nor one day. For many days and nights neither sun nor stars appeared; we cast with our own hands the tackling out of the ship; a heavy tempest lay on us; all hope that we should be saved was taken away. In fine, the ship was lost, the crew perished. (94)

This metaphoric shipwreck is reminiscent of several instances in the *Odyssey* recounted by Wilson's article, primarily the initial shipwreck that deprives Odysseus of his crew and the shipwreck that lands him on the shores of Scheria, home of the Phaeacians. As in the *Odyssey,* shipwreck in *Villette* seems to represent the workings of fate, singling out Lucy as a survivor, upon whom "self-reliance and exertion were forced . . . by circumstances" (95), and a sufferer, deprived of a home she can never reclaim. But just as Odysseus's homesickness can be viewed as an essentially heroic quality, so too does Lucy's unsatisfied longing for home serve as perhaps the greatest testimony to her strength and resilience.

There is, of course, another shipwreck that haunts the pages of *Villette*—the one that ends M. Paul's life and leaves Lucy in a permanent state of suspended hope for his return. Although his death deprives Lucy of the companion who might end her homesickness, I suggest that M. Paul's absence locates the poignancy of homecoming in the hopeful expectation of return. In this sense, the ending of *Villette* is not unlike the conclusion of the *Odyssey,* for the reunion between Penelope and Odysseus famously closes with the hero's anticipation of yet another journey and the prophecy of his death. Similarly, *Villette,* in a frustrating resistance to closure, finds Lucy anxiously awaiting M. Paul's arrival after his three-year absence. But the anticipation of Odysseus's last journey only intensifies his moment of intimacy with Penelope, and it is in the space of M. Paul's absence that Lucy stakes her claim on their mutual devotion. "I thought I loved him when he went away; I love him now in another degree; he is more my own" (595), Lucy states, withholding the truth of M. Paul's death from the reader. By concluding her odyssey with her lover's unfinished voyage, Lucy leaves her story with both the anticipation of a return and the memory of a love that transcends moments of meeting in space and time. Locating herself in this emotionally charged space between expectation and arrival, Lucy—and, by extension, Charlotte—concludes her narrative with the suggestion that the journey is what ultimately gives meaning to the idea of return, and the hope of home must lie suspended in the indefinite distance between desire and destination.

Lucy Snowe's sense that ownership comes most fully not from possession but rather from the deeper intimacy allowed by imagination might very well apply to Charlotte Brontë's relationship with the ancient Greeks. Although irked by insecurities about her classical knowledge—like Lucy Snowe—Charlotte was able to use her scattered Greek knowledge to formulate her aesthetic philosophy and, at the end of her life, to speak of emotional experiences that she could not otherwise articulate. The deeply personal uses to which she put her knowledge exemplify the malleability of the Greek sources available to the common reader in the early and mid-nineteenth centuries. While these sources offered knowledge that was fragmentary and often contested, they also exposed the instability of Greek knowledge, questioning just how much was and could be known about a dead language and ancient civilization. For writers such as Charlotte Brontë who might easily have felt daunted by their lack of formal classical training, such instability—and the contentions underlying it—lent validity to their unique interpretations of Greek literature and myth. For women writers more confident in their classical knowledge, debates about the place of ancient Greece vis-à-vis Victorian culture offered a forum for expressing viewpoints that opposed dominant social and cultural ideologies. The aesthetics of fragmentation that Charlotte Brontë developed as a form of personal expression can, I suggest, provide the foundation for an alternative historiography that reimagines the past's relationship to the present.

Heretical Humanism

Romola and Hellenism's Distaff Legacy

CHAPTER THREE

Marian Evans's first trip to Italy was, for several reasons, an escape from England.[1] She had just completed her third novel, *The Mill on the Floss* (1860), and the painful memories of familial estrangement revisited for that book together with her anxieties about its reception were draining her emotionally. In addition, although the success of her two earlier novels had improved her public reputation, she still bore the social stigma attached to her common-law marriage with George Henry Lewes.[2] Submerged in centuries of history, Italy provided a haven distant from England in time as well as space and offered Marian new horizons toward which she might expand her mind and senses. Devoting the trip to self-improvement, she immersed herself in her new environment, recording detailed observations of the art, architecture, and scenery encountered during the three-month journey that she later recalled "seem[ed] to divide one's life in two by the new ideas [it] suggest[ed] and the new veins of interest [it] open[ed]."[3] What seems to have struck her in all the cities she visited was the fusion—and sometimes jarring contrast—between the various historical periods that had left their marks on the landscape: "the mixture of ruined grandeur and modern life";[4] the contrast of ancient and Renaissance art; the amalgamation of Greek concepts with Roman forms. Fleeing the immediate pressures of her life, Marian acquired on her journey a broader awareness of how the past seeps into the present and, conversely, how modernity frames and shapes history. As Margaret Harris and Judith Johnston remark in their preface to *Recollections of Italy, 1860*, "There is a consciousness in [Eliot's] journals of history being constantly remade: in her fiction [after the journey], there is an engagement with the layers of previous civilisations and with competing histories (individual and collective)."[5] Marian's increasing awareness of an ongoing historical dialogue and its implications for her work was especially strong in Florence, which etched itself into her mind and would have a determinative impact on the direction of her career. "I am thrown into a state of humiliating passivity by the sight of the great things done in the far past," she wrote to her friend and publisher John Blackwood during her three-week stay in the city. "[I]t seems as if life were not long enough to learn, and as if my own activity were so completely dwarfed by comparison that I should never have courage for more creation of my own."[6] Recognized as one of the world's greatest centers of art and learning, Florence heightened the tension between high ambition and subsequent self-doubt that were habitual to Marian's thinking. However, her intimation of the latter's triumph was somewhat premature, for a week later, in a letter to Major William Blackwood, John's brother, Marian confessed that Florence "has stimulated me to entertain rather an ambitious project. . . . It will require a great deal of study and labour, and I am athirst to begin."[7] The endeavor, as many critics agree, would turn out to be the most challenging of her career, testing not only her intellectual and imaginative capacities but also the strength of her belief in a larger cultural and historical vision that opposed some of the most cherished values of her own time.

Taking more than two years to complete, *Romola* was published in the *Cornhill Magazine* between July 1862 and August 1863. Established in 1860 by George Smith with William Thackeray at the editorial helm, the *Cornhill* was one of the first successful magazines to combine high literary quality with a cheap selling price. Integrating criticism with poetry, high-quality illustrations, and fiction ranging from Trollope to the sensation stories of Wilkie Collins and Charles Reade, the *Cornhill* appealed to diverse interests and provided an ideal forum for George Eliot's experiment of molding rigorous scholarship into a popular form.[8] The only one of Eliot's novels to be set entirely in a foreign country and distant century (Renaissance Florence),[9] *Romola* departed considerably from her previous fictional outings and marked a turning point in Eliot's career: "Of necessity, the book is addressed to fewer readers than my previous works, and I myself have never expected—I might rather say *intended*—that the book should be as 'popular' in the same sense as the others," she wrote in a letter to her friend Sara Hennell in July 1862, after the publication of *Romola*'s first installment and while she was still struggling to complete the novel. "If one is to have freedom to write out one's own varying unfolding self, and not be a machine always grinding out the same material or spinning the same sort of web, one cannot always write for the same public" (*Letters*, 4:49). Eliot's shift of focus here indicates her attempt to incorporate the convictions she had developed in her work as a cultural critic and independent scholar into her relatively new occupation as a novelist. But while her comment might imply that she was abandoning the common reader to situate herself decisively within elite, intellectual realms, it is perhaps more accurate to see *Romola* as attempting, like the *Cornhill Magazine,* to blur the boundaries between high intellectual and popular culture. Indeed, because the novel was commissioned by George Smith to boost falling sales of the *Cornhill,* Eliot wrote knowing that her audience would have to be a broad one, approaching her work with expectations of an experience similar to *Adam Bede* and *Mill on the Floss,* which were securely grounded in familiar contexts. That she delivered *Romola* to her readers in the face of such expectations suggests her insistence on the relevance of her historical research to the broader human experience and, subsequently, her implicit challenge to the intellectual elitism attached to humanism's traditional association with educational privilege. Her disappointment in the final result, despite the praise of readers such as Trollope and Browning and despite her initial defense of her intentions to Sara Hennell, reveals that Eliot may not have been satisfied with reaching so selective an audience: the book's lack of general appeal to some extent reflects its falling short of its author's greatest aspirations.[10]

One of her most important aspirations was to discriminate those ideas and sentiments that have transcended space and time to aid human progress from (as she states in an 1851 article for the *Westminster Review*) those "terms and conditions which, having had their root in conditions of thought no longer existing, have ceased to possess any vitality, and are for us as spells which have lost their virtue."[11] Taking the measure of her own age, Eliot saw that transhistorical values such as faith, morality, and sympathy were imprisoned within religious, political, and educational institutions and ideologies that persisted not because they contributed to human progress but because they upheld empty traditions and maintained the forms of social hegemony through which individuals defined themselves. *The Mill on the Floss* comically noted this phenomenon in its portrait of the Dodson family, in whose company Maggie, with her superior intellect and sensitivity, is tragically isolated, her potential suppressed: "There were particular ways of doing everything in that family: particular ways of bleaching the linen, of making the cowslip wine, curing the hams, and keeping the bottled gooseberries; so that no daughter of that house could be indifferent to the privilege of having been born a Dodson, rather than a Gibson or a Watson."[12] In this ironic description of Mrs. Tulliver's provincial beliefs, faith in the Dodson name and its traditions cancels out the possibility of individuality, no matter how insignificant or pointless the tradition. Irony aside, Eliot saw the persistence of tradition qua tradition on a broader social level as a threat to the advancement of humanity. With her critic's perception, she maintained that the release of living ideas from dead forms depended on a history of human thought and belief that would distinguish between the transient and the transcendental. The writer of such a history must possess a "nature which combines the faculty for amassing minute erudition with the largeness of view necessary to give it a practical bearing; . . . a wonderful intuition of the mental conditions of past ages with an ardent participation in the most advanced ideas and most hopeful efforts of the present."[13] As the writer of *Romola,* Eliot attempted to accomplish this dual feat of historical and intellectual negotiation by transplanting the living ideas of the past into the organic form of the novel. Rooted in the soil of popular culture, which guarantees its vitality and relevance to the present, the novel, in Eliot's hands, becomes an instrument of historical redemption. Thus, while *Romola* may have drawn a more exclusive audience than much Victorian fiction, it also largely destabilizes the institutional values upon which high-culture authority rests by recognizing the affinity between the most exalted moments of the distant past and the most common experiences of the present.

Romola thus reformulates an institution fundamental to Victorian England's concept of its cultural and historical identity: the humanist legacy that Eliot, along with most of her contemporaries, traced to ancient Greece. The turn away from Rome and toward Greece as the cultural and intellectual foundation of secular modernity was a mid-eighteenth-century phenomenon that began in Germany and was seeded in England with the translated works of Winckelmann, Lessing, Goethe, Schiller, and Hölderlin. British hellenophilia continued to develop in response to the arrival of the Elgin Marbles in England at the beginning of the nineteenth century and to the Greek Revolution, which began in 1821 and inspired considerable British support. John Henry Newman's concept of "liberal education" and Matthew Arnold's vision of Greece as the epitome of "sweetness and light" established the nineteenth-century Hellenic revival firmly upon humanist foundations and an institutional ideal. Newman's and Arnold's visions of Greece as a basis for educational and cultural reforms bear two implications that Eliot's novel calls into question. First, in idealizing Greek culture as an example of intellectual freedom and self-discipline, humanistic Hellenism enacts an erasure of Greece's historical reality, which, as archaeologists and historians were beginning to reveal, differed considerably from Newman's or Arnold's apotheosized conceptions. Second, the confinement of Greece's legacy within an institutional context implicitly defines Hellenism, and the humanism based upon it, as an exclusively male legacy from which women, who did not have access to higher education until the late nineteenth century, were essentially excluded.[14]

As a woman whose opinions were respected in elite, male, intellectual circles, Eliot occupied a unique position from which to critique dominant cultural values and assumptions. Indeed, her intimacy with the governing theories and debates of her time and her friendships with such leading Hellenists as George Grote and Richard Claverhouse Jebb undermine any facile notion of a binary opposition between orthodox and heretical Hellenism. Rather, Eliot's ideas about the Greeks drew from the theories of her male associates, while her special sensibilities as a woman in a male-dominated field led her to expand the heretical implications of their theories. For though Eliot's privileged associations might put some doubt on her marginality to mainstream ideas, she nevertheless approached the most erudite discussions with a consciousness of her anomalous position as a woman occupying traditionally male terrain and with sensitivity to the fact that most women lacked either the education or the opportunity to participate in similar conversations. In *Romola,* she used both her privileged social position and her gendered sensitivities to challenge the entrenched notion that Hellenism belonged exclusively within institutional and masculine contexts. She did so first by distinguishing between two strands of Greece's modern legacy. The first of these strands comprises the textual and material artifacts that form the foundations of institutional discourse and whose recovery and transmission Eliot explored in the intellectual context of the Florentine Renaissance, the period to which nineteenth-century historians had traced the scholarly revaluation of classical works fundamental to the Victorian definition of humanism.[15] *Romola* identifies this strand of historical interaction with the forceful seizure of another's property, authority, or autonomy—practices characteristic of male dominated institutions. The second strand of Greece's legacy is far less tangible and constitutes on the one hand the need for a sense of historical and personal continuity and on the other the imaginative and moral capacity to fulfill this need. Eliot viewed this second form of historical legacy as an innate human desire to which all individuals have a natural right of ownership but to which women are particularly sensitive. Largely excluded from male-dominated institutions, with their acquisitive approach to historical succession, women remain grounded in the emotional, familial, and moral relations that Eliot saw as both elemental to ancient Greek society and opposed to traditional humanist values of self-discipline and rationality. In *Romola,* women become the bearers of a historical legacy obscured by male competitive and material interests and possess the power to redeem an age in danger of losing itself to the egotism and destructive principles of an institutionalized historiography. Written at a critical moment of negotiation over Greece's role in the constitution of modernity, *Romola* uses the stage of the Florentine Renaissance to argue that Hellenism belongs not only to the rationalist, implicitly male, upper-class humanist ideology represented by scholarly and political institutions but also to a common humanity whose bonds transcend temporal, spatial, and sexual boundaries.

Eliot and the Problem of Historical Synthesis

Eliot's concern with modernity's relationship to the ancient past and the special role of popular fiction in mediating this interchange began well before *Romola*'s conception. Her 1856 article "Silly Novels by Lady Novelists," written for the *Westminster Review* two years before *Scenes from Clerical Life* was published, demonstrates her belief in the novel's—and woman author's responsibility to cultural and intellectual history:

> [P]erhaps the least readable of silly women's novels, are the *modern-antique* species. . . . [W]hat can be more demonstrative of the inability of literary women to measure their own powers, than their frequent assumption of a task which can only be justified by the rarest concurrence of acquirement with genius? The finest effort to reanimate the past is of course only approximative—is always more or less an infusion of the modern spirit into the ancient form,—
>
> Admitting that genius which has familiarized itself with all the relics of an ancient period can sometimes, by the force of its

> sympathetic divination, restore the missing notes in the 'music of humanity,' and reconstruct the fragments into a whole which will really bring the remote past nearer to us, and interpret it to our duller apprehension,—this form of imaginative power must always be among the very rarest, because it demands as much accurate and minute knowledge as creative vigor.[16]

Eliot's use of the term *modern-antique* can be traced back to the "ancients versus moderns" debate dating to the late seventeenth and early eighteenth centuries. Originating in France and most famously satirized by Jonathan Swift's *Battle of the Books* (1704), this debate revolved around the question of whether modern science was superior to the knowledge of the Greeks and Romans. Eliot's formulation of the modern-antique reflects the more conciliatory tone that the discussion had acquired during the later eighteenth and early nineteenth centuries, when Rome and, later, Greece became cultural models upon which modernity could base its own cultural and artistic aspirations. For Eliot, the ancient past not only serves as a cultural model but also performs the vital function of providing the present with a sense of historical continuity, or the knowledge that ideas and beliefs have a foundation in and relevance to the human condition beyond the distinctive circumstances of one particular moment in time and space. Anticipating Mikhail Bakhtin's theory of novelistic polyglossia, Eliot believed that the novel, as a form shaped by the currents of its own age, has the special capacity to serve as a conduit for this historical dialogue and bears a unique obligation of cultural recovery that must not be taken lightly. The novelist who endeavors to reach into the dark spaces of antiquity must have not only the factual knowledge to piece together fragmentary relics of the distant past but also the sensitivity to gauge the temper of her own age to ensure the relevance of her historical material in a contemporary context. As if setting a challenge for which she felt herself uniquely qualified, Eliot's criteria for the modern-antique novel assign this popular genre the crucial tasks of cultural documentation and historical synthesis.

Romola was the closest Eliot ever came to writing a modern-antique novel, and as such, it proved the ultimate measure of her powers of historical synthesis. Set in fifteenth-century Florence, the novel is centrally concerned with exploring the Renaissance's reformulation and adaptation of ancient Greek ideas and literature as the foundation of a humanist tradition inherited by the Victorians. Ironically, while her "Silly Novels" essay had outlined the difficulties of reconstructing antiquity, it was the "modern" part of her modern-antique novel that gave Eliot the most trouble, testing her capacity to adapt the analytical rigor of scholarship to a popular narrative form. The effort made *Romola* one of the most difficult projects of her career. "The writing of *Romola* ploughed into her more than any of her other books," wrote Eliot's second husband, J. W. Cross, after her death. "She told me she could put her finger on it as marking a well-defined transition in her life. In her own words, 'I began it a young woman—I finished it an old woman.'"[17] Eliot's difficulty arose largely because she found herself riveted to the historical facts that she had earlier associated with the calcified forms imprisoning history's living legacy. A research trip to Florence in April 1861 and months of cramming information about the Renaissance only increased her doubts about her capacity to write convincingly of an era with such established historical import. "At present [Marian] remains immovable in the conviction that she *can't* write the romance because she has not knowledge enough," Lewes wrote to John Blackwood in the winter of 1861. "'Now as a matter of fact I know that she has immensely more knowledge of the particular period than any other writer who has touched it; but her distressing diffidence paralyses her. . . . When you see her, mind your care is to discountenance the idea of a romance being the product of an Encyclopaedia."[18] In her studious efforts to acquire factual knowledge, Eliot inadvertently deadened her creative energy, becoming a victim to the very paralysis that she had earlier anticipated in her critical work.

The inhibiting influence of her Renaissance setting on Eliot is evident from the novel's exhaustive reproduction of names, dates, events, and physical details, which give *Romola* a ponderous weight that both evoked admiration from readers for her laborious research and alienated others by its excessive erudition. In contrast, Eliot's incorporation of Greek mythology, literature, and history seems almost effortless, integrated into the flow of her narrative and extending the novel's interpretive possibilities beyond the imposing banks of factual detail. Just where these interpretive channels lead are traced in the final sections in this chapter. For now, I will supply some historical context for Eliot's vision of Greek antiquity as an instrument of imaginative release. This vision is rooted in her independent study of the language and of Greek literature. Although she compared university education in *Adam Bede* to the Eleusinian Mysteries, Eliot more than compensated for her lack of formal classics training by becoming fluent in Greek and Latin. According to the American philosopher

 John Fiske, Eliot was "thoroughly acquainted with the Homeric question [and] seems to have read all of Homer in Greek."[19] In addition, as her biographer Gordon Haight records, she spent a good portion of the years 1856–58 poring over the Greek tragedians. "Her imagination was soaked in Greece," states Richard Jenkyns, "and nothing was more natural to her than to use Greek literature as part of the small change of social intercourse" (113). Eliot's hellenophilia undoubtedly drew much of its passion from her study of German philosophy, upon which the Greeks famously wielded a "tyrannical" influence from the eighteenth century onward, and certainly her translation of David Friedrich Strauss's mythic reconstruction of the Gospels, *Das Leben Jesu,* in 1844 forced her to hone her Greek skills during a pivotal moment in her life.[20] Acquired in studious independence, sharpened through the translation of a work that challenged the Christian foundations of her upbringing, and daily practiced through leisure readings and casual conversation, Greek, for Eliot, was associated from the outset with heretical impulses against religious orthodoxy, against academic rigidity, and against the conventional limitations imposed upon her sex.

In addition to reflecting the attitude of German Romantics such as Goethe and Strauss, Eliot's handling of Greek material drew from a historical theory that surfaced in the mid-nineteenth century and created new possibilities for interpreting Greek antiquity's relevance to the modern imagination. This theory began with George Grote's vastly influential *History of Greece,* the first two volumes of which were published in 1846 and the last two ten years later. In opposition to late-eighteenth and early-nineteenth-century mythographers who regarded myths as containing reliable historical facts about the archaic world, Grote argued that myths were back-formations of civilizations existing well after the time period in which the stories took place and that even if these myths do contain historically accurate information, modern scholars are unable to separate these facts from fantasy: Greek myths "do not take their start from realities of the past, but from realities of the present, combined with retrospective feeling and fancy, which fills up the blank of the aforetime in a manner at once plausible and impressive. What proportion of fact there may be in the legend, or whether there be any at all, it is impossible to ascertain and useless to inquire."[21] Grote's argument extends the ancient-modern dynamic backward in time by suggesting that even the Greeks, to whom modernity traces its origin, were driven by the need for a sense of historical continuity and satisfied this need by imagining their past. This reformulation of Greek history as a function of psychological need and metaleptic imaginative projection allowed the extension of Greece's legacy from the external context of culture to the internal realm of human thought and desire. "Grote had provided a useful finite concept of myth and imagination for writers who were profoundly troubled by the difficulty for creative imagination in human experience limited strictly to the realm of sensations," writes Frank Turner, examining Grote's widespread influence on Victorian thought. "Grote had demonstrated that human beings so circumscribed could create, and in the legendary age of Greece had created, a mental realm of beauty and fanciful animation that answered to the deeper needs of the human situation."[22] By integrating psychological insight into historical theory, Grote expanded Greece's humanistic legacy from the arena of cultural acquisition to that of innate, emotional inheritance.

As a member of Eliot's and Lewes's intellectual circle, Grote's work had a profound influence on both writers: Eliot would extend Grote's theory beyond the scholarly boundaries of mythography to reveal its relevance to the larger history of the human imagination and thus its importance to the layman as well as the scholar. Even before taking extensive notes from Grote's *History* in her *Middlemarch* notebooks, Eliot's thinking about the mythic past seemed compatible with Grote's, as is apparent from her rearticulation of his ideas in her 1851 review of Robert William Mackay's *Progress of the Intellect, as Exemplified in the Religious Development of the Greeks and Hebrews,* which likewise showed the influence of Grote's theories:[23]

> That allegorical elements exist to a considerable extent, in the divine, if not in the heroic myths of Greece, there is strong evidence, both presumptive and internal; and the allegorical interpretation, on the lowest estimate of its soundness, is far superior to the pragmatical or semi-historical, which, in endeavouring to show a nucleus of fact in the myths, exhibits an utter blindness to the mental state in which they originated, and simply substitutes an unpoetical fable for a poetical one. But owing to the manysidedness of all symbols, there is a peculiarly seductive influence in allegorical interpretation; and we observe that all writers who adopt it . . . acquire a sort of fanatical faith in their rule of interpretation, and fall into the mistake of supposing that the conscious allegorizing of a modern can be a correct reproduction of what they acknowledge

> to be unconscious allegorizing in the ancients. . . . [T]he exuberant religious imagination of the Greek . . . would generate myths having relation rather to the human symbol than to the real phenomena of its cosmical prototype. Hence it appears to us, that any attempt extensively to trace consistent allegory in the myths must fail. Nor need we regret it, since our interest in the subject is of a different nature from that of the ancient philosophical interpreters, who, living at a period when the myths still constituted the popular religion, were under the necessity of bringing them into accordance with their own moral and religious views. It is enough for us if we have sufficient insight into the myths to form an approximate conception of the state of mind which produced them, and to assign them their true rank in the scale of religious development.[24]

Grote's ideas about the unknowability of the archaic age are apparent in Eliot's comments on Mackay. However, while his history celebrates the transpiring of the "mythopoeic age" to one commanded by reason and intellectual progress in the fifth century BC, Eliot's reformulation, resembling the thought of the German Romantics, expresses an enthusiastic, even nostalgic, admiration for the richness of the mythopoeic imagination. Her insistence on the incompatibility of these myths with historical, pragmatic, or even allegorical interpretations releases the myths from the scholarly, scientific, and religious frameworks that restrict meaning. Expanding on the implications of Grote's theory for the history of the human psyche, Eliot envisioned the mythopoeic imagination as not only designating a stage in humanity's development but also constituting a legacy that has the capacity to expand the boundaries of the modern mind. As we will see, her integration of Greek mythology into *Romola* forms an alternative view of history that corresponds to this expansive vision and challenges the linear chronology of her Renaissance setting. The historical and mythical elements of her novel mark two distinct historical trajectories that connect modernity to the ancient past and testify to the importance of the mythopoeic imagination in supplying narrative continuity where concrete knowledge fails.

Eliot's struggle to reconcile acquisitive and imaginative knowledge in *Romola* had a decisive influence on her views of historical synthesis, as is apparent from her reflections on the novel after its completion: "[W]ith regard to . . . my whole book, my predominant feeling is—not that I have achieved anything, but—that great, great facts have struggled to find a voice through me, and have only been able to speak brokenly,"[25] she wrote to R. H. Hutton after reading his largely favorable review of her novel in the *Spectator.* The "great, great facts" that Eliot speaks of in this letter are quite different from the encyclopedic knowledge that she had sought to acquire in preparing for *Romola.* They gesture rather toward what she called elsewhere in the letter "that religious and moral sympathy with the historical life of man which is the larger half of culture." She more clearly defined this sympathy some five years later in a letter to a young admirer, Clifford Allbutt: "[T]he inspiring principle which alone gives me courage to write is, that of so presenting our human life as to help my readers in getting a clearer conception and a more active admiration of those vital elements which bind men together and give a higher worthiness to their existence; and also to help them in gradually dissociating these elements from the more transient forms on which an outworn teaching tends to make them dependent" (*Letters,* 4:472). It is interesting to note the contrast between Eliot's expression of her artistic philosophy in this letter and her ideas in "Silly Novels." In both, she expresses her belief in the importance of conveying a transhistorical truth, but while the musical analogy of the earlier essay imagines a seamless fusion between past and present, the letter focuses on the interstices between definitive historical moments. These interstices signify the sense of incompletion that drives each generation to reach back into the past for a sense of continuity and suggest the impossibility of a seamless reconstruction of the past. The shift in Eliot's views is not so much one of ideology as one of perspective: the critic, in her distanced objectivity, may be able to envision holistically, an ideal composition; the novelist, who has laboriously pieced together collected facts with imagined characters, must see the resulting unity as an arrangement of fragments, whose ultimate form, like a mosaic, depends on the lines of jointure. While maintaining the ideal of historical synthesis, Eliot's concept of this idea after *Romola* suggests that the transcendent element of humanity may be precisely the experience of fragmentation that continually leads us to reimagine ourselves in terms of the past.

Rupture and Continuity: The Meanings of Greekness

> The great river-courses which have shaped the lives of men have hardly changed; and those other streams, the life-currents that

> ebb and flow in human hearts, pulsate to the same great needs, the same great loves and terrors. As our thought follows close in the slow wake of the dawn, we are impressed with the broad sameness of the human lot, which never alters in the main headings of its history—hunger and labour, seed-time and harvest, love and death. (*Romola,* proem)

Romola's dual task of historical synthesis and cultural recovery is immediately revealed in its proem, which traces the two distinct historical strands that Eliot saw interwoven into the tapestry of every age. The first strand consists of objects and events belonging to a specific moment in time and space; the second comprises spiritual and physical needs that all people share and that draw individuals from all ages into a common sense of historical continuity. The overlapping pattern of these two historical threads appears in Eliot's introduction to her novel's setting. On the one hand, the first words of her proem locate the work in a very specific historical moment: "More than three centuries and a half ago," she began, "in the mid spring-time of 1492 . . . "[26] This temporal designation is accompanied by a steady stream of physical detail that further grounds the work—the landscape that surrounds Florence, the great dome of the city's Old Palace, the church of the Santa Croce, the Ponte Vecchio arcing across the Arno with its decorative burden of shops, the Pitti Palace, only half constructed at the end of the fifteenth century. On the other hand, and in counterpoint to the solidity of these descriptions, Eliot also identified Florence as representing a transhistorical legacy of which the city's artistic achievements are but a visible reminder: this "world-famous city" seems "to stand as an almost unviolated symbol, amidst the flux of human things, to remind us that we still resemble the men of the past more than we differ from them, as the great mechanical principles on which those domes and towers were raised must make a likeness in human building that will be broader and deeper than all possible change" (2). The architecture that represents, for the modern reader, some of the finest accomplishments of the Renaissance past are significant to humanity not only as physical monuments of a specific age but also as reminders of historical continuity. Thus, while she may be directing us back to a distant moment in space in time, that place, Eliot suggested, shares the pulse of our most basic experiences and desires.

Eliot's sense of a spiritual connection between her own age and the Renaissance is literally embodied in the fifteenth-century ghost resurrected in the proem to lead the reader from the contemporary world back to his own time. In tracking the reminiscences of her spirit guide, Eliot reveals not only that modernity is the inheritor of the Renaissance's spiritual and material legacy but also that this dual bequest was passed down from an earlier age. The Renaissance spirit "was duly tinctured with the learning of his age, and judged not with the vulgar, but in harmony with the ancients; he, too, in his prime, had been eager for the most correct manuscripts, and had paid many florins for antique vases and for disinterred busts of the ancient immortals" (5). While modernity may look to the art and architecture of the Renaissance for a sense of historical continuity, the Renaissance discovered inspiration for these creations in the relics of the ancient past. These relics—which the spirit identifies specifically with the Greek of Homer, Plato, and Aristotle—not only contributed to the progress of human thought but also represented the persistence of intangible spiritual forces impervious to change. "For the Unseen Powers were mighty," her Renaissance ghost reflects. "Were not all things charged with occult virtues?" The intermingling of scholarly pride and superstitious fear in the mind of the Renaissance spirit, contemplating his ancient inheritance, signifies, for Eliot, that the fifteenth century was not simply an age of intellectual advancement but "a strange web of belief and unbelief; of Epicurean levity and fetishistic dread; of pedantic impossible ethics uttered by rote, and crude passions acted out with childish impulsiveness; of inclination towards a self-indulgent paganism" (6). Throughout the novel, the strains of superstition pulsing throughout the Renaissance are revealed in such scenes as the Bacchanalian celebration of St. John the Baptist, featuring a representation of the Christian saint outfitted in the tiger skins of the Greek god of wine and revelry. Even Savonarola's bonfire of the vanities, while purporting to destroy both physically and spiritually the legacy of a corrupt, pagan past merely replaces old rituals with new symbols and arouses the same superstitious frenzy in the masses. By gesturing toward these events in her proem, Eliot makes the argument that the Renaissance inherited from the ancient past not only the material and ideas upon which to construct its edifice of cultural achievement, as Walter Pater would later celebrate in his *Renaissance,* but also the passion, irrationality, and mythopoeic mentality associated with the primitivity of earlier ages.[27] Contesting the Victorian persuasion that the Renaissance, the ultimate model of humanist endeavors, had filtered the primal from the progressive elements of the ancient past, Eliot argued that if modernity is fully to claim its position in the history of human thought, it must acknowledge not only the achievements of the past but also the tumultuous and conflicting impulses that underlay their creations. Embodying the energy of his own age as well as of the ancient past, the Renaissance spirit of Eliot's proem leads the reader on a journey both backward in time and inward to the mythopoeic regions of his own psyche.

This journey begins with Tito's arrival in Florence. A shipwrecked stranger of Greek origins, Tito awakens from a dream at the outset of the first chapter, and his initiation into his new surroundings launches the reader's introduction to the novel's epochal setting. Following Tito's recovery from sleepy daze to consciousness to increasing awareness of his historical context, the opening of *Romola* draws a literal parallel between the Florentine Renaissance and the process of Greek reawakening. Indeed, referred to only as the "Greek" or the "stranger" throughout the first three chapters, Tito embodies a puzzle that unites the nature of his origins and the import of his immediate surroundings in a single question of identity that propels the narrative forward. The significance of the mysterious Greek to his Renaissance moment and vice versa is revealed through the juxtaposition between Tito's arrival in Florence and the death of Lorenzo de Medici.[28] This occurrence has thrown the city into a state of stunned chaos, but Tito has heard neither of Lorenzo nor of his death. "What Lorenzo?" Nello the barber responds, shocked by Tito's ignorance. "There is but one Lorenzo, I imagine, whose death could throw the Mercato into an uproar, set the lantern of the Duomo leaping in desperation, and cause the lions of the Republic to feel under an immediate necessity to devour one another. I mean Lorenzo de Medici, the Pericles of our Athens—if I may make such a comparison in the ear of a Greek" (30). Comparing the Renaissance fervor of spiritual and cultural rejuvenation to Pericles' similar project in fifth-century BC Athens, Nello's analogy points to two major accomplishments of the Italian Renaissance that owed their success greatly to the interests and support of the Medicis: the revival of Greek culture and learning—epitomized by Periclean Athens—and the recovery of ancient Greek manuscripts. Trained as a scholar and "dipped over again [in Greek dye] by long abode and much travel in the land of gods and heroes" (30), Tito, newly wakened from his shipwrecked daze and ready to establish himself in his new environment, incarnates the possibilities for a rebirth of the Greek Golden Age, whose cherubic image Tito identifies in the artist Piero's sketch.[29]

However, while Tito's economic worth and practical survival hinge on his Greek learning and Greek possessions, upon which rest his chances

for patronage, his innate Greek heritage, as Nello cautions, could very
well get in the way of his Renaissance aspirations. "[L]et me hint to you that your being a Greek . . . is not in your favour," Nello tells Tito.

> Certain of our scholars hold that your Greek learning is but a wayside degenerate plant until it has been transplanted into Italian brains, and that now there is such a plentiful crop of the superior quality, your native teachers are mere propagators of degeneracy. . . . [W]e Florentines have liberal ideas about speech, and consider that an instrument which can flatter and promise so cleverly as the tongue, must have been partly made for those purposes; and that the truth is a riddle for eyes and wit to discover, which it were mere spoiling of sport for the tongue to betray. Still we have our limits beyond which we call dissimulation treachery. But it is said of the Greeks that their honesty begins at what is the hanging point with us, and that since the old Furies went to sleep, your Christian Greek is of so easy a conscience that he would make a stepping-stone of his father's corpse. (37)

Nello here makes a distinction between Greek learning and Greekness that clarifies the values and terms through which the Renaissance conceives its ancient legacy. His comment suggests that "Greek learning" constitutes a body of knowledge whose significance is determined solely by the forms through which it is received, processed, and transmitted. Nello's perspective is consistent with Renaissance humanism's intense interest in the collection and transcription of Greek texts and its general regard for the classics as an instrument of social exchange. Paul Oskar Kristeller points out that "classical studies in the Renaissance were rarely, if ever, separated from the literary and practical aim of the rhetorician to write and to speak well."[30] Nello's attempt to market Tito's Greek knowledge to potential sponsors exemplifies this practical mentality, demonstrating that Greek learning is regarded as valuable less in what it reveals about the culture and people of the past than in how it contributes to defining the social and cultural stratifications of the present. Tito's knowledge of Greek, a rare and much-coveted commodity during the Renaissance,[31] adds to his market value and strengthens his chances of social ascent. Tito's Greekness, in contrast, holds inherent meaning as a racial identification that attaches the value of Greek to a specific history and personal past rather than an exchange value. In juxtaposing the intrinsic value of Greekness and the exchange value of Greek learning, Eliot poses a question that is central not only to an evaluation of the Renaissance in particular but also to historical legacy in general: to what extent can a body of knowledge surrender the contingencies of its past to the contemporary circumstances of its exchange and still maintain its validity as an intellectual legacy?

This question had particular relevance for Eliot's own time as discussions over England's rights to ancient Greek artifacts and ideas arose on several fronts. The most volatile and earliest of these involved debates over Lord Elgin's, and later England's, right to the Parthenon marbles. In his 1811 poem "The Curse of Minerva" and later his 1812 *Childe Harold's Pilgrimage,* Byron inveighed against the "plunderers" who "could violate each saddening shrine, and bear these altars o'er the long-reluctant brine."[32] Even after England had purchased the marbles from Elgin, the debate over rightful ownership continued. One visitor to Greece commented, "That the Elgin Marbles will contribute to the improvement of Art in England, cannot be doubted. They must certainly open the eyes of British artists, and prove that the true and only road to simplicity and beauty is the study of nature. But had we a right to diminish the interest of Athens for such motives?"[33] Arguments against British ownership of the marbles escalated after Greece won independence from Turkish rule in 1831. "The Manes of ancient Greeks are as if offended by Lord Elgin's spoliation of art," the new king of Greece wrote to the British parliament, "and blessedness will not smile on new-born Hellas ere they have been atoned for and their sculptures shine again at the front of the holy temple."[34] But such nationalistic arguments as these against England's claim to Greek art and ideas contended with evolving theories that justified ancient Greece's legacy to Victorian England on philosophical grounds. In a series of articles and sermons collected in the *History of Rome* (1838–43) and in his *History of the Peloponnesian War by Thucydides* (1857), Thomas Arnold, following Giambattista Vico's theory of parallel ages, argued for an intrinsic connection between Periclean Athens and nineteenth-century England: "The period to which the work of Thucydides refers belongs properly to modern and not to ancient history."[35] His son, Matthew Arnold, followed his father's lead in his 1857 inaugural lecture as professor of poetry at Oxford, which stated that the works of Aeschylus and Sophocles contained "all the fulness [*sic*] of life and of thought which the new world has accumulated. This new world in its maturity of reason resembles our own."[36] Both of these arguments divorce the issue of intellectual and artistic legacy from that of nationalism, establishing Victorian England's right of ownership through the appeal to a humanist tradition that transcends space and time.

While Eliot certainly shared the Arnolds' conviction in a transcendent element of history to which all humanity has right of claim, she also saw the danger of abstracting intellectual tradition from its historical and social contexts. *Romola* voices this concern by examining the contesting values behind the Renaissance interest in Greek learning. As evidenced by Nello's distinction between Tito's Greekness and his Greek knowledge, the Florentines' renewal of the ideas and relics of the ancient Greek past depends on a process of rationalization that essentially negates the intrinsic history and substance of the Greek nation. The nature of this simultaneous act of recovery and repudiation is revealed in Tito's later account of the rapaciousness set loose after the 1453 fall of the Greek empire: "[O]n every memorable spot in Greece conquest has set its seal, till there is a confusion of ownership even in ruins, that only close study and comparison could unravel. High over every fastness, from the plains of Lacedaemon to the straits of Thermopylae, there towers some huge Frankish fortress, once inhabited by a French or Italian marquis, now either abandoned or held by Turkish bands" (67). Tito's resentment on behalf of his ancestral motherland might apply not only to the destructive appropriation of Greece's physical remains but also to the Florentines' (and Victorians') claim to the Greeks' intellectual legacy. For just as contests over ownership of physical territory and objects literally destroy the land itself, so too does the Florentine pride in the "superior quality" of its Greek learning constitute an act of historical suppression. In both cases, the interest is not to preserve Greece as a nation with its own unique past but to use its destruction as a foundation for another authority.[37] As suggested by Nello's warning to Tito, the discrediting of the modern Greeks as morally deficient justifies the transferal of their legacy to another race: Greek learning must find a new form of expression because the Christian Greeks have ceded their moral right to their inheritance. Though Nello later ascribes the prejudice against Greeks to the particular doxology of Greek Christianity,[38] the bias against Greekness (as portrayed by Eliot) goes beyond "religious scruple," as Nello would have it. By asserting an unbreachable divide between ancient and modern Greece, Florentine scholars, in Nello's account, institute a system of self-vindication that enacts the very destruction it seeks to correct.

 The blind hypocrisy in such a system of moral self-validation is demonstrated by Nello's advice to Tito. On the one hand, the barber criticizes the Greeks for their treachery and dishonesty, thereby vindicating Florentine perfidy as both morally superior and more cunning. On the other hand, he advocates to Tito a behavioral ethics of *sprezzatura*, or social dissimulation, so that the Greek stranger may prosper in Florentine society.[39] "Oil your tongue well when you talk of the ancient Latin writers, and give it an extra dip when you talk of the modern," he tells his young protégé. "A wise Greek may win favour among us" (38). The "wisdom" that Nello talks of here is not book learning but an understanding of the vanity—and venality—inherent in human nature, at least in its Renaissance manifestation. Success in the marketplace of Florentine scholarship is based not on knowledge of ancient texts and languages per se but on proficiency in the sophistical parlance of economic exchange. On the former might rest an appreciation for the past in its historical context. The latter asserts its intellectual legacy by obliterating the very values it claims to inherit. Tito's social and economic prosperity depends on his severing his acquired knowledge from the personal and moral ties that bind him to the past. This severance, as the novel later reveals, entails a betrayal of the moral obligations that bind Tito to his adoptive father and teacher, Baldassarre—the source of his Greek possessions, his learning, and even his life. In Tito's initiation into the secular world of Florentine scholarship, the concept of renascence is established as an assertion of historical discontinuity and cultural imperialism.

Greek Knowledge and Moral Sympathy

Tito's initial encounters in the *mercato* present a bleak view of Renaissance intellectual history as one that authorizes the destruction of the past as a condition of cultural progress and personal advancement. This view of history as erasure and conquest is juxtaposed against that of the blind, reclusive scholar Bardo de Bardi, whose personal investment in Greek learning directly opposes the economics of the mercato. Whereas the merchants who first introduce Tito to Florentine politics regard Greek scholarship as a saleable commodity disconnected from personal history, scholarship for Bardo becomes a substitute for human interchange and a guarantor of his personal legacy. "For me, Romola, even when I could see, it was with the great dead that I lived; while the living often seemed to me mere spectres—shadows dispossessed of true feeling and intelligence,"

Bardo tells his daughter. "I forsook the vulgar pursuit of wealth in commerce that I might devote myself to collecting the precious remains of ancient art and wisdom, and leave them . . . for an everlasting possession to my fellow citizens" (51). Removed from a social and economic rationale that insists on the separation of human and intellectual history, Bardo's static existence attempts to ensure the inseparability of his name and personal accomplishments and the legacy of his material possessions. However, Bardo's disavowal of the people, ideas, and values of his own time is just as detrimental to the current of human progress, Eliot suggested, as the commercial ethos that would barter the integrity of the past for present gain. Without what Eliot called in her Mackay essay an "ardent participation in the most advanced ideas and most hopeful efforts of the present,"[40] the scholar who would bequeath to the future the ideas and achievements of the past can only offer a collection of lifeless forms whose vitality has long since dissipated.

Bardo's statement of his aspirations at the novel's outset demonstrates how the rejection of his historical moment points to the futility of the scholar's conservative endeavors while blinding him to the disingenuousness of his professed philanthropy and devotion to scholarship. "I cannot but regard the multiplication of these babbling, lawless productions [of the present time] . . . as a sign that the glorious hopes of this century are to be quenched in gloom," Bardo laments to Nello, who has brought Tito to the Bardi house in a bid for patronage. "[T]hey have been the prologue to an age worse than that of iron—the age of tinsel and gossamer, in which no thought has substance enough to be moulded into consistent and lasting form" (62). While professing a strong desire to preserve intellectual history for the sake of his fellow man, Bardo's misanthropic pessimism about his own age sabotages his goal by condemning mental labor to insubstantiality. Conceived in isolation from the currents, interests, and works of his own age, Bardo's dream "that men should own themselves debtors to the Bardi Library in Florence" (57) merely institutes a condition of stagnation whereby intellectual history will be eternally tethered to the increasingly obsolete values to which he has devoted his life. The preservation of his scholarship contributes less to intellectual progress than to a personal economy of accumulating losses. Mistaking personal desire for civic concern, Bardo's visions of the future testify to an individual's struggle for immortality against annihilating historical forces.

But while Eliot might have looked critically upon the futility of Bardo's scholarly project, she nevertheless acknowledged the validity of his desire for personal continuity: the manifestation of the need for historical continuity at the level of individual experience, encompassing an individual's need both to understand one's history (that is, the source of one's ideas and being) and to feel the impact of one's ideas and being on others, both in that time and in the future. In Bardo's relationship with Tito, Eliot demonstrated that the fulfillment of this desire for personal continuity ultimately lies not in the study and preservation of inanimate manuscripts but in the personal interactions and sympathy that scholarship can enable. The impact of such a personal exchange on an individual's sense of continuity is exemplified in Bardo's effect on Tito. In direct contrast to Tito's "market" value, which rests on the distinction between his Greekness and Greek learning, Tito's contribution to Bardo's vision depends on the identification of his acquired knowledge with his personal experience. "You must recall everything, to the minutest trace left in your memory," Bardo urges Tito as the latter begins to reveal something of his personal past for the first time since his arrival in Florence.

> You will win the gratitude of after-times by leaving a record of the aspect Greece bore while yet the barbarians had not swept away every trace of the structures that Pausanias and Pliny described: you will take those great writers as your models; and such contribution of criticism and suggestion as my riper mind can supply shall not be wanting to you. . . . [Y]es, I will spend on you that long-accumulated study which was to have been thrown into the channel of another work—a work in which I myself was to have had a helpmate. . . . But who knows whether that work may not be executed yet? For you, too, young man, have been brought up by a father who poured into your mind all the long-gathered stream of his knowledge and experience. Our aid might be mutual. (67)

Bardo's interest in preserving the remnants of the Greek empire along with its literature and his appreciation for Tito's personal experience of Greece as well as Tito's Greek scholarship all contrast with the earlier sentiments of Nello, whose advice for Tito's ascension in Florentine society echoes the destructive principles of the "barbarians" that Bardo disdains. Insisting on the interconnection of personal history and acquired knowledge, Bardo not only encourages a holistic vision of history but also reanimates a sense of moral integrity that Tito is in imminent danger of abandoning through his betrayal of his adoptive father, Baldassarre. Bardo values Tito's personal history not only because it bears witness to a Greek world that the reclusive, blind scholar had believed destroyed but also because it testifies to a principle of filial devotion that Bardo's son, Dino, had betrayed in deserting his father. As the apparently faithful product of another father's labor, Tito represents not only the possible completion of Bardo's scholarly ambitions but also the reparation of a shattered faith in personal obligation. The transcription of Tito's Greek learning and experiences thus affirms an ethos of interpersonal commitment in which intellectual legacy is inextricable from the history of human relationships invested in its production.

Baldassarre's relationship with Tito demonstrates the reliance of personal continuity on what Eliot called on numerous occasions "moral sympathy." This was a transhistorical element of human existence that she used to describe both an individual's compassion with his fellow man and, as she wrote in her Mackay essay, "an expansion of one's being, a pre-existence in the past" (269). Scholarship and the transmission of knowledge can provide the foundation upon which such moral sympathy is constructed, but without moral sympathy, the transmission of knowledge loses all meaning, leaving the desire for continuity unfulfilled. It is Baldassarre's failure to recognize the importance of cultivating such moral sympathy with Tito that underlies, at least partly, the disastrous loss of his sense of continuity. "[Baldassarre] was constantly scrutinising Tito's mind to see whether it answered to his own exaggerated expectations," Tito remembers of his schooling by his adopted father.

> [A]nd age—the age of a thick-set, heavy-browed, bald man beyond sixty, whose intensity and eagerness in the grasp of ideas have long taken the character of monotony and repetition, may be looked at from many points of view without being found attractive. . . . [W]hen he was seven years old, Baldassarre had rescued him from blows, had taken him to a home that seemed like opened paradise. . . . And he had been docile, pliable, quick of apprehension, ready to acquire . . . a radiant presence for a lonely man to have won for himself. . . . [T]he pleasure of looking at him made amends to one who had watched his growth with a sense of claim and possession. (99)

For Baldassarre, even more than for Bardo (with whom there is a mutual exchange of knowledge), Tito serves an intensely egotistical purpose: he both represents the recovery of an intellectual prowess lost to the progress of time and enables an illusion of control over the forces dictating that loss. With a mind and character that Baldassarre has shaped with his own teaching, Tito becomes for Baldassarre a material possession that is synonymous with the old man's self-integrity and sense of power. Tito's importance to Baldassarre's mental stability and self-confidence is emphasized by the old man's simultaneous loss of his son and his mind. "Would any believe that he had ever had a mind filled with rare knowledge, busy with close thoughts, ready with various speech?" Baldassarre reflects with dismay as he searches for Tito and struggles to recover his lost Greek knowledge.

> It had all slipped away from him—that laboriously-gathered store. Was it utterly and for ever gone from him . . . [o]r, was it still within him, imprisoned by some obstruction that might one day break asunder? . . . [O]nce or twice . . . he had seemed momentarily to be in entire possession of his past self . . . seemed again to see Greek pages and understand them, again to feel his mind moving unbenumbed among familiar ideas. . . . [He had harbored a hope] that he might find his child, his cherished son again; might yet again clasp hands and meet face to face with the one being who remembered him as he had been before his mind was broken. . . . "[A]t least I shall meet eyes that remember me. I am not alone in the world." (267–69)

Baldassarre's thoughts here directly equate the loss of his knowledge with the disappearance of his son. Tito, the Greek, has become equated in Baldassarre's mind with the entirety of his intellectual capacities, and his adoptive son's absence translates for Baldassarre into a mental fragmentation that can only be rectified by the recovery of the personal relationship through which his knowledge has been transferred. The experience of fragmentation reveals that Baldassarre's work of recovering and preserving the ancient past served the far more critical task of self-reproduction while the devastation of Tito's desertion impresses the futility of scholarship without moral sympathy. In the wake of Baldassarre's losses, Tito's acknowledgment of his father comes to surpass in importance whatever scholarly knowledge he may have inherited, promising the recovery of a self-integrity destroyed by the dissolution of Baldassarre's mental empire.

Though the effects of Baldassarre's amnesia directly contrast with Bardo's encyclopedic memory of the words and world he can no longer

see, both suffer the discontinuity and impotence of an intellectual sover-
eignty dissociated from moral sympathy. Baldassarre's relentless pursuit of Tito emphasizes the primacy of the very personal desire for continuity that both nourishes and is obscured by the claims of the intellect. The novel exposes the deceptive veneer of intellectual conceit through juxtaposing Baldassarre's loss of his Greek learning with the awakening of the Furies—those spirits of vengeance from Greek mythology that protected friendship and other relations of mutual obligation.[41] Stripped of his scholarship and openly rejected by Tito, Baldassarre is reduced to a primal hatred that constitutes its own form of renascence. Baldassarre's awakening after a moment of mental clarity is described with a churning mix of emotions.

> The first moments were filled with strange bewilderment: he was a man with a double identity; to which had he awaked? to the life of dim-sighted sensibilities like the sad heirship of some fallen greatness, or to the life of recovered power? Surely the last, for the events of the night all came back to him: the recognition of the page of Pausanias, the crowding resurgence of facts and names, the sudden wide prospect which had given him such a moment as that of the Maenad in the glorious amaze of her morning waking on the mountain top.
>
> He took up the book again, he read, he remembered without reading. He saw a name, and the images of deeds rose with it. . . . There were stories of inexpiable crimes, but stories also of guilt that seemed successful. . . . If baseness triumphed everywhere else, . . . it would never triumph over the hatred which it had itself awakened. . . . Baldassarre felt the indestructible independent force of a supreme emotion, which knows no terror, and asks for no motive, which is itself an ever-burning motive, consuming all other desire. And now in this morning light, when the assurance came again that the fine fibres of association were active still, and that his recovered self had not departed, all his gladness was but the hope of vengeance. . . . It was not any retributive payment or recognition of himself for his own behoof, on which Baldassarre's whole soul was bent: it was to find the sharpest edge of disgrace and shame by which a selfish smiler could be pierced; it was to send through his marrow the most sudden shock of dread. (336)

 Baldassarre does not retain his momentary lucidity. The "magical black marks" fade once more into obscurity, leaving the learned man unable to defend his claim to scholarly recognition against Tito's public denunciations of him as a madman. But while Tito's accusation of madness may deny Baldassarre's intellectual power, it also identifies with unconscious irony the potent rage that will eventually resolve itself in his murder. For though Baldassarre may be unable to recuperate his scholarly reputation, the loss of his knowledge proves the evanescence of the intellectual conceits with which he has identified his power. The exhilaration of the awakening described in the above passage derives not from the old man's recovery of his ability to read Greek but from an emotional arousal independent of the textual record inscribed in Pausanias's history. The "facts and names" on the page serve only to trigger an array of mythic images that, through the "fine fibres of association," lead Baldassarre from emotional awakening to moral resolve. The unreliability of his intellect has driven Baldassarre to regard his regained mastery over language as merely a means of accessing a more primal and enduring emotional need. The novel's equation of the maenads[42] and the Furies in the context of Baldassarre's "mad" quest for vengeance suggests that his rejection of a rational world also delivers the disgraced scholar to a mythopoeic consciousness that, while more primitive in its operation, allows him to see beyond the seductive but false promises of scholarly authority to the more pressing force of moral sympathy—and, in Tito's case, moral betrayal.

Having lost his hope of being recognized for the scholar and father he once was, Baldassarre comes to embody an elemental emotion that both transcends his personal attachments and redefines the boundaries of his existence. Baldassarre's "maenadic" rage unveils an aspect of his being that forms a "double-identity" with his rational mind. Baldassarre "was not mad; for he carried within him that piteous stamp of sanity, the clear consciousness of his shattered faculties; he measured his own feebleness," states the narrative after Tito's initial refusal to recognize his father. The idea of an intellect trapped within a body alludes to an earlier image in the novel that frames Baldassarre's transformation as an essentially human condition. For Baldassarre's situation recalls that of the doomed Actaeon, whose story Romola was reading to Bardo from Nonnus's *Dionysiaca* when Nello first brought Tito to the Bardi house.[43] In the myth, the young hunter had the misfortune of seeing the goddess Artemis naked. As punishment, he was transformed into a deer with the consciousness of a man. Bardo asks Romola to read the passage from Nonnus containing Actaeon's lament as he is devoured by his dogs: "I have the alien shape of a beast, yet a man's feeling is in me! Do beasts ever lament their own death? They live without thought, and know not their end. . . . I drop intelligent tears, under the brows of a beast."[44] The parallel between Baldassarre and Actaeon is significant not only in identifying Baldassarre with Bardo in their shared subjection to forces beyond their rational control but also in defining humanity as a function of this subjection. Actaeon's intellect testifies to his humanity not because it can alter his fate but because it recognizes his powerlessness to mitigate his suffering. Nonnus's mythic imagery thus unites Bardo and Baldassarre in a narrative of human experience wherein each attempts to make sense of his relationship to the world through visions of intellectual prowess that, though deceiving in their illusions of control, testify to a spiritual need for personal continuity and moral sympathy that underlies their common humanity.

Romola's Mythopoeic Imagination

Baldassarre's relationship with Tito emphasizes that the significance of intellectual legacy rests not only in the transferal and preservation of scholarship but also, and more important, in the intangible bonds of moral sympathy formed through the exchange of ideas. Baldassarre's intellectual conceits prevent him from recognizing this fact until he can no longer recover Tito's loyalty. Similarly, Romola's inability to ever belong to a scholarly enclave, thus being denied its attendant conceits, is the reason that her character remains sensitive to the underlying spiritual needs and moral claims obscured by Tito's, Bardo's, and Baldassarre's ambitions. "I constantly marvel at the capriciousness of my daughter's memory, which grasps certain objects with tenacity, and lets fall all those minutiae whereon depends accuracy, the very soul of scholarship," Bardo informs Tito during their first meeting. "[T]hou [Romola] art endowed beyond the measure of women; but thou hast withal the woman's delicate frame, which ever craves repose and variety, and so begets a wandering imagination" (64, 69). For Bardo, Romola can never be an adequate substitute for his lost son, Dino, because, as a woman, she lacks the rationality and focus necessary for intellectual labor. Like Actaeon, her intellect is trapped within an inferior frame, and though her mental capacity exceeds that of most women, it cannot be weighed on a scholarly scale. However, because of its very exclusion from conventional systems of intellectual measurement, Romola's expansive imagination creates a distinct system of values through which the novel's other characters can be judged, and it lays out an alternative mapping for the novel's account of history.[45] This map traces the internal legacy of the mythopoeic imagination: that element of the human psyche that George Grote attributed to archaic Greek myth-making faculties but that Victorians after him extended to explain a transhistorical human capacity to account for experiences beyond the limits of rational understanding.

The nature of this alternative, mythopoeic history is apparent from Romola's initial reaction to Tito, which reveals a concept of spiritual regeneration contrasting the politically and culturally based accounts of rebirth associated with the idea of renaissance in the novel's first chapters.

> Romola's astonishment could hardly have been greater if the stranger had worn a panther-skin and carried a thyrsus; for the cunning barber had said nothing of the Greek's age or appearance. . . . Tito's bright face . . . seemed like a wreath of spring, dropped suddenly into Romola's young but wintry life, which had inherited nothing but memories—memories of a dead mother, of a lost brother, of a blind father's happier time—memories of far-off light, love, and beauty, that lay embedded in dark mines of books, and could hardly give out their brightness again until they were kindled for her by the torch of some known joy. . . . The finished fascination of his air came chiefly from the absence of demand and assumption. It was that of a fleet, soft-coated, dark-eyed animal that delights you by not bounding away in indifference from you, and unexpectedly pillows its chin on your palm, and looks up at you desiring to be stroked—as if it loved you. (59)

Romola's spiritual reawakening at her first sight of Tito juxtaposes with both Nello's and Bardo's interest in the Greek stranger. For Nello, Tito represents a concept of cultural renewal dependent on the asseveration of Greek knowledge from historical contingencies. For Bardo, Tito's foreign travels and knowledge of ancient civilizations allow Bardo to pursue his work of transcription in continuing disregard for the ideas and needs of his own time and place. The interests of both in Tito's acquired knowledge form disconnective views of history that regard Greek legacy as largely a project of material acquisition and exchange. Romola's response to Tito, in contrast, is independent of his scholarly value and is grounded in her need to connect an importunate spiritual hunger with a dispossessed past. Daily experiencing the vacuity of an existence dissociated from sensuality and imagination, Romola has inherited a legacy of bright memories that has little relevance to her immediate life. For Romola, this disconnect between past and present translates into the splitting of knowledge from existence wherein "light, love, and beauty" have become abstractions divorced from perception and desire. Like shadows flickering before Plato's imprisoned cave dwellers, the memories that crowd Romola's consciousness are as removed from her experiential reality as the ancient worlds bound in her father's books. Satisfying Romola's craving for a sense of continuity, Tito reattaches the memories of love and light that are the distant history of Romola's existence to the immediate sensations that are its substance. In connecting Romola's knowledge of her past with her present experience, Tito not only enables an act of historical recovery but also restores Romola to the most elemental aspects of her being.[46]

Romola's image of Tito as the god Dionysos, with his panther skin and thyrsus, traces her experience of personal continuity to the operation of a mythopoeic imagination that has the capacity to transport her beyond the sensual limits of her experience, momentarily releasing her from the mordant, book-lined boundaries of her life. The nature of this mythopoeic imagination can be seen in the contrast between Romola's and Bardo's responses to Nonnus's *Dionysiaca,* which Romola was reading to Bardo just before Tito's arrival. Bardo's interest in the mythic compendium seems primarily focused on the superiority of his textual emendations in comparison with those of his contemporaries, on the book's exact location in his library, and on his aspiration to "gather, as into a firm web, all the threads that [his] research had laboriously disentangled" (51)—a project as ambitious as Nonnus's voluminous work and prefiguring Casaubon's similar project in *Middlemarch.* The contents of the myths, however, have little significance for Bardo's life. In contrast to Bardo's material aims of collation and codification, the fragmentary images of the god that Romola projects onto Tito reveal her inclination to connect the contents of the myths to her living experience. Just as he was for the ancient Greeks, Dionysos for Romola is a spiritual being—a god of fertility, natural forces, and mystical experiences wholly alien to the organized, rational world that she and her father inhabit. Abstracted from its textual history, the mythology of the Greek god has been absorbed into Romola's imagination as a visual vocabulary of the primal needs for love, nurturance, and sympathy that have been suppressed in her since her early childhood but persist in her adult psyche.

Surfacing as a cognitive framework for her emotional response to Tito, Romola's mythopoeic imagination not only aids in the achievement of personal continuity, putting her immediate sensations in vibrant synchrony with her memories, but also reveals that beneath her "proud self-dependence" courses an impulse for human connection that links Romola's life to a larger chain of being. "A girl of eighteen imagines the feelings behind the face that has moved her with its sympathetic youth, as easily as primitive people imagined the humours of the gods in fair weather; what is she to believe in, if not in this vision woven from within?" (68). The equation between Romola's youth and the state of humanity in its "primitive" stages suggests that the desire for moral sympathy is not merely a product of adolescent fantasies but constitutive of what Eliot called in her letter to Hutton "the historical life of man." Reflecting the face and function of an archaic faith, Romola's mythopoeic projections testify to the persistence of spiritual needs throughout time and within individuals even as systems of thought evolve. Demonstrating the expansive capacity of the mythopoeic imagination, Romola's impulsive response to Tito opens up new possibilities of experience. "Romola . . . felt that this new acquaintance had with wonderful suddenness got within the barrier that lay between them and the alien world" (60), the narrative states as Tito begins to tell Bardo of his recent travels throughout the Mediterranean. For Romola, the "alien world" is not merely the larger universe of scholarly research whose news Tito brings to Bardo's insular library but the unfamiliar territories of her own nature. Her image of Dionysos—the "twice-born" god—reflects personal desires ungovernable by a regime of intellectual rationality while at the same time representing a cyclical, recuperative view of history that values the persistence of mythopoeic faculties and counteracts even as it coexists with a linear account of human progress marked by rupture and appropriation.[47]

The same mythopoeic consciousness that links Romola to humanity at large sensitizes her to the spiritual needs of those around her, and throughout the novel, she seems to have the unique role of translating into spiritual (and ultimately redemptive) terms the outward expression of other characters' desires. While she confesses to Tito that she has "not the gifts that are necessary for scholarship" (68), Romola also fully recognizes other "gifts" to which her father is blinded by the rigidity of his intellectual values: "Romola did not make [her] self-depreciatory statement in a tone of anxious humility, but with a proud gravity" (68). Her response to Bardo's lament for his "right to be remembered" gives further insight into the nature of her perceptions:

> Romola was moved with sympathetic indignation, for in her nature too there lay the same large claims, and the same spirit of struggle against their denial. She tried to calm her father by a still prouder word than his.
>
> "Nevertheless, Father, it is a great gift of the gods to be born with a hatred and contempt of all injustice and meanness. . . . There is strength in scorn, as there was in the martial fury by which men became insensible to wounds." (56)

Romola can never share her father's ambition for social and intellectual recognition. Yet her exclusion from such aspirations opens her to the broader moral concerns underlying Bardo's indignation at the rapaciousness and dishonesty of modern scholars. Directing her father's attention away from the specific context of scholarship while at the same time validating his anger against injustice, Romola's reference to a martial law of the emotions credits his outrage with a substantive value independent of the sociopolitical framework through which it is expressed. Her comparison of Bardo's rage at the degeneration of scholarly principles with the fury of pagan warriors translates the old man's egotistical concerns into a transcendent sense of integrity that belongs to human nature.

Romola's ability to redeem the moral integrity of human desire is perhaps most significant in her relationship with Tito, in whom Romola inspires a longing for self-integrity that transcends his aspirations toward social recognition and intellectual achievement. Romola's influence on Tito is apparent in their initial interactions as fellow assistants to her father:

> [Romola and Tito] were the best comrades in the world during the hours they passed together round the blind man's chair: she was constantly appealing to Tito, and he was informing her, yet he felt himself strangely in subjection to Romola with that simplicity of hers: he felt for the first time, without defining it to himself, that loving awe in the presence of noble womanhood, which is perhaps something like the worship paid of old to a great nature-goddess, who was not all-knowing, but whose life and power were something deeper and more primordial

> than knowledge. . . . [H]e could only fancy and wish wildly—what he knew was impossible—that Romola would some day tell him that she loved him. . . . [Romola's love] was the topmost apple on which he had set his mind. (95)

In a mutual act of spiritual awakening, Tito's sense of Romola as "a great nature-goddess" and the "fancy" and "wild wish" that she inspires in him mirror Romola's initial response to him as a Dionysian deity. Both visions function on a mythopoeic level of cognition (and recognition) that transcends the context of their intellectual interactions. Like Romola's Dionysian associations, Tito's mythopoeic visions suggest an inward, spiritual self-expansion enhanced by the concluding allusion to an image from Sappho: "As the sweet-apple reddens on the bough-top, on the top of the topmost bough; the apple-gatherers have forgotten it—no they have not forgotten it entirely, but they could not reach it."[48] The Sapphic reference emphasizes the contrast between the two kinds of memory that are at work in Tito's relationship with the Bardis—the knowledge of facts that is the essence of Bardo's scholarship and a "deeper and more primordial" knowledge that escapes definition but for its living embodiment in Romola. The first kind of memory is directed toward the production of a material work: Tito's recollections of his experiences and knowledge of Greek are tools in the work that will ultimately enable his social recognition. In the second instance, memory serves in the constitution of self-integrity—that moral self-certainty resistant to external persuasion. Like Sappho's apple, this sense of self-integrity is in danger not so much of being forgotten as of being dismissed as a goal too difficult to attain. The apple exists independent of the gatherer's gaze, its ripening reality standing as accusation against the mind's capacity for self-deception. As the "topmost apple" of Tito's aspirations, Romola represents a hope of self-recovery that is also, for Tito, a promise of moral salvation.

Tito does win Romola's love, but the self-integrity that her love represents drifts increasingly out of reach as Tito learns to pander his scholarship for social acceptance, choosing the path of sophistry advised by Nello over his innate moral attraction to Romola. The opposition between sophistical and mythopoeic mentalities is shown as Tito turns his intellect not only toward political flattery but also toward an emotional manipulation of Romola that ultimately undermines his highest aspirations. "I want a very delicate miniature device taken from certain fables of the poets, which you will know how to combine for me . . . in the form of a triptych," Tito tells Piero di Cosimo, commissioning a gift for Romola just before their marriage.

> The inside may be simple gilding: it is on the outside I want the device. A story in Ovid will give you the necessary hints. I want [the triumph of Bacchus and Ariadne] treated in a new way. . . . The young Bacchus must be seated in a ship, his head bound with clusters of grapes, and a spear entwined with vine-leaves in his hand: dark berried ivy must wind about the masts and sails, the oars must be thyrsi. . . . [L]eopards and tigers must be crouching before him. . . . But I want to have the fair-haired Ariadne with him, made immortal with her golden crown—that is not in Ovid's story, but no matter, you will conceive it all—and above there must be young Loves, such as you know how to paint, shooting with roses at the points of their arrows. (184)

Tito's triptych seems at first to mirror Romola's vision of her betrothed as a "rich dark beauty which seemed to gather round it all images of joy—purple vines festooned between the elms . . . all objects and all sounds that tell of Nature revelling in her full force" (177). Both scenes depict a world of natural harmony, abundance, and celebration. But while Romola's images of natural abundance and growth are the spontaneous outpourings of a passion previously repressed under her father's stoic regime,[49] Tito's triptych is a carefully planned, artificial device, purchased with money from the sale of Baldassarre's ring and designed to take advantage of Romola's naïveté and emotional vulnerability.

The textual source of Tito's triptych enhances the subversive subtext of his design. For the episode from Ovid's *Metamorphoses* from which Tito instructs Piero to draw his inspiration is one that illustrates Bacchus's vindictive rage after he is captured by sailors:

> The ship stands still upon the waves, as if held dry in dock. The sailors in amaze redouble their striving at the oars and make all sail. . . . But ivy twines and clings about the oars, creeps upward with many a back-flung, catching fold, and decks the sails with heavy, hanging clusters. The god himself, with his brow garlanded with clustering berries, waves a wand wreathed with ivy-leaves. Around him lie tigers, the forms

(though empty all) of lynxes and of fierce spotted panthers.
The men leap overboard, driven on by madness or by fear.[50]

In Ovid's description, the natural world serves as a form of entrapment and deception—a world woven of illusory images through which the god enacts his destruction. By combining this display of malicious force with the story of Bacchus's rescue of Ariadne, Tito's triptych perverts his original feelings for Romola. Rather than envisioning Romola as a "great nature goddess," the painting depicts Tito as a deity to be worshipped—exerting control over his captive with false visions that lure her into submission even as the vines bind the oars of the sailor. Drawing on these textual implications undetected by Romola, the triptych symbolically betrays Romola's initial belief in Tito as a salvational force, marking the demoralization of her "primordial" life by Tito's cunning as well as the destruction of his aspirations to deserve her love.

Though Romola initially believes in the outward tale of rescue depicted in Piero's painting, her eventual realization of Tito's deceptions precipitates a moral conflict that Eliot expresses through two mythopoeic images. "The crowned Ariadne . . . felt more and more the presence of unexpected thorns" (243), the narrative states as Romola senses Tito's abandonment of Bardo. The allusion here to Jesus's crown of thorns is apparent, suggesting, as Felicia Bonaparte has pointed out, Romola's suffering under Tito's betrayal and anticipating her similar self-sacrificial role as "Madonna Antigone" when she returns to Florence at Savonarola's prompting.[51] But although the symbolic resonance between Christ and Madonna seems clear, representing Romola as a moral ideal, the relationship between Romola's representation as Ariadne and her personification as Antigone is less so. Conventional accounts of the Cretan and Theban princesses seem to assign them distinctly opposing fates and discrepant value systems. Ariadne's betrayal of Minos is the moral antithesis of Antigone's devotion to Oedipus, whom she follows into exile. Ariadne's betrayal by Theseus and her seduction by Bacchus suggest her victimization by and subjection to the will of male authority figures, while neither Creon's threats nor Haemon's love can overcome Antigone's will.[52] However, as suggested by Romola's depiction as both Ariadne and Antigone in Piero's paintings, these two figures are combined in Eliot's novel through their mutual representation of a woman torn between inner desires and external demands. These images present a much more ambiguous morality than the Christian iconography with which they are combined. The mythic Ariadne forced by the realization of her husband's betrayal to "violently rend . . . her life in two" (318) evolves into the tragic figure of Antigone, battling to maintain her moral idealism against an opposing social obligation. Juxtaposing Christian values of self-sacrifice, this mythopoeic association represents a spiritual dilemma that transcends religious and temporal boundaries.

The exact nature of this spiritual dilemma and the particular significance of Sophocles' tragedy to *Romola* might be adduced from Eliot's 1856 essay "The *Antigone* and Its Moral," written with the play's 1850 London performance in mind.

> It is a very superficial criticism which interprets the character of Creon as that of a hypocritical tyrant, and regards Antigone as a blameless victim. . . . The best critics have agreed with Bockh in recognizing this balance of principles, this antagonism of valid claims; they generally regard it, however, as dependent entirely on the Greek point of view, as springing simply from the polytheistic conception, according to which the requirements of the Gods often clashed with the duties of man to man.
>
> But, is it the fact that this antagonism of valid principles is peculiar to polytheism? Is it not rather that the struggle between Antigone and Creon represents that struggle between elemental tendencies and established laws by which the outer life of man is gradually and painfully being brought into harmony with his inward needs. . . . Wherever the strength of a man's intellect, or moral sense, or affection brings him into opposition with the rules which society has sanctioned, there is renewed the conflict between Antigone and Creon.[53]

For Eliot, Antigone exists both as an individual torn between two moral responsibilities and as a representation of what Eliot called in her article the "impulses of affection and religion" on a transhistorical plane. As an individual, Antigone must wrestle with her sense of spiritual duty and the civil obligations that prohibit Polynices' burial.[54] However, Antigone is also a symbolic entity, representing the transcendent, moral, and spiritual needs in humanity. Romola, like Antigone, possesses this dual identity of struggling individual and transcendent principle in Eliot's novel—she is both a woman fighting to bring her "inward needs" into harmony with her social situation and, like Antigone, a representative of the innate impulses within humanity.[55] This symbolic and transcendent aspect of Romola's character prompted objections from friends and critics, with Sara Hennell remarking in a letter to her friend that "in Romola you have painted a goddess, and not a woman."[56] But it was perhaps Eliot's aim to create in her heroine both a woman of her own time and a figure transcending time. Romola's identification with Antigone's symbolic aspects testifies to Eliot's faith in the persistence of humanity's moral needs, but this portrayal also concedes to the partialness of these needs within a larger social reality that demands their compromise.[57]

Romola's representation of moral needs that are an essential—if component—element of human motivation is most clearly illustrated in her relationship with Tito upon her return to Florence, after she has discovered his nefarious personal and political deeds. "I am more bound to you than to anything else on earth," Romola informs her husband, explaining why she returned to him even after learning of his betrayal of Bardo (413). The comment ostensibly refers to the sense of spousal obligation impressed upon her by Savonarola. But for Romola, the spiritual union symbolized by their marriage identifies her faith in the "law of the affections" with her husband's moral sense. "If we are united, I am that part of you that will save you from crime" (405), she appeals to him, suspecting his part in the plot against Savonarola. On a mythopoeic level, Romola is not only Tito's possession, fulfilling her obligations to him as a wife, but also a distinctly female "inward need" that Tito wants to obliterate from his consciousness. In reminding her husband of their union, Romola identifies herself with the "highest apple" that represented Tito's initial desire for simplicity and self-integrity—virtues that are ever more elusive as Tito becomes inextricably entangled in Florentine politics.

The evolution in Romola's mythopoeic significance to Tito establishes a final link between the moral and primitive aspects of spirituality in the novel. While driven at the outset of his courtship by a sense of reverence, Tito's sense that Romola embodies a "life and power deeper . . . more primordial than knowledge" merges with the reprimand of his conscience as he cements his betrayal of Baldassarre. "The terrible resurrection of secret fears, which, if Romola had known them, would have alienated her from him for ever, caused him to feel an alienation already begun between them—caused him to feel a certain repulsion towards a woman from whose mind he was in danger" (249). Tito's fear of Romola's "mind" here both foreshadows Romola's discovery of his betrayal of Baldassarre and associates Romola's powers with a form of justice that Eliot explicitly associates with the Eumenides (or Furies) of Greek tragedy early on in the novel: "'It is good,' sing the old Eumenides, in Aeschylus, 'that fear should sit as the guardian of the soul, forcing it into wisdom—good that men should carry a threatening shadow in their hearts under the full sunshine; else, how shall they learn to revere the right?' That guardianship may become needless; but only when all outward law has become needless—only when duty and love have united in one stream and made a common force." (116) Directly after the quotation of these lines from the final play of Aeschylus's trilogy,[58] Tito's mind is described as "destitute of that dread which [is] . . . the initial recognition of a moral law constraining desire." But though Tito does not possess the moral aspect of this fear within himself, his terror of Romola testifies to the impact of her struggle toward moral perfection upon even the most venal of her associates and, more broadly, to the potential of this struggle in driving humanity's outward pursuit of justice. "Romola retained one sort of power over him—the power of dread" (403), the novel states, opposing Romola's Fury-driven "wisdom" with Tito's "acute mind," accustomed to taking "the only rational course in making [all parties] subservient to his own interests" (402). Assuming her tragic role in the "great drama of human existence," Romola, with her preternatural power, becomes the voice of the "elemental tendencies" guarding man's soul against the rationalism that would drive him ever further from his humanity. Her ultimate failure to save Tito from both moral degradation and physical destruction affirms the unresolved struggle between inward affection and outward persuasion that guarantees the relevance of the Greeks' legacy not only to the greater vision of mankind's civil and intellectual perfection but also to the sense of inward self-coherence without which grand visions can remain only in the realm of illusion.

"I liked being shaken and deafened by [the clang of the bells]: I fancied I was something like a Bacchante possessed by a divine rage" (280), Romola confesses to Tito early on in their courtship during Florence's celebration of the French departure from the city. Romola's enjoyment of her momentary madness is prophetic of her later realization that though "the law was sacred . . . rebellion might be sacred too" (468), as she devotes herself to an "irrational" pursuit of moral rectitude against her husband's personal and political deceptions. By at once embodying the Furies and attempting to protect Tito from their vengeance, Romola becomes a living testimony to the survival of archaic—and elemental—moral laws within humanity despite the intellectual and spiritual projects of Renaissance humanism. Indeed, though Tito's primary self-defense against Romola's prosecution of his actions is that she cannot assert any authority in political, social, and intellectual arenas from which she is inherently excluded because of her sex, it is precisely because of her alienation from these formal institutions of power that Romola becomes the bearer of the sympathetic bonds essential to the construction—and continuation—of humanity. "You are so constituted as to have certain strong impressions inaccessible to reason," Tito informs Romola. "And if . . . you succeed in holding me up to infamy, you will have surpassed all the heroines of the Greek drama." This statement simultaneously dismisses Romola's moral sense as mere "play" (482) and rejects the forces that preside over Greek tragedy as antiquated, obsolete concepts of justice operative only in the realm of imagination and delusion. But the archaic forces of vengeance assert themselves into Tito's reality when he becomes a victim both of his father's rage and of "that Masque of the Furies, called Riot" (541). Tito's calculated ascension within the ranks of political, social, and academic institutions ultimately entangle him in a fatal web woven of his lies and self-deceptions. Meanwhile, Romola's ability to extricate herself from the political and social institutions to which she never legitimately belonged leads to a regeneration of her sympathetic faculties. She returns to Florence as the guardian both of Tito's personal legacy, through raising his son, Lillo, and of the larger legacy of the Renaissance, through instilling in Lillo the scholarship she learned from her father. As a product of scholarly learning refracted through Romola's mythopoeic mind, Lillo represents the possibility of a renascence that merges the legacy of Greek scholarship with the moral truth of Greekness that exceeds the grasp of rational knowledge.

In *Romola,* George Eliot anticipated a future in which women's creativity would be recognized as having a definitive impact on the shape of intellectual history. This impact, Eliot argued, has operated throughout history on an interpersonal level, but it has been overlooked as a historical force because of the valuation of gender-biased institutional and acquisitive knowledge. Although women's minds work differently from men's, this difference held a salvational potential, Eliot believed, for an age in which intellectual legacy was jeopardized by a humanistic legacy whereby ancient knowledge was reduced to an instrument of egotism and social privilege.

CHAPTER FOUR

The Daimon Archives

Jane Harrison and the Afterlife of Dead Languages

In her autobiography, *Reminiscences of a Student's Life* (1925), Jane Harrison reverently recalls the day George Eliot came to visit her room at Newnham College. "At Cambridge great men and women began to come into my life," she writes:

> Women's colleges were a novelty, and distinguished visitors were brought to see us as one of the sights. Turgenev came . . . Ruskin came . . . Mr. Gladstone. . . . And then last, but oh, so utterly first, came George Eliot. It was in the days when her cult was at its height—thank heaven I never left her shrine! . . . She came for a few minutes to my room, and I was almost senseless with excitement. I had just repapered my room with the newest thing in dolorous Morris papers. . . . I remember she said in her shy, impressive way, "Your paper makes a beautiful background for your face." The ecstasy was too much, and I knew no more. Later, in London, I met, of course, many eminent men, but there never came again a moment like that.[1]

Embellished with her characteristic self-dramatization, Harrison's account of her meeting with Eliot identifies the novelist as a forerunner to the first generation of women venturing into the world of academia. Some thirty years older than Harrison, Eliot reached the pinnacle of her career when the debate about women in higher education was at its height and offered support—in the form of advice, books, and money—to Barbara Bodichon and Emily Davies when they were establishing Girton, the first women's college to be affiliated with Cambridge University.[2] In 1874, when Harrison entered Newnham College, the second women's college at Cambridge, Eliot had already gained an international reputation as a novelist and was one of the few prominent female voices conversant with the nation's leading scholars and intellectuals.[3] But what drew the aspiring classicist to the celebrated novelist was not so much Eliot's prestige as her unorthodox ideas. One of these ideas that had particular resonance for Harrison was Eliot's belief that women could make unique contributions to social and intellectual progress not despite but because of their innate differences from men and their historic exclusion from male-dominated institutions and value systems. Harrison took for her raison d'être Eliot's conviction, forcefully expressed in *Romola,* that women's expansive imaginations allowed them a special sensitivity to their own and humanity's spiritual needs for continuity and moral sympathy. As indicated in the almost maenadic fervor of the above-quoted passage from her memoirs, Harrison felt a spiritual connection with Eliot that went far beyond the recognition of their mutual positions in the advancement of women's education. Mingling feminine reserve with an unapologetic conviction in her controversial ideas, Eliot awakened in her young devotee a passion that Harrison would later devote to her study of ancient Greece—a study that would deliberately transgress institutional boundaries by insisting on the personal investment that individuals have in their visions of the ancient world.

A self-proclaimed disciple of Eliot, Harrison built a career around promoting controversial ideas; her life exemplifies how an individual can affect scholarship through the sheer force of her personal convictions and the allure of her visionary imagination. Helping to pioneer the integration of archaeological, ethnological, and sociological theories into Hellenic studies at the turn of the twentieth century, Harrison devoted herself to rescuing classics from what she called the "hortus siccus"[4] of a literary and linguistically based study that was closed off from scientific advancements. Science, Harrison believed, was uncovering a more complex and multifaceted view of the ancient world than that represented by the ideals of Victorian humanistic Hellenism. However, beneath Harrison's stated effort to reveal previously neglected truths about archaic Greece lay a highly individualized epistemology informed by her chronic sense of peripherality in the academic world where she spent almost the whole of her life.[5] Intensely conscious of her deficiencies in literary-linguistic knowledge, Harrison mitigated her alienation from nineteenth-century classical scholarship by asserting the privileged insight of her "sympathetic imagination."[6] This was a creative, personal form of cognition that, much like Grote's theories of the mythopoeic age of Greece, denied the complete comprehensibility of the ancient world and defied both the analytical principles of "pure scholarship," which at Cambridge meant rigorous linguistic and grammatical analysis of texts (as opposed to the broader literary-interpretive approach at Oxford), and the rationalist foundations of "scientific method."[7] Motivated on the one hand by a sense of her inadequacies as a traditional scholar and on the other by an opposition to institutional conventions, Harrison's narrative of the ancient Greek world is inseparable from the narrative of her own experience of knowing.

Based on her self-determined, heroic alienation from what she termed "sound scholarship," Harrison's narrative of ancient Greece is a legacy of the nineteenth-century popular imagination. For despite their institutional context, Harrison's ideas about Greece are energized by a personal vision that deliberately challenged the conventions of humanistic Hellenism. As in the cases of Charlotte Brontë and George Eliot, Harrison's accomplishments demonstrate how individuality can be experienced through manipulation of the boundaries that define a body of knowledge. But because of her prominent place in academia, Harrison's influence also shows that entire categories of knowledge can shape themselves in response to an individual. Identifying with the "daimones" that she believed to have governed the natural cycles of death and rebirth in the archaic world, Harrison initiated a crusade for spiritual renewal in Greek scholarship by deliberately undermining the ideological, religious, and institutional foundations of classical tradition and by sublimating her desire for scholarly legitimacy into a quest for the redemptive transformation of her field into a body of knowledge with crucial relevance for her own and future ages. Harrison's unique relationship to ancient Greece thus not only illuminates the contesting ideologies determining the role of Greek scholarship at the turn of the twentieth century but also validates her conviction that it was precisely the methodological and ideological conflicts between individuals' definitions of "knowing Greek" rather than any one resounding truth about the Greeks that would ensure the survival of Greek scholarship into modernity.

Harrison's formulation of the "sympathetic imagination" and her campaign to save Greek from traditional scholarship lie in a personal history of desire, rebellion, and exile that began with her childhood reading of the Gospels. "The apparatus of religion interested me," Harrison wrote in *Reminiscences of a Student's Life* (19).[8]

> I followed the prayers in Latin, and the lesson in German, and the Gospel in Greek; this with some misgivings as to the "wholeheartedness" of this proceeding.[9] A keen impulse was given to my study of the Greek Testament by the arrival of a new curate. He was fresh from Oxford and not, I think averse to showing off. Rashly in one of his sermons he drew attention to a mistranslation. This filled me with excitement and alarm. I saw in a flash that the whole question of the "verbal inspiration of the Bible" was at issue. That afternoon I took my Greek Testament down to the Sunday School and, eager for further elucidation, waylaid the hapless curate. I soon found that his knowledge of Greek was, if possible, more slender than my own. (27)

Harrison's joyful appreciation for the mistranslatability of the New Testament laid a solid stone in the foundation of her avid protests later in life against interpreting the ancient Greek world within the prescribed boundaries of doctrinal Christianity. Though she early questioned her stepmother's fervent Evangelicalism, she could give herself "whole-heartedly" to the Bible precisely because the mystery of its language held out the possibility of challenging religious authority. The knowledge of Greek offered a way of transforming what she was beginning to reject as an overly dogmatic system of faith into an intellectual challenge. Harrison presented this early substitution of a devotion to the mysteries of language for Christianity as the inspirational beginning of her academic career as a skeptic of theological doctrine and a lover of Greek. Her aversion toward the institutional rigidity of the former only cemented her devotion to the personal liberty of the latter. "To realise the release that Aristotle brought, you must have been reared as I was in a narrow school of Evangelicalism," she wrote in *Reminiscences* of her study of the *Ethics* at Newnham. "The notion of the *summum bonum* as an 'energy,' as an exercise of personal faculty, to one who had been taught that God claimed all. . . . I remember walking up and down in the College garden, thinking could it possibly be true, were the chains really broken and the prison doors open" (80–81). The contrast between the "narrow school" of religion and the spiritual and mental freedom of reading Aristotle in Newnham's gardens emphasizes Harrison's dissociation of Greek knowledge from institutional constraint. Even if Aristotle was required reading, his Greek appealed to the "personal faculty" of the intellect, by which Harrison meant the freedom of imaginative interpretation. This highly individualized faculty was capable of defying interpretive conventions and opening up unknown worlds that came to house Harrison's gods.

Harrison's early insight into the power that Greek held and her later attraction to Greek philosophy were counterbalanced, however, by the limited classical education available to girls in the mid-nineteenth century and by her awareness that women could not participate in the discursive arena where Greek scholarship mattered. Even after establishing her considerable reputation as a Hellenist, Harrison's descriptions of her relationship with Greek resonate with longing for an unattainable dream. Reflecting on her early love of Greek in a paper first read before the London Sociological Society and the Cambridge Branch of Suffragists in 1913, she wrote,

> [T]he dear delight of learning for learning's sake a "dead" language for sheer love of the beauty of its words and the delicacy of its syntactical relations, the joy of tracking out the secret springs of the human body irrespective of patient and doctor, the rapture of reconstructing for the first time in imagination a bit of the historical past, that was, that in a few laggard minds still obscurely is, unwomanly. Why? . . . "I do not see how Greek grammar is to help little Jane to keep house when she has a home of her own." . . . [T]he child understood [her aunt]: she was a little girl, and thereby damned to eternal domesticity; she heard the gates of the temple of Learning clang as they closed.[10]

Images of gates and barriers resurface in many of Harrison's writings on her scholarly career. Sometimes these doors shut in her face, and sometimes they open up a vista of opportunity before her. But always in these images, Harrison is standing at the threshold, accepting neither exile nor invitation. On the one hand, this insistent liminality indicates the lasting impact that her lack of early Greek education had on her confidence as a scholar, contributing to her sense of alienation from the academic institutions that legitimate scholarship. On the other hand, these images also resonate with the excitement of one who has learned to appreciate liminality and no longer wants to relinquish the thrill of desire for the comfort of possession. For Harrison, the very seductiveness of learning lies on this borderline between the confidence of knowing and the rapturous fantasy that comes from not knowing. The "secret springs of the human body" are alluring because they *are* secret and thus subject to the will of the mind. "I am moving about in worlds half unrealised,"[11] she wrote in 1901, as she began the most productive period in her career. By that time, she could claim the indefinite space between imagination and reality as her intellectual arena, but this world of half unreality became "a home of her own" only after Harrison's experience of exile.

From the outset of her education, Greek was both a homeland and a land of exile for Harrison. When she entered Newnham in 1874 and could indulge her longing to learn Greek,[12] the language remained frustratingly elusive and continued to hold the aura of the unknowable. "Greek literature as a specialism I early felt was barred to me," she wrote in *Reminiscences*. "The only field of research that the Cambridge of my day knew of was textual criticism, and for fruitful work in that my scholarship was never adequate" (82–83).[13] Harrison's sense of her "inadequacy" was no doubt strengthened by the unexpected second she received in her Classical Tripos examinations in 1879, the year before the exam was divided into two parts and two years before women were formally admitted into university examinations.[14] The divided Tripos would have allowed students to receive independent scores on a special field (ancient philosophy, history, or archaeology), reducing the focus on linguistic knowledge. The undivided Tripos consisted primarily of translation and composition papers (ten out of fourteen). Later testimonies from two of Harrison's teachers indicate that her disappointing results were attributable almost solely to her lack of early language training. "I was one of the examiners for the Classical Tripos in the year when she took the paper (as the custom then was) by private arrangement," wrote A. W. Verrall, Harrison's mentor and the first professor of English at Cambridge. The comment was part of Verrall's letter recommending Harrison for the coveted position of the Yates Professorship in Archaeology at University College in 1888. "She was declared to merit a place at the top of the second class, and this in spite of early training necessarily unsuitable, and an examination which gave no scope to her special faculties."[15] Verrall's statement implies that Harrison would have earned a first in Part II if this had been available in 1879 (that is, in her specialization of archaeology, in which the focus was on the history of art, monuments, mythology, and religious beliefs). But if institutions evolve, an individual's history is bound to a particular moment in this evolution. Though Verrall added in his recommendation that Harrison's Greek was "more than sufficient for the purpose of scientific Archaeology," that he felt it important to excuse her Tripos performance nine years after the fact indicates the lasting effect of these results on Harrison's career. She did not receive the Yates that year, and when she reapplied for the position in 1896, the issue of the Tripos exam again arose. Her former teacher S. H. Butcher wrote, "I cannot recall any pupil who showed a more subtle appreciation of language; and her rapidity, not only in acquiring, but in assimilating knowledge, indicated very exceptional qualities of mind. Had she begun classics a little earlier, she could not have failed to reach the standard of a high first-class in the Classical Tripos. As it was, her scholarship was marked by the literary sense and clear intelligence that she brought into all branches of it."[16] Harrison was again passed over for the Yates, and although historians still debate over the reasons for this rejection, the record of her achievements would always testify that she had come to Greek too late. However much she compensated for her lack of early Greek training in later years, her sense of her merit as a scholar would always balance on the divide between her love of Greek and her sense of its unknowability.[17]

Harrison's years away from Cambridge only exacerbated the tension between her love of Greek and her sense of exile from the institutions in which Greek knowledge was primarily housed. In 1879, she was passed over for the first Newnham lectureship in classics, which was given instead to her younger friend Margaret Merrifield (later Mrs. A. W. Verrall), whom Harrison had urged to take the Classical Tripos. The loss of the lectureship meant an unforeseen departure from Cambridge and the beginning of an almost twenty-year study of ancient Greek art and archaeology outside the context of a home institution. Although these years of traveling, research, and lecturing at the British Museum, schools, and universities put her in contact with leading scientists, artists, and literary figures of the day, Harrison's lingering "hurt pride" over her dismissal from Newnham prevented her from fully inhabiting the role of a "populist for Greek art" that she adopted during these years.[18] Her memory of lecturing during this time is tinged with irony:

> In those days I met many specimens of a class of Victorian who, if not exactly distinguished, were at least distinctive and are, I think, all but extinct—British Lions and Lionesses. The Lionesses first—that was the name we gave them at Newnham. They were all spinsters, well-born, well-bred, well-educated and well off. They attended my lectures on Greek Art. Greek Art was at that time booming and was eminently respectable. At home they gardened a great deal; they, most of them, had country houses. Their gardens were a terror to me, for I never could remember the names of the plants. . . . Above all, they kept a vigilant eye on the shortcomings of local officials. (*Reminiscences*, 51–52)

Written in 1925 after twenty-four years establishing her reputation as a Cambridge Hellenist, Harrison's *Reminiscences* barely conceals her lingering distaste for her stint as a public intellectual. The opposition between "we at Newnham" and "them" in their frightening country gardens sprinkles bitterness into bemusement. The terms *specimen, class,* and *extinct* turn the scientific gaze of the reabsorbed Newnhamite on the socialites' "vigilant eye." It is a staring contest across the decades that implicitly questions the meaning of being "well educated." In Harrison's view of knowledge, what matters is not whether or even what one has learned but whether one chooses to make a life of learning—a life that can only thrive "in institutions renouncing the rank egotism of Home Life."[19]

The fact that Harrison did choose the academic life and yet was thrown to the lions explains her ambivalence toward both popular and institutionalized knowledge during her London years. Although her lectures earned her a celebrity status that she could not have had if she had stayed at Newnham, her social prestige also demeaned knowledge that demanded institutional recognition. "What people want who attend lectures on Greek subjects is not a deep insight into these subjects," Harrison told an interviewer for the *Pall Mall Gazette* in 1891.

> They want to know something, not very much, of the life and manners of a highly cultured and intellectual race of olden times. It is curiosity rather than a desire for thorough knowledge that prompts them. . . . They are sincerely interested, but only superficially, and that fact the lecturer in Greek subjects to general audiences should never forget. . . . [The popular lecturer] must be prepared to generalize a good deal, which is apt to result in

> much personal demoralization. . . . He often must feel that his attitude towards his subject and his audience is intellectually a somewhat squalid one.[20]

The distinction implied here between Harrison's "thorough knowledge" and the "curiosity" of her audience takes a deliberate stab at her interviewer's assumptions. For the *Pall Mall* interviewer had come to ask her about the "topic of the day, Greek at the Universities," which had arisen (again) in 1891 when a grace was proposed to appoint a syndicate to "consider the expediency of . . . the abolition of Greek as one of the subjects for the Little-Go."[21] The interviewer's underlying assumption is that there is parity between the popular interest in Greek art and Greek scholarship. "Of course, Miss Harrison . . . with your enthusiasm for Greek you are all for retaining the study of the language in the Universities?" the interviewer asked. Harrison did "confess to a pretty strong prejudice in favour of 'compulsory Greek,'" but the interviewer made the fatal fault of assuming that Harrison's "enthusiasm for Greek" was on a par with either the crammers for the Little-Go or with the Lionesses who attended her lectures. In her reply, Harrison emphasized that knowing the Greek necessary for the Little-Go did not a "real Greek student" make and suggested that to parallel such general knowledge with her specialized field of study was as much an insult to her intelligence as the superficial interests of the Lionesses were demoralizations of her person. Harrison must have been particularly sensitive to this insult given that by 1891, there was an increasing sentiment in Cambridge that even the linguistic knowledge needed for Part I of the Tripos was insufficient for a true classical education.[22] Having specialized in Greek art for some twelve years and contributed to the accretion of knowledge that was unsettling the regime of "pure scholarship," Harrison no doubt felt that her "deep insight" transcended the understanding not only of the Lionesses but also of her interviewer. Exactly what her "insight" entailed, she did not reveal, but the very act of withholding it from the interviewer suggests that she was as distant from her general audiences as was the "intellectual race of olden times." Her smug coyness insinuates that Harrison did enjoy toying with her fame as, in the words of the *Pall Mall Gazette*, "the lady to whose lectures during the last ten years the revival of popular interest in ancient Greece is almost solely due."[23] But her flippant responses also indicate her awareness of the elusiveness of her public appeal and her careful guardianship over her knowledge from the "squalor" of public lecture hall and press.

 However much Harrison resented the assumptions of her public, its regard for her as an authority on the "Greek question" at Cambridge gave her leverage to criticize institutional policy in a forum that honored her opinions certainly more than might have the university. In addition to disillusioning the press about her sympathy with the popular audience, Harrison also used the *Pall Mall* interview to take a stab at the institution she was apparently supporting.

> [I have] first, . . . a secret sympathy with all good old crusted educational abuses; next, the thing in my own education I am most thankful for is that much abused examination, the London Matriculation. It compelled me to learn some smattering of elementary chemistry. . . . [P]rofessionally it was all so much lost time; but the different look of the world, the imaginative opening out of things, that came of realizing such a thing as chemical combustion is a possession forever. Is there no counterpart for the scientific man? . . . I find it hard to believe that anyone can be brought into contact with a thing so fine, so subtle, as the Greek language without carrying away with him some haunting remembrance of beauty, some vision of leisurely culture, of a society of men whose keenest delight it was to think exactly and express with a perfect fitness.[24]

Harrison's idealization of the Greek language resonates deceptively with many of the pro-Greek arguments coming out of the university. "Every one who knows something of Greek knows something of the noblest of literatures," argued the provost of King's College in a senate discussion of the proposed syndicate.[25] If Harrison agreed with the loftiness of Greek literature and language, she was also skeptical enough about the touted virtues of compulsory Greek to parody her idealizing tendency by comparing Greek's "haunting remembrance" to the lasting impressions of chemical combustion. But beneath her self-conscious irony lies a satiric commentary on the argument of the pro-Greek supporters within Cambridge, which rested largely on a defense of the university's reputation as a foundation of "pure scholarship" and a guardian of "culture."[26] The feelings of J. K. Stephen exemplify the conservative rhetoric, which Harrison reiterated during the interview in her own tongue-in-cheek fashion. Stephen's views in a senate discussion of 1891 were summarized by the *Cambridge University Reporter*: "He . . . believed that there was a certain feeling against Greek outside the University and inside: a feeling which allied itself with the natural desire of scientific men to increase the importance of their own studies: and this feeling they ought to be ready to meet in a combative spirit. The ancient learning of the Greeks and Romans was an inheritance of which the University ought to be proud, and which they ought to guard most jealously against the encroachment of other studies."[27] Professor Richard Jebb seconded the opinion that "at the present day a popular pressure from without was often a pressure which it was the bounden duty of the Universities to withstand."[28] There are two sets of boundary markings etched out by the pro-Greek camp. One separates the opinions of those inside the university from those without. The other distinguishes the "scientific" from the literary scholar. These apparently clear-cut oppositions, however, are confused by the underlying implication that those who objected to compulsory Greek—such as "scientific men"—were *naturally* outsiders threatening the classical inheritance that *true* university insiders were duty-bound to defend. The reality, however, was that science was becoming an increasingly legitimate field of research both within and outside of the university. The designation of scientists as "outsiders" only demonstrates the confusion of categories, redefinition of boundaries, and rhetorical sleights-of-hand endemic in the compulsory Greek debates.

Harrison's interview with the *Pall Mall Gazette* exemplifies her exploitation of the categorical confusions provoked by the debates to introduce a new vision of potential cooperation between scientific and literary sensibilities. Instead of supporting either side of the argument, Harrison's suggestion that Greek offers the "imaginative opening out of things" for the scientifically inclined and, implicitly, that science provides the same for the literary scholar, sidesteps altogether the questions of educational principle. Instead, the destabilization of disciplinary boundaries as manifested in the compulsory Greek debates offered Harrison a chance to legitimate her hybrid professional interests and to assert the "insider" status of her "outsider" scholarship. For however useless chemistry may have been to Harrison, by 1891 she was far closer to the scientific than to the literary scholar. Among her scientific forays were her work with Wilhelm Dörpfeld in his archaeological excavations in Athens in 1888,[29] the writing of *Mythology and Monuments of Ancient Athens* with Margaret Verrall (née Merrifield) in 1890,[30] and twice standing for the Yates, one of the most coveted professorships in archaeology.[31] The accumulation of professional achievements on her resume gave her confidence and argumentative leverage to promote the equality of archaeological research with literary, "pure scholarship" at the university. "The study of Greek language and literature has long reigned supreme and well-nigh alone at Cambridge," she wrote in an 1884 article for the *Magazine of Art*, welcoming the new cast museum at Cambridge. "Some of us are tired of hearing that Greek art is the handmaid of Greek literature. . . . Indeed, if one is to be chosen as handmaid, let it be literature."[32] In light of her strengthening opposition to the values that had contributed to her departure from Cambridge, Harrison's support of compulsory Greek goes far beyond the romantic idealism that her answer to the *Pall Mall* interviewer might too easily suggest. Rather than endorsing the purist, conservative platform, her argument develops a concept of knowledge that merges the scientific and literary imaginations and deliberately resists the institutional boundaries that compulsory Greek was meant to reinforce.

Archaic Religion and the Prolegomena

When Harrison was invited back to Newnham in 1898, she had already acquired a reputation as both a public luminary and a specialist in classical art and archaeology.[33] Her declared area of specialization upon her return to Cambridge, however, was archaic Greek religion, which in 1879 was placed in Part II, Group D of the Tripos, along with art and archaeology. Ancient religion was an emerging field of study at Cambridge and had less of a discursive basis than other sections in the second part of the Tripos, which also included philosophy, history, and philology.[34] According to one speaker in an 1892 senate discussion of the Tripos, "Archaeology [is] a subject of immense extent and of vague definition. [He] did not know how candidates were to prepare for it."[35] Vague as the entire field might have been, the combination of archaeology and religion into one field made the subject even murkier by positing an incongruous analogy between the examination of material culture and the study of the spiritual and imaginative life of a people.[36] To what extent do artifacts speak for themselves and how far can implications be drawn? Upon whose authority ought the truth be judged? By posing these questions, Group D (art, archaeology, and religion) became a category not only for testing Greek knowledge but also for debating what knowing Greek meant. In associating herself with a specialization rife with inherent ideological oppositions, Harrison placed her scholarship on treacherous political terrain indeed but also located herself in an ideal position for manipulating the boundaries by which knowledge was being redefined.

The foundations for Harrison's institutional resistance lay in her ideas about Greek art, the primary focus of her research between 1880 and 1898, when she returned to Newnham. As an alternative to the literary specialization for which she felt unqualified, the study of non-language-based archaic media (for example, vase paintings, statues, and monuments) helped Harrison formulate a science of not knowing Greek in reaction to institutionalized knowledge. The subversive foundations of this science are exemplified in a series of articles she wrote for the *Magazine of Art* in 1884, in which she analyzed various myths through their artistic depictions. Contrasting the works of the Attic vase painter with more-sophisticated poetic representations of myths, she wrote that the latter operates "on a lower emotional plane. . . . [While in the vase painting] we had 'understatement,' reserve, the suggestion rather than the expression of pathos. . . . Throughout much is left to the imagination."[37] For Harrison, the superior resonance of archaic art lies in its comparative lack of clarity. While Catullan or Alexandrian poetry might be more emotionally expressive, archaic art is more impressive because its obscurity awakens the viewer's imaginative faculties. "Archaic art loved telling a story" (296), Harrison wrote in her *Prolegomena to the Study of Greek Religion* in 1903. Stemming from her interest in archaic Greek art, the *Prolegomena,* written during her first years back at Newnham, transferred her philosophy about Greek art to the field of archaic religion, taking full advantage of the creative freedom granted to specialists in a field without a formal discourse.

Punctuated with assertions about the inscrutability of archaic religion, the *Prolegomena* sets out to undermine the possibility of reaching a state of perfect knowledge and suggests that the true spiritual basis of Greek society lies in mystic cults antithetical to the well-known Olympian deities. The book's meanderings through what one reviewer called "fanciful," "misleading," "specious" argumentation and its "wandering thoughts" and "merry jests"[38] all aim to expand the mind's conceptual parameters beyond the boundaries of literary and artistic evidence. The truths it proffers about Greek religion derive their force and conviction not from the plethora of texts, paintings, and sculptures it cites but from the surprising narrative twists and conclusions unfolding from Harrison's creative imagination. For example, in speaking of archaic rites addressed to "those below, who are black and bad and malignant," she wrote, "We know what was done, though we have no English word fully to express that doing.

 This fact may well remind us that we have lost not only the word but the thought, and must be at some pains to recover it. . . . I do not deny that the word can be translated if we are content to vary our rendering in each various case. . . . No one word carries the whole field. It is this lost union of many diverse elements that has to be recovered and is nameless" (58–59). The idea of a nameless recovery is strikingly oxymoronic, especially in a textbook.[39] The admission calls into doubt the author's didactic purposes. But for Harrison, archaic religion was valuable precisely because its unknownness allows for a variability of truths that escape linguistic capture and permit an intimacy of knowledge formed through an individualized vocabulary. Through the irrecoverability of its language, archaic religion presented Harrison with an academic field wherein the consciousness of her inadequate linguistic training could be transformed into an epistemology of loss and a rationale for imaginative recovery. She wrote in the *Prolegomena,*

> [I]t is only by a somewhat severe mental effort that we realize the fact essential to our study that *there were no gods at all,* that what we have to investigate is not so many actual facts and existences but only conceptions of the human mind, shifting and changing colour with every human mind that conceived them. . . . There is no greater bar to that realizing of mythology which is the first condition of its being understood, than our modern habit of clear analytic thought. . . . The first necessity is that by an effort of the sympathetic imagination we should think back . . . into the haze of . . . primitive [conceptions]. (164)

The "sympathetic imagination" that Harrison asserted was essential for understanding archaic religion is a reformulation of the "scientific instinct" that she deemed necessary for the study of Greek art earlier in her career. Resisting "clear analytic thought," Harrison's version of scientific investigation into archaic religion emphasizes the investigator's ability to reinhabit the primitive mentality of the archaic Greek and to discover the truth of archaic thought through identifying it with one's own imaginative capacities. Her conception, then, is not unlike George Eliot's idea in *Romola* of the persistence of the mythopoeic imagination. Eliot, however, suggested this idea within a fictional context. Harrison sought scientific legitimation for it within the imposing realm of academia. Announcing her reentry into the gates of learning, the *Prolegomena* is, nevertheless, as much Harrison's reflection on the personal, spiritual foundation of knowledge as on what is known about the Greeks.

Several prominent classicists responded to the *Prolegomena* with skepticism and some with outright dismissal. W. H. D. Rouse, who had received a double first in his Classical Tripos exams and had been made a fellow of Christ's College, stated in the *Classical Review* that "several suggestions [in the *Prolegomena*] seem more fanciful than true" (465). He continued: "[Harrison] acknowledges herself [that] the processes are not clear: links are wanting in the chain, and the reader is left with the feeling that there is too much assumption" (468). Instances where Harrison's fancy takes flight are abundant throughout the text. For instance, in a section entitled "The Placation of Ghosts," she refuses to translate the problematic word *enagizein,*[40] stating that her rationale was to "avoid all danger from misleading modern connotations" (59). She then proceeds to use this untranslatable term throughout the rest of the chapter to draw together her interpretations of vase paintings and literary works, "vary[ing] our rendering [of the word] in each various case" (59). Not bothering to date her sources and hypothesizing at length about the motives of artists as well as of their creations, she conducts an animated discussion that follows its own narrative logic and chronology, operating on principles of probability rather than fact. Indeed, in speaking of one piece of literary evidence in this discussion, she states, "Whether or not [the author's] story is [a] matter of fact or not is of little moment; it was felt to be probable, or else it would never have been narrated" (74). Launched from assertions about the untranslatability of Greek terms and about the probable feelings of ancient authors, this and other discussions in the book engage in word plays and guesswork that inscribe Harrison's study of religion within a personal narrative space that refuses institutional and social categorization while at the same time forming itself against their boundaries. Contemporary critics have emphasized that such reliance on imagination and laws of probability has made Harrison a more powerful influence in literary and artistic circles than in academic ones. As Frank Turner notes, Harrison's efforts to link religion to ritual and art expresses "a fuller appreciation of the unity of life and of the connectedness of things than either traditional rationalism or traditional Hellenistic humanism could afford. In that respect she struck a responsive chord with one of the major impulses of early twentieth century intellectual life" (128). Also attractive to early twentieth-century thinkers was Harrison's emphasis on the importance of female deities and matriarchal cultures to archaic societies. In her study of Harrison's influence on James Joyce, T. S. Eliot, and Virginia Woolf, Martha Carpentier suggests that Harrison's scholarship helped to clear new pathways for the female literary imagination by providing a "new understanding of the powerful female archetypes so prevalent in primitive Greek ritual and drama, leading to a younger generation of writers whose 'sympathies' could be 'almost entirely with Clytemnestra'—mother, lover, powerful queen, and vengeful witch."[41] Although Carpentier's arguments about Harrison's influences are at times tenuous, especially as there is little concrete evidence of Harrison's relation to Joyce and Eliot, Harrison's friendship with Woolf and her influences on the Bloomsbury Group certainly indicate that the imaginative projection that, for many classicists, discredited Harrison's work as serious scholarship helped to establish important foundations for the reconceptualization of ancient history and its relation to the twentieth-century popular imagination.

Critical attention to Harrison's influence on literary and artistic figures tends, however, to obscure her considerable impact on her own academic context. In her own time, Harrison's advocacy for the importance of the imagination in understanding Greek religion was fundamental to what became for her a spiritual mission to reinvigorate an institution that she felt was "losing touch with life and reality" in the same way as the Olympians of the Golden Age, whose "luminous perfection" (363) robbed them of any spiritual value, as she argued in her *Prolegomena*. Recognizing that journal articles and reviews were vital to the circulatory system of ideas nourishing the classical community, Harrison injected hers like hypodermic shots, intended to jolt the system into reaction and life.[42] One of the most potent drugs in her arsenal was her conviction that the scholar's personality and motives were as valuable as the scholar's theories, and she was willing to go to great lengths to expose these motives. A case in point is her admittedly "intemperate review"[43] of the third and fourth volumes of Lewis Farnell's *Cults of the Greek States* (1896). The review condemned the noted Oxford Hellenist for taking the "canonical Olympians [as] his Aristotelian categories." Farnell's association of Greek cults almost exclusively with familiar Olympian gods—rather than with the mystery deities that Harrison studied—earned him the accusation of having a "medieval method and spirit" that disregards "all the apparatus of novelty [and] great stores of new learning." The target of Harrison's criticism was not so much Farnell's ideas as the spirit in which they were conceived: Farnell's book was written "because he or his possible readers think that something ought to be said." In contrast to this satisfaction of public demand is the work produced through purely egoistic motives:

> [T]he book written under the impulse of a new idea, is like a live thing, begotten he knows not how, in the writer's brain; he has only partial control over the form it takes, probably he does not want to write at all, he would rather sit and dream; but this live thing stirs and flutters, haunts him by night and day, goads him almost to madness, till at last he can bear it no more, and willy-nilly he brings it to birth in a book—. . . It is practically sure to be overfocussed, that is part of the intensity of first vision, but the reviewer need not and does not criticize the method and form of the book as distinguished from its content, because in a live thing "body and soul are one."[44]

Beginning with a prolonged, transparent reference to Harrison's own writing methods, the article is as much a proposal to change the critical criteria of the field as it is a review of Farnell's book. For Harrison, ideas are, and must be, organic entities, born not only of rational contemplation but also of passion and pain. Only through this grueling process of live birth can the idea survive and exert a vital force on the world beyond the individual mind. Ironically, while she argues here for the birth of ideas through natural genesis rather than design, the language of her critique is craftily provocative.

Not surprisingly, the review caused an immediate reaction among classicists. Farnell was away when it was published, and Percy Gardner, a professor of classical archaeology at Oxford with whom Harrison was friendly, rose to his colleague's defense, accusing Harrison of unjustly using her personal prejudice for the "superstition" of the "Athenian rabble" as criteria for judging "a master of his subject."[45] "[T]he notice . . . is neither review nor criticism, but a call to repentance," wrote Gardner in the *Cambridge Review*. "Miss Harrison's criticism merely amounts to saying 'he followeth not with us.'" Harrison regretted upsetting Gardner, but she stuck to her belief about what constituted valuable scholarship and made no effort to deny that her notice was "in some sense, a 'call to repentance.'"[46] Accepting the role of redeemer, Harrison argued not only that the individual book must be born from a purely egoistic impulse in order to live but also that this impulse guaranteed the life of scholarship. In contrast to Gardner's statement that "a scientific work is not a poem nor a dream of a new social system" (482), Harrison accepted wholeheartedly the social burden of individual genius. The true scholar takes on the risks of "overfocus" and "intensity" to ensure the impact of the idea on scholarship as a whole. Farnell's sin, in Harrison's eyes, lay in his explicit refusal to accept personal risk. "It has been my object to restrict myself as far as possible to the statement of the facts, and not to wander too far into the region of hypothesis and controversy," he stated in his preface to the first volume (1896). "One's work thus incurs the risk of a dryness and coldness of tone; and the risk is all the greater because, while Greek mythology was passionate and picturesque, Greek religion was, on the whole, sober and sane. An emotional exposition of [Greek religion] may be of great value for the purposes of literature; but for the purposes of science it is best to exhibit the facts, as far as possible, in a dry light."[47] Farnell's "sober and sane" view of Greek religion refutes the atheistic ideology that Harrison set out forcefully in her *Prolegomena*. But more alarming for Harrison than this ideological opposition was Farnell's calculated intention of avoiding controversy. His exposition of dry facts was a deadly antidote to her vision of a living idea. His professed "risk" was merely a disguise for personal cowardice. Ironically creating a controversy from Farnell's deliberate avoidance of conflict, Harrison's exposition of the myth-making mind of the scholar attempted to reassert the vital interdependency between the "passionate and picturesque" and the scientific-analytical mentalities.

Demonizing John the Baptist

Harrison's most provocative assault on institutional tradition took place in the winter of 1916–17, while England was in the midst of the Great War. The debate it provoked in the academic community offers a telling glimpse into both Harrison's motives and her larger impact on classical scholarship, as well as into the precarious status of Greek study as the Victorian age drew to a decisive close. The debate was initiated by Harrison's article "The Head of John Baptist," which proposed a novel approach to Salome's dance for the Baptist's head in the Gospels. The article was published in the December issue of the *Classical Review*, one of the most widely read and respected journals in the field of classical studies.[48] "No one, I suppose, reads the story of the daughter of Herodias and the Head of John Baptist without a sense of sudden jar," the article begins. "In the Old Testament it might stand; in the New its licentious savagery seems an outrage. But for the familiarity of Holy Writ we should probably long ago have asked what lies behind."[49] With a flourish of the first-person plural, Harrison set out with the confident assumption of her readers' repressed disapprobation of the Gospels story. Seeking first to expose and then to answer this desire for moral justification, she proceeded to defamiliarize Holy Writ by comparing the Gospels episode with narratives in ancient, Eastern, and Russian mythology and then to suggest that Christian "savagery" might find vindication as an adjunct of "sacred" primitive and pagan rituals:

> *The dance of Herodias' daughter with the Head of John Baptist is, mutatis mutandis, the ritual dance of Agave with the head of Pentheus.* It is the dance of the daimon of the New Year with the head of the Old Year, past and slain. . . . John the Forerunner has kept some savage elements expurgated from the sacred legend of his Prototype, and these elements rightly understood are not so repulsive as they seem. The loathsome story of the Head and the dance is redeemed at once from its squalour of amorous license and dressed in a new ritual dignity.

Any reader of the *Classical Review* would have immediately recognized the reference to the finale of Euripides' *Bacchae,* in which the crazed Theban princess appears triumphantly clutching the severed head of her son, believing it to be that of a lion she has hunted down and killed.[50] The attribution of savagery to this gruesome scene is readily comprehensible, as might be the desire to find a mitigating metaphorical explanation. What seems more dubious is that Agave's Bacchic frenzy might redeem Christian scripture. Indeed if the article's naturalistic explanation for Salome's dance (that is, as a New Year's celebration) vindicates the story from any charges of "licentiousness," it also undermines Christian rationale by identifying biblical personae as "daimones." "[T]he legend of John Baptist was marked by various daimon traits," Harrison argued, and Salome was possessed by the "intense religious need [for] ritual . . . rejoicing . . . over the dead daimon." The term *daimon* refers generally to gods or spirits of the dead, but Harrison's use of the term was loaded with critical connotations calculated to inspire controversy.

In the *Prolegomena,* Harrison had defined *daimones* as amorphous "potencies" with greater spiritual influence than the familiar Olympian "anthropomorphic divinities ('theoi')" (587). In her 1912 book *Themis,* she had developed the term into the intensely disputed concept of the "Eniautos-Daimon." "I am well aware that no such conjunction as Eniautos-Daimon exists in Greek," she wrote in the introduction to *Themis*:

> I did not set out to invent any such word, nor did I even foresee its employment; it simply grew on my hands from sheer necessity. . . . A word was wanted that should include . . . the whole world-process of decay, death, and renewal. I prefer "Eniautos" to "year" because to us "year" means something definitely chronological, a precise segment as it were of spatialized time; whereas *Eniautos*, as contrasted with *etos*, means a *period* in the etymological sense, a cycle of waxing and waning. This notion is, I believe, implicitly though not always explicitly, a cardinal factor in Greek religion. Beyond it, to anything like our modern notion of non-recurrent evolution, the Greek never advanced. I prefer the word *daimon* to "spirit" because . . . *daimon* has connotations unknown to our English "spirit."[51]

As an expression of what Harrison believed to be an "implicit factor in Greek religion," the Eniautos-Daimon is a doubly displaced entity with no historical existence beyond Harrison's desire to bridge a spiritual and verbal chasm between spatially and temporally remote civilizations. Emerging out of "necessity" in the kind of live birth that Harrison had described in her Farnell review, his formation as an "unknown" concept of collective belief embodies the creative force of an imagination that insists on its individuality by refusing to accept available beliefs and categories. As the ultimate embodiment of Harrison's creative ethos, the Eniautos-Daimon not only represents a concept of cyclical time in the archaic Greek mind but also argues for an alternative sense of historical continuity for the modern mind—one that cannot be found in the records of history and literature but rather must be imagined in the interstices of measured time and metered translation.

Harrison's subversive use of mythology as an interpretive framework for the Bible finds an early precedent in ideas first expounded by eighteenth-century Enlightenment philosophers for whom "parallels between Christian and pagan myths . . . [suggested] that Christianity was neither historically unique nor morally pure."[52] In the nineteenth century, David Friedrich Strauss's *Life of Jesus*, published in 1835 and translated into English by Mary Ann Evans in 1846, heightened the tension between Christian historiography and ancient mythology by arguing for the mythical foundation of events in the Gospels. George Grote's *History of Greece*, the first two volumes of which were likewise published in 1846, further destabilized Christian assumptions by suggesting the unreliability of New Testament myths as historical sources. These and other works by such prominent mythographers as Friedrich Max Müller and James George Frazer testify to the inextricable connection between mythography's development as a scientific field of inquiry in the nineteenth century and concerns for the status of Christianity.[53] Whether seeking to undermine or defend its authority, mythographers could not escape the necessity of reconciling their theories with Christianity. As Frank Turner puts it, Victorian mythographers "recognized that what they said about Greek myths and religious experience might bear directly on Christianity and the moral and intellectual life derived from it" (83). As the century progressed and mythography became the foundation for later fields such as anthropology and sociology, the informed mind had increasing difficulty in testifying its faith without at least grappling with the problem of alternative religious practices throughout time and space. Harrison, then, was hardly unique in seeking to destabilize the authority of one of the central texts underlying the institutional legitimacy of classical studies, whose primary function at Oxford and Cambridge was, traditionally, to prepare the nation's religious leaders.[54] But her John the Baptist article and its threat of replacing Christian teleology with savage ritual as the spiritual foundation of intellectual tradition came at a particularly sensitive moment, when the pressures of war had newly reinforced the partnership of church and state and had made adherence to Protestantism a bounden duty of British citizens.

The lead article in the *Classical Review*'s first February issue indicates the impact of Harrison's sacrilege on a sensitive academic community: "Miss Harrison's amazing article on the Head of John Baptist in the December number of the *Classical Review* seems to me to call for some plain-spoken criticism. It is confused and confusing, and in its use of certain texts most grossly misleading."[55] Harrison's critic was M. R. James, recent vice-chancellor of Cambridge, provost of King's College, antiquarian, medievalist, and specialist in Apocryphal studies. Launching into a sardonic denunciation of Harrison's imprecise identification of sources, her neglect of crucial historical background, her self-contradictory, muddled argumentation, and in particular, her imprecise knowledge of ancient Greek, James pointedly questioned the soundness not only of Harrison's thesis and ethics but also of her scholarly credentials. Proceeding from a pointedly *ad feminam* attack, he concluded his article with a scathing indictment of the entire field of academic study that Harrison's article represents:

> [I]s this Comparative Mythology? Or is it tolerable under that or any other name?
>
> I have often viewed with very grave suspicion the way in which comparative mythologists treat their evidence, but it has not often happened that I have found them gathering it in fields with which I was at all specially familiar. I hope Miss Harrison's use of "Apocryphal Scriptures" is not an average sample. Her article cannot, I feel sure, be the result of very careful thought, and I regret to see that a researcher of her experience can allow herself to make public crude and inconsequent speculations of this kind, which go far to justify those who deny to Comparative Mythology the name and dignity of a science.
>
> I believe it to be a science, but only in the making. I also believe that one of the worst services that anyone responsible for the direction of young students can do them is to encourage them to make it the subject of dissertations, or to propound any theory concerning it. Loose thinking, exaggeration of resemblances, ignoring of differences, and downright falsification of evidence, are only a few of the evils which a premature handling of it fosters in its votaries.

At once alarmed and dismissive, James's condemnation of Harrison seems to violate the pacifist principles he had set forth in his vice-chancellor's speech at the outset of the war, when he had urged the university to "confine our controversies within the narrowest limits, and be ready if necessary to postpone them altogether."[56] That he had, in his own words, "dipped [his] pen in gall and flayed"[57] a fellow scholar indicates that there was far more at stake than textual misinterpretation in the territorial dispute over the expansion of classical studies.

James's nearly line-by-line critique of Harrison's article and his skepticism about the legitimacy of her field register a mounting concern for the repercussions of scholarly activities on wider political affairs—affairs from which the university had, until the Great War, maintained a dignified detachment.[58] But the war prompted an urgent reassessment as well as a rigorous refortification of academic values even as the walls between the "dignity" of knowledge and the savagery of experience eroded. Beneath James's denunciatory rhetoric lies a preoccupation shared by many in the much-depleted Cambridge community with reasserting the moral principles that on the one hand justified England's participation in the war and on the other clarified the duty of those who remained at home, in James's words, to "keep alive that fire of education, religion, learning and research which will in God's good time outburn the flames of war."[59] In the search for ideological stability, scholarship assumed a spiritual burden that was measured and weighed by the terms of opposition and resistance dictating international relations. "Even if ruin should overwhelm this University, it may be found to the last a home of sound learning and religious education," preached the Reverend F. J. Foakes-Jackson in October 1914.[60] The sermon emphasized that adherence to Christian faith was part of the scholar's arsenal against the enemy. "[Germany] is waging with fierce concentration unredeemed by generosity one of the first absolutely non-moral wars of history," Foakes-Jackson continued after acknowledging the bond of "mutual study and encouragement" previously shared between England and Germany. Condemning the latter's "historico-critical school" for "attacking the Church, the Creed and the Bible, till all faith has disappeared," he asserted that "such a state of things [as an academic attack on Christian faith] is inconceivable in England. Christianity is either false and therefore to be eradicated or true and therefore to be cherished at all costs. To regard it as a corpse to be dissected seems even worse than to hate it as a pernicious error. . . . [W]e can only accord to the German at war the admiration Milton compels us to feel for Satan and his fiends." Regarded in light of this polarizing religious rhetoric, Harrison's virtual autopsy of the beheaded Baptist was tantamount to claiming allegiance with the arch-enemy himself—a comparison that James did not fail to suggest in his article.[61] By treating the scriptures as myth and appealing to German authorities to back her argument, Harrison's article flippantly disproved Foakes-Jackson's patriotic pronouncement of the secure Christian foundations of British scholarship. In the same irreverent spirit, her statement that John is Jesus's "double . . . so far as [the] daimon aspect goes" blatantly defied the principles of T. R. Glover's well-attended 1916 Michaelmas lectures, entitled "Jesus as a Historic Personality," which had stated that "it is the acme of bad criticism . . . and profoundly unsatisfactory to make of Jesus only an archaic figure."[62] Far from speaking for the academic community as the first lines of her article propose, Harrison's "daimonization" of John and Jesus opposed a common effort within the university to promote Christian faith as an antidote to world catastrophe. Indeed, at a time when many in the nation had begun to think the war a divine punishment for their abandonment of Christian principles,[63] Harrison's article was another step in the wrong direction of self-destructive atheism. James's characterization of her methodology as "evil"—even demonic—contributed to an academic evangelicalism that emphasized the need for systematic discrimination. The "exaggeration of resemblances, ignoring of differences" fostered by the mythological mindset threatened the framework of the nation's—not to mention the university's—moral stability.

Energized by the war's sudden disruption of academic traditions, the exchange between Harrison and James exposes the broader social, political, and religious resonance of Greek scholarship by the early twentieth century. While this debate may appear to be a conflict between an old-school conservative and a new-fangled liberal, Harrison's calculated insubordinance and James's harsh rebuttal suggest that broader political considerations were underpinned by the deeply personal investment that each held in Greek knowledge. The private significance of the affair is witnessed by the fact that Harrison's article lingered in M. R. James's mind long after he had exhausted his "gall" in the *Classical Review.* Some three months after publishing his initial reaction to Harrison, James took up *The Bacchae* in a train back to Cambridge from the National Club in London. A letter to his friend Gordon Carey, then stationed at the front, indicates that it had been some time since he had looked at the play:

> This afternoon in the train I read the Helen, Electra & Bacchae of the poet Euripides. The Bacchae is really rather horrible: a great fuss is made of it, but the behaviour of the incarnate god to Pentheus (who . . . is the man who wants to keep the home together & does represent the things that make life possible) is flagitious. I ought I suppose to have read what Verrall has to say about it: if I have, I have forgotten it. Very likely he has said that Pentheus is the man with whom Euripides really sympathizes.[64]

That James picked up *The Bacchae* after he had written his condemnation of Harrison testifies to the haste with which he had penned his protest as well as to the profound impact that her words had on him—one that was greater than an objection to unsound scholarship could nullify.[65] His identification with "the man who wants to keep the home together" suggests that his officious response to Harrison was rooted in a deeper fear that she was undermining his personal sense of stability and threatening "the things that make life possible." Just what these "things" are, James does not specify, but his meaning can be gathered by examining the opposing "parts" he and Harrison took in their interpretations of Euripides.

The Bacchae had been one of Harrison's favorite tragedies since the *Prolegomena*. Using the tragedy as a primary source of evidence, she had identified Dionysos with "'a return to nature,' a breaking of bonds and limitations and crystallizations, a desire for the life rather of the emotions than of the reason. . . . This notion of a return to nature is an element in the worship of Dionysos so simple, so moving and in a sense so modern that we realize it without effort" (444–46). Harrison's interpretation of Dionysos as a nature god representing emotional liberation from rational boundaries as well as her sense of his modernity derived, in part, from the popularity of this concept in late-nineteenth-century literature, art, and philosophy. Nietzsche had written about the "Dionysian principle" in *The Birth of Tragedy* (1872).[66] Walter Pater had celebrated the nature god and suggested his relevance to the modern spirit in "Study of Dionysus" (1876), noting that "Shelley's *Sensitive Plant* shows in what mists of poetical reverie such feeling [of nature-worship] may still float about a mind full of modern lights, the feeling we too have of a life in the green world, always ready to assert its claim over our sympathetic fancies."[67] Pater's appreciation for the aesthetic merits of Dionysian worship was shared by classicist painters such as Frederic Leighton and Lawrence Alma-Tadema, whom Pater admired and for whom Dionysos and his Bacchante followers became symbols of their break from the moralistic, Ruskinian ethos of the Pre-Raphaelites.[68] Closer to Harrison's field, J. G. Frazer had discussed Dionysos's role as god of agriculture, the corn, and trees in *The Golden Bough*,[69] and Harrison's colleagues A. W. Verrall and William Ridgeway had both written about Dionysos as a nature god.

For Harrison, however, the most influential Dionysian commentary came not from mythography or anthropology but from literary scholarship. One of the central inspirations for the *Prolegomena* was Gilbert Murray's discussion of *The Bacchae* in his 1897 *History of Ancient Greek Literature*, in which he wrote that

> there is . . . a certain tone of polemic against "mere rationalism" which has every appearance of coming from the poet himself. . . .

> Reason is great, but it is not everything. There are in the world things not of reason, but both below and above it; causes of emotion, which we cannot express, which we tend to worship, which we feel, perhaps, to be the precious elements in life. These things are God or forms of God: not fabulous immortal men, but "Things which Are," things utterly non-human and non-moral, which bring man bliss or tear his life to shreds without a break in their own serenity.[70]

Finishing her *Prolegomena* in 1902, Harrison asked for and received permission from Murray to quote this passage at the end of the book, for, as she confessed to him, it has "been a sort of theological (mythological) Alpha and Omega to me and was long before I knew its inadequate author, in fact it first really started the plot of my book [the *Prolegomena*] 4 years ago."[71] Harrison and Murray remained close friends throughout her tenure at Cambridge, partly because of their shared passion for Euripides, but Harrison put her passion to revolutionary ends that exceeded the realm of aesthetic vision or philosophical ideal, adopting the polemic against "mere rationalism" as her own practical ethos. Whereas Murray's comments are conditioned by his tone of interpretive conjecture, Harrison drew on a popularized, aestheticized image of Dionysos to make a definitive statement about archaic Greek society and to institute a change in critical discourse. The image of Dionysos provided Harrison with a vehicle for transporting the languages of classicist aestheticism and literary interpretation to scientific discourse as ammunition against the withering sanity and sobriety of institutional tradition.

Harrison's interest in Dionysos as a figure of spiritual rejuvenation for the modern world (and, in particular, classical scholarship) expands on Pater's regard for the god and his maenadic followers as revitalizing inspirations for modern art.[72] Though she would become increasingly disenchanted with the violent elements of Dionysian worship, Harrison maintained the conviction throughout her career that the emotionality and mysticism of Dionysian faith constituted an essential element of historical continuity between the ancient and modern religious experience. In a letter of 1907, she reported on getting "stormy" with her friend A. W. Verrall for siding with Pentheus,[73] as James had rightly predicted. In her 1916 article on John the Baptist, she tempered her once-passionate partiality for Dionysos the god but maintained the justice of Pentheus's murder by interpreting it as an aspect of nature's inevitable cycle of death and re-birth. According to this view, Dionysos—who has been killed and resurrected[74]—acts as an agent in the life cycle by causing the king to be slaughtered by his mother, Agave. Harrison's interpretive framework dissociates the three figures from the themes of vengeance and guilt that govern Euripides' play to argue for a universalizing concept of cyclical renewal. Rather than being placed antagonistically toward each other, Pentheus, Dionysos, and Agave are collapsed into a common denominator of "daimonic" forces. The removal of individual motivation thus allows identification of the beheaded Baptist both with Pentheus and with his enemy Dionysos—as well as with numerous other legendary murder victims. For Harrison, the "life-history of the year daimon" absorbed the identities of "such figures as Tammuz, Adonis, Osiris, Orpheus, Dionysos"[75] (as well as John the Baptist and his "double," Jesus Christ) into representatives of the "stages of the year itself, or rather the fertility of the year." Sharing the "life-history" of the year-daimon, Dionysos, Pentheus, John, and Christ are all personifications of humanity's "intense religious need" for a sense of historical continuity. As suggested by ritual celebrations of death, this sense is felt at its keenest in the moment of destruction, when individuality dissolves into process.

Although James shared Harrison's concern for the *Bacchae*'s broader philosophical implications, his reading of the tragedy opposes the life force to the destructive elements that Harrison deified. In contrast to her regard for the divine elements that represent death's inevitability, James's sympathy with Pentheus privileged the individual's resistance to death, however futile the effort. This difference in philosophical perspective was rooted in personal experience. Burdened by the responsibilities of a spiritual and political leader in wartime, James might very well have identified with Pentheus's disgust at the Bacchic revelry of the Theban women and his desire to squelch the new faith introduced by Dionysos.[76] James's defense of the Theban king's attempt to maintain order indicates a momentary clearing of his increasing sense of personal obscurity as the war progressed.[77] Indeed, *The Bacchae* seems to have impelled James to articulate a more personal response to Harrison's article in a different public forum. In a sermon preached at the church of St. Edward the King in Cambridge on October 28, 1917, James revealed his Penthean efforts to resist both the physical disruption of the war and the spiritual threat of those such as Harrison who, Dionysos-like, would undermine traditional belief systems. "Is it merely an interesting, or even a not very interesting piece of ritual that is here presented to us?" he began.

> A minor scene in what people are fond of calling the liturgical drama? Certainly we can make it so: we can note the special features of the service: Collect, Epistle and Gospel, and Lesson . . . and think no more of the matter . . . but it is possible and reasonable to deal differently. . . . [M]inor things . . . in the course of centuries have tended to become in the eyes of many mere pieces of ritual and drill. . . . [But] some are able to expend themselves with complete sincerity upon the observance as it is laid down and to find in it a living meaning, and, what is more a channel still open for communication between their souls and the Infinite. To these the acts and processes of ecclesiastical worship are by long practice natural. The child is always speaking to his Father in this special language: its surroundings and idioms are . . . sacred in his eyes. . . . Others, who are many in these days and in this country, are on the whole inclined to be suspicious of observances.[78]

"The Head of John Baptist" attends this sermon like the proverbial pink elephant. James's emphasis on the personal significance of rituals implicitly rejects Harrison's focus on the mere act of repetition. As seen in her interpretations of Salome and Pentheus, the prescribed acts and formulaic proceedings of ritual distance individuals from the "squalor" of personal motivation. Religious feeling arises from the dissipation of individuality into what Harrison called a "mystical oneness with all things."[79] Religion, for Harrison, is essentially an experience of self-estrangement. For James, in contrast, rituals are important insofar as they can assume an individualized meaning and help the individual establish personal intimacy with God. Rituals have a concentrative rather than a diffusive force, such that the "oneness" achieved through religious experience constitutes a private communion that shuts out all others. James's rhetoric re-creates this exclusive religious atmosphere by arguing, rather tautologically, that those who regard Christian ritual as mere "drama" are spectators, not true participants, of worship. Their own doubt casts them as outsiders to the sacred "surroundings and idioms" of the faith and disqualify them from interpreting the "special language" of Christian ceremony—not to mention the words of scripture that are the written representations of that language. James's use of the oppositional terms *some, many,* and *others* serve as much to mark off sacred space from those such as Harrison who are "suspicious of observances" as to define this space for "natural" believers who hardly need his explanation.

However much rituals may serve as merely the outer walls around a sacred space accessible to a privileged few, these institutional boundaries are nevertheless essential in preserving the "living meaning" within. James stressed the crucial role of the public institution in preserving private worship in a seemingly tangential remark on the Christian celebration of the dead that allusively argues against Harrison's interpretations of death rituals.

> I am led [from discussion of Saints Simon and Jude] to . . . turn . . . to the feast of All Saints [when] we shall recite . . . the names of the Cambridge men who have fallen. . . . These are public rites: but there are others. Upon that day each of us will have his own roll of honour: . . . people of whom all that you could find to say would resolve into this, that they stayed at home and were Christians there. . . . The sum of the matter is that their lives [versus those who have gone off to fight] may have been so inconspicuous that when you too have passed out of sight, they will not be remembered at all, and yet these lives mean more to you than anything else in the world. . . . Love of the work we are doing will carry us a long way, no doubt, but if we cannot see that it is part of a greater thing than itself, part of a cause or an institution worthy of love, there will come a day when it will appear unreal and not worth doing.[80]

James's final remark on the necessity of committing to a larger, impersonal institution that transcends any one life seems at first to contradict his emphasis throughout the sermon on the overriding importance of private relations. His point, however, was not to endorse one above the other but to invest institutional relations with the force of devotion that one might hold for a loved one or for God. It is only as a beloved being that the institution can compensate for the reality and sense of self-worth threatened by the loss of a beloved individual. As with the desire for personal communion with God, the love of an institution is rooted in a fundamental human longing for the tangible, the known, the real that constitutes the life-instinct. According to this view, the horror of *The Bacchae* lies not so much in the play itself as in a reading of it that associates the life-instinct with the erasure of individual values and that sanctions a death resulting from self-disguise, misrecognition, loss of self-consciousness, and the sacrifice of tangible, "real" relations to the illusion of Dionysian mysticism. The instinct for self-preservation against these Dionysian threats is what drove James's defense of academic traditions—traditions that, for him, were inseparable from the life-sustaining force of personal faith. On July 31, 1917, he wrote to Gordon Carey, "The available people here are few. . . . [T]here is not much to diversify existence. In fact were it not for work having to be done & work that can be done in the way of research . . . I should be puzzled."[81] For James, work meant the meticulous task of collating, translating, and commenting on obscure Apocryphal manuscripts as well as writing and delivering sermons.[82] If his letter implies that such tasks are mere "diversions," they are nevertheless functionally equal to what James called "the undoubted value of discipline and regularity" afforded by ecclesiastical observance. Both involve a methodical process aimed at maintaining familiar structures of meaning when the inescapable awareness of the unknown and unknowable makes existence itself "appear unreal and not worth doing."

Harrison wrote her provocative article on John the Baptist partly to ensure that the preservation of individual existence would not result in the ossification of knowledge and thus threaten the life of scholarship. Like James, she invested research with a sacred value, but whereas for him academic work derived its ultimate worth from institutions "larger than itself," she regarded knowledge as a vital being in its own right, independent of institutional structures and deserving the undiluted commitment of its worshippers. "[T]he world of things to be known is my god, I *value* them intensely; so they become my religion,"[83] she wrote to her friend Francis Cornford, opposing her religion of "things to be known" to his devout Christianity. In continually reaching beyond familiar structures to horizons of the unknown, the scholar's research aspires, in Harrison's view, toward the same goal of self-estrangement with which she associated Dionysian ritual. "Gods and theology are always . . . a temporary phase, always perforce fabricated, and only to be broken," she wrote in 1915. "[T]hey are husks, shells, that the swelling kernel of religion must always break through; and by religion I mean . . . just that commerce with the unseen and unknown that we have by virtue of our 'free ideas.'"[84] Harrison's equation of the life of thought (that is, of "free ideas") and the religious impulse for mystical communion directly opposes James's emphasis on the basic human need to know and be known. His Christian God and his research were familiar and "loved" for their familiarity, whereas for her, religion was "the beckoning, sometimes almost the threatening, of the unseen . . . the not fully known."[85] This contrast between a religion of love and one of fear explains why James's institutional reinforcements during the war were for Harrison the hardened husks and shells that suffocate the vital, spiritual impulse of scholarship beyond the reassurance of the known. "War, if it cannot, and shall not, slay, can most grievously wound learning,"[86] she wrote in 1914, anticipating the cessation of research as international turmoil shifted previous priorities. She expressed her concern again a month later in her "Epilogue on the War": "Learning, and still more research, is a hard mistress; she will have your whole heart or none of you."[87] Christianity threatened Harrison's religion of the "unseen and unknown" by diverting the hearts and minds of the scholars around her. Indeed, she had registered with surprise the resurgence of religious belief at the war's outset, noting that "it is very funny now-a-days . . . the importance of people being simple and rather stupid and doing their duty at home and having a religion. . . . I knew this Catholic reaction was on in France, but I did not know that Jacques and Gwen [Raverat] and Rupert [Brooke] etc., were all in it here."[88] Harrison's light, somewhat scornful observation here in 1914 disguises her mounting anxiety over the death of scholarly work—a death heralded by the onset of a regime of simplicity, stupidity, and Christian complacency.

Having contemplated an article on "my favorite saint—John Baptist" at least since 1914,[89] Harrison finally published it just at the moment when she felt that her god of "things to be known" was threatened by the common desire for a known God. Going against her friends' return to religion and duty and performed in full recognition of the institutional commandments she was breaking, it was as much an attempt to salvage her faith as James's sermons were delivered in the name of his Christian God. Indeed, the amalgam deity of Dionysos and the Christian saint represented Harrison's personal crusade on behalf of her belief that the "swelling kernel of religion must always break through." On the one hand, this image of rupture identifies Harrison with Dionysos as a destructive force. On the other hand, Harrison's comparison of Dionysos with John the Baptist emphasizes that the Greek god is also a mystic who, like the Baptist, is associated with acts of initiation and salvation. As Harrison wrote in her *Prolegomena,* Dionysos "came into Greece . . . [j]ust when [the Olympian gods] were losing touch with life and reality, fading and dying of their own luminous perfection [and brought] an impulse really religious . . . Mysticism" (363–64). Just as John the Baptist is a "Forerunner" of Jesus who, as the opening lines of Harrison's article suggest, occupies an ambiguous space between the Old and New Testaments, so too is Dionysos an outsider to established faith who ultimately represents purgation and enlightenment.[90]

Just how Dionysos's role as religious salvationist applied to Harrison's spiritual mission lies in her perception of the contrast between the Greek god and the Christian saint. For though her article might collapse John and Dionysos into the year-daimon, Harrison held distinct attitudes toward them as mythic-historic individuals. For her, John is an ultimately defeated figure with whom she identified when she felt particularly discouraged, unappreciated, or misunderstood.[91] He is the "lone voice in the wilderness" who, as she states in her article, is "obscured by the figure of Him to whom he was Forerunner." Dionysos, in contrast, is a triumphant god—the hero of a play that she called in 1912 "the document of the New Birth."[92] Even as Dionysos's identification with John had brought out the Greek god's beneficent aspect, so too did John's association with Dionysos restore to the Baptist his powers as an agent of change. By emphasizing John's "daimonic"[93] force and provocatively identifying him with Jesus, Harrison challenged the deathly luminosity of the Christian God, who had become a rationalized and thus nonreligious fabrication like the despised anthropomorphic Olympians. The article thus transforms John the Baptist into a Dionysian force for Harrison's own time. Encompassing both the self-sacrificial fervor of the Baptist and the epiphanic triumph of Dionysos, Harrison's daimon reinhabits the Gospels to shock and thus to revitalize a scholarship "fading and dying" of its own "limitations and crystallizations" (*Prolegomena*, 444).

If the composite daimon of Dionysos–John the Baptist is the totem of Harrison's religion of the unknown, the Greek language is the clay of its creation. As the shared language of sacred and secular texts, Greek naturally spans that dangerous liminal space between scholarship and sacrilege. Its commonality in Euripides, the Gospels, and Apocryphal manuscripts enables the analogies that justify the "life-history" of the year-daimon and allows Harrison to break through the barriers between Christian and pagan belief. Her adaptation of Greek as the language of her own religion of scholarly mysticism is exemplified in her John article by a citation of an obscure Greek passage in an eleventh-century manuscript, of which she confessed, "The words are not very easy to translate, for we have no exact equivalent for *thriambeutheinai*." The untranslatable phrase led her to conclude that "a triumphal dance with the head seems almost implied" and thus to link Salome's dance with Agave's and both with the daimon's life-history. The unknowability of the Greek here allowed Harrison to venture across the barrier between pagan and Christian texts and to justify the use of her sympathetic imagination as an instrument of scholarly interrogation. James's correction of her grammar identifies the narrative impulse behind Harrison's treatment of Greek. "*Thriambeuo* is surely not a very hard word to render," he wrote. "[I]n the active it means to lead in triumph, . . . in the passive, to be led in triumph, or to be triumphed over." James's demagogic tone suggests that Harrison's inability to construe was attributable not to the obscurity of the passage but either to Harrison's inadequate linguistic expertise or to an all-too-suggestible narrative imagination. "[C]an Miss Harrison point to any document earlier than the nineteenth century in which the princess is represented as being enamoured of John?" queried James. "And again, if it is so, 'to speak of the love of Salome for the Baptist is to put the loathsome performances of Flaubert and Oscar Wilde in place of the Gospel story.'" By pointing out Harrison's indiscriminate amalgam of primitive myth and modern fiction, James recast the accusation of "amorous license" from the biblical narrative to the irresponsible, morally dubious exegete. His defense of the Gospels' sovereignty firmly resituates the blame of licentiousness on Harrison's romanticizations.

James's accusation, however, is ironically double-sided. For although his quotation marks attribute the mention of Flaubert and Wilde to Harrison, the latter made no direct mention of either author. James is the one who made the explicit association with Flaubert's *Salaambô* and Wilde's *Salome*. This may be a small technical slip, but it is a telling one. If James's criticism centers on Harrison's overly facile blend of history and fiction, the slip of his pen here—not to mention his reading of Euripides—demonstrates just how fluid are the boundaries between Gospel truth and narrative invention. Challenging these boundaries, Harrison's use of Greek might very well warrant the *Cambridge Review*'s claim that "while Miss Jane Harrison, not Salome, leads the dance; no doubt the walls of Jericho (if not already down) are showing some more cracks."[94]

Afterlives of the Eniautos-Daimon

In conceiving the Eniautos-Daimon, Harrison did not merely invent a god and spearhead a school of thought. She also shaped a critical rhetoric that had to recognize and contend with the instability of discursive boundaries and by doing so contribute to Harrison's fight for scholarship in the face of seemingly greater catastrophes. Unlike the European war, Harrison's was a battle whose goal was not the victory of one side or the other but the perpetuation of conflict itself as a vital fuel for what James called the "fire of education, religion, learning and research." The two published responses to James's article emphasize the obscurity of victory when the battle lines seem to dissolve in the fighting.[95] Harrison's letter was, as she purported, "a polite, formal acknowledgment of my errors."[96] The acknowledgment was short, falsely deferential, and pointedly curmudgeonly. "I should like to thank Dr. James for his kind—if not too kindly—correction of my inaccuracies," she began. "'Apocryphal Scriptures' and 'late Byzantine legends' are to me new seas into which I am but just plunging, so I am doubly grateful to be set right at the outset." Having paid due homage to the superior knowledge of the provost, who was twelve years her junior, Harrison came to the main point of her letter:

> The details in which he is good enough to correct me nowise invalidate, or even affect, my argument. . . . I propose, therefore, to continue unabashed my "crude and inconsequent speculations."
>
> As to the general desirability of Comparative Mythology as a subject for students, I would leave that question in hands more judicious than my own. I am no educationalist. To me the keenest joys of science—as of sport—are always perilous, and I hope to die commending perilous joys to a generation better equipped, and I trust more valorous, than my own.

Harrison brandished this dramatic combat rhetoric with the rebellious glee of Dionysos and the self-sacrificial fervor of the martyr-saint, willing to die for her beliefs.[97] Playing up the roles of soldier and victim, she loaded her defense with an insistent self-referentiality that draws attention to James's inappropriate personal attacks. Meanwhile, her language casts the fighting spirit of experimental science in a heroic light that implicitly identifies James as an overscrupulous Pentheus whose unsporting cowardice is as much a threat of intellectual degeneracy as the "premature handling" of a "science in the making."[98]

Harrison's letter to Gilbert Murray, shortly after she read James's diatribe, emphasizes that she was less concerned about the fate of her poor Baptist than about maintaining the intensity of her sport. "*Please* . . . will you look at the Provost's outbreak over the Head of John Baptist—I knew somebody wld [*sic*] rage and swell," she wrote, confessing to full precognizance of the objections her article would ignite and suggesting that provocation was at least half the goal. "You can say J.B.'s head is all nonsense if you like—tho [*sic*] it isn't! . . . If you haven't time for all please read just the end of the Provost's article—and *please* answer it, it really affects the Humanities."[99] Murray responded by writing a companion letter to Harrison's that argued both on her behalf and on behalf of the "Humanities." At this point, Murray was not only a well-known Hellenist but also a prominent figure in matters of national education: he had joined the National Board of Education in 1916 and had been proposed as education minister. In addition to his qualifications on the educational front, Murray's authority on the texts involved in the debate rested, in part, on his position as Regius Professor of Greek at Oxford and his contributions to the *Biblical Encyclopaedia* on the philosophical background of the New Testament. The tone of his letter was diplomatic, but Harrison wrote to him afterwards, "you have pierced to the Provost's real motive—it is a general attack, though levelled at me."[100] Murray's letter began, "'Very outspoken criticism' may no doubt at times be desirable, but I cannot see that the errors of fact or faults of method which the Provost of King's has pointed out in Miss Harrison's article . . . are sufficient to justify the tone of his condemnation." James's personal hostility is thus at odds with the requisite objectivity of "fact" and "method" that his article purports to defend. Clearly, if James wanted to argue on grounds of professionalism and scholarly conduct, Harrison could find a champion to defend her position without sacrificing her composure in counterattack.[101]

Murray, however, was far more than an auxiliary arms-bearer for Harrison or an apologist for "premature sciences." Though Harrison may have felt compelled to speak only for herself, Murray set out to prove more generally and as an "educationalist" that the "perilous joy" of the sympathetic imagination can—and must—coexist with philological scruples: "[There are] two passages of Greek, where the Provost differs from her. But here, I must confess, her interpretation seems to me to be probably right, and certainly defensible. . . . I should precisely agree with Miss Harrison that a 'triumphal dance with the head seems almost implied.' Observe the 'almost.' The Provost wants it to mean 'was exposed in triumph.' . . . Quite possible; though unlikely in point of language. And surely unnecessary in view of the passage quoted by the Provost himself." While engaging the linguistic technicality insisted on by the provost, Murray's defense of Harrison also argues that translation—especially of an ancient language—is inherently an act of interpretation. Meaning stems as much from context and implication as from precise lexicographic rendering; it is guided as much by narrative possibility as by the certainties of "fact" and "method." Indeed, James's seemingly authoritative translation is, Murray pointed out, as much a function of what he wanted it to mean as Harrison's is a reading based "on her own facts." At least Harrison had the self-awareness and humility to admit an "almost" into her reading, while the provost's translation errs more self-damningly on the side of pomp and superfluity. Whatever linguistic superiority James wanted to assert has thus been not merely summarily squelched by a specialist whose credentials trump his own but exposed as a rhetorical pretension that discredits his scholarly objectivity and defense of institutional dignity.

Murray was not the kind of person who would pull rank, however. His letter sincerely questions the authority of those who supposedly have earned the "name and dignity" to pronounce judgment on "fields with which [they are not] at all specially familiar." The weakness of James's defensive offense becomes more clear in Murray's addressing the contentious issue of Salome's supposed desire for John. "It had never occurred to me that any student of mythology would so interpret Miss Harrison's argument," wrote Murray, suggesting that the idea of Salome's lust for John stemmed not from any confusion on Harrison's part between history, the Gospels, and modern fiction but from the biases of a man so foreign to "the surroundings and idioms" of mythology—or so eager to adopt a mythological mindset—as to allow for the complete reduction of historical fact to imaginative conception.

> He evidently thinks Miss Harrison has said something both paradoxical and offensive, something which justified him in using every art of polemic to destroy so noxious a view. I believe he imagines—though I hesitate to ascribe such a view to him, and offer him sincere apologies if I am wrong—that Miss Harrison means that John the Baptist was a Year-daemon and not a historical person; or, even more strangely, that, to quote his own words: "There were love passages between Herodias' daughter and St. John (on her side only) and that when she was repulsed the motive *spretae iniuria formae* came into play, and she demanded John's head out of spite."

Whether or not Harrison did indeed want to challenge the historicity of biblical personae, Murray's argument stresses that the faults of offensiveness and paradox lie as much with James as with Harrison. In fact, it completely reverses the indictment of trespass: James, who willingly admitted his ignorance of comparative mythology, had no right to criticize its ways—indeed, risked his own values of conduct and integrity by doing so. For not only does his attack present itself as unprofessional, but his misreading of Harrison's article exposes both his unfamiliarity with the conventions of myth criticism and an imagination that seemed all too eager to collapse a biblical persona into a linguistic conjunction that Harrison elsewhere identified as her own rhetorical invention. Could James have been shadowboxing against his "noxious" inclinations to move from historical to mythological personae?[102] This implicit question surfaces in Murray's statement that although "Miss Harrison never suggested that the Gospel story itself is derived from the Year-myth. . . . I do not for a moment mean to imply that a scholar should be debarred from making such a suggestion, if the argument seemed to him to lead that way." Such an extension of the year-myth to modern narrative certainly does seem likely in James's case, because the explicit juxtaposition of Wilde's dramatic retelling with the biblical tale appears not in Harrison's article but in James's—a point Murray was careful to emphasize in his use of direct quotation.

Murray's article uses James's misreading of Harrison to expose the provost's own imaginative inclinations and, by doing so, suggests that comparative mythologists' approach to antiquity does not merely constitute a legitimate method of historical inquiry but might serve as a model for modern scholarship. While Murray might acknowledge the specialized discourse of each disciplinary field, his counterindictment of James also recognizes the impossibility of confining knowledge within rational, objective boundaries or judging it according to institutional hierarchies. By implicating James in the flights of personal fancy that James denounced in Harrison, Murray pointed out the impracticability of rigid discriminations between legitimate and illegitimate knowledge. His final remarks directly question James's assumption of insider privilege: "If we mythologists are to blame for the excessive hostility which we seem to arouse, I venture to suggest that it is chiefly not for the reasons alleged by the Provost, but for a quite different one. It may be true that, like other groups of inquirers, we sometimes fall into a sort of shorthand language which is perfectly intelligible to other mythologists, but is apt to be misinterpreted by outsiders. If that is so, it looks as if we and our readers both ought to be more careful." By defending the right of mythologists to cultivate their own "shorthand language," Murray emphasizes the formation of new boundaries between splintering disciplinary fields and challenges those who would deny multiplicity of perspective to any field of inquiry. There is no longer one inside or one outside; instead, there are multiple interiorities. A single concept of "scientific dignity" can no longer assert proprietary authority over all forms of knowledge.

Indeed, the principles of comparative mythology assume applicability to scholarship in general precisely because they emphasize the fluidity of the boundaries that control the relationships between scholars and their subjects and between scholars in different fields. Fields of knowledge are fertilized by the processes of reception and projection, of reading and misreading that guarantee the continuing vitality of the university. Harrison expressed this view in her 1913 essay "Scientiae Sacra Fames": "Science today is . . . more co-operative, more democratic. The several departments, once sharply sundered, now work in conjunction; there is a sense of the whole towards which each is tending. A University that used to be split into faculties is now—though specialization is intenser than ever—conscious of its unity, its interrelations. That consciousness may yet save our older Universities, spiritually moribund, though they are."[103] Such a vision of institutional unity seems at first hopelessly idealistic given the territorial squabblings between specializations. But for Harrison, these territorial disputes *are* the keenest evidence of the growing consciousness of interrelations. She believed that continuing debates about the significance of the ancient world would ensure not only the survival of classics as a modern discipline but also the vibrancy of all fields of learning.

For Harrison—a woman haunted by the conviction that she was not a "sound scholar"—the very fact of her increasing prominence within the scholarly community, however intentional and controversial, presented a puzzle as intriguing as primitive ritual. "I fell to laughing consumedly at myself," she wrote to Murray of the experience of writing the preface to *Themis*. "[W]hat an absurd mind I have. There is no harm in having an absurd mind only it gives you such a lot of trouble setting it straight."[104]

Letters such as this register her surprise that she should have become the guiding light for the men of the Cambridge Ritualists, a group that began to form around Harrison's anticategorical ethos.[105] Indeed, it is largely the curious fact of Harrison's influence on her acolytes rather than any specific theory of the Cambridge Ritualists that has ensured the group's historical longevity. "We can now see how remarkable it is for Jane Harrison to stand out in this band of geniuses," wrote Stanley Edgar Hyman in 1962 in commemoration of the fiftieth anniversary of *Themis*'s first publication. "Murray was a far better Greek scholar, Cornford had a much more rigorous and logical mind, Cook was always more fertile of ideas. But Miss Harrison . . . had a power of imaginative understanding that went beyond any of them. . . . [She] inspired them, collaborated with them, and set them tasks in the intellectual revolution that produced a dozen major books between 1903 and 1941."[106] Indeed, the Eniautos-Daimon catalyzed the kind of revolt against familiar categories and knowledge that Harrison had intended to provoke. Murray and Cornford both contributed chapters to *Themis,* taking the familiar forms of tragedy and the Olympic Games and "daimonizing" them out of recognition. J. A. K. Thomson's *Studies in the Odyssey,* A. B. Cook's *Zeus,* and Murray's *Hamlet and Orestes: A Study in Traditional Types* followed in the next three years.[107] All of these familiar title figures (Odysseus, Zeus, Hamlet, and Orestes) are interpreted by their authors, either directly or indirectly, as representatives of the Eniautos-Daimon. That a person's legacy as a scholar should be based on the power of an imagination that Harrison herself often admitted bordered on madness is an idea that questions the very legitimacy of institutional authority. The phenomenon suggests the ambiguous division between the field of knowledge and that of belief, between scholarship and religion.

"Miss Harrison is the Scholar Gipsy of Hellenic studies," stated the *Classical Review* of *Themis.* "In this book we find her ranging 'still untired' the accustomed fields and . . . plunging into the dark and devious coverts of savage anthropology. . . . [T]he road to Truth is paved with good heresies; and if indeed *Themis* embodies one, it is of the very best kind—at once brilliantly suggestive and a direct incitement to controversy."[108] Other reviewers were not as enthusiastic about Harrison's heretical forays. "The book seems to have been written in a white heat," wrote Lewis Farnell in his review of *Themis,* "and it is Miss Harrison's theory that books should be so written. . . . A white heat of mind is good for poetry and art; but we may doubt if a scientific treatise . . . is best composed in such a mental atmosphere. . . . We do not find in *Themis* the great tradition of Cambridge scholarship."[109] No doubt taking the opportunity to retaliate against Harrison's review of his book some six years previously, Farnell intended his criticism to discredit Harrison's scholarship and to make her an embarrassment for her home institution. Ironically, however, his criticisms only help to articulate Harrison's emphasis on the need for imaginative projection as the life force of classical scholarship against the restrictive boundaries of the "great tradition." This spirit of disruption and invention is at once classified and daemonized in *Themis*. Shaped by her beliefs, preferences, and hands, the divine Eniautos-Daimon must always be eclipsed by Harrison's creative genius, its historical reality overwritten by her narrative intervention, its mythological origins circumscribed by her imagination.

Afterword

The First World War and the Death of Heresy

Despite the ardent efforts of Jane Harrison, M. R. James, and others in the academic community to maintain, each in his or her own way, the vibrancy and relevance of classical learning through the years of the First World War, the event had a damaging and irreversible impact on the Hellenism that had shaped nineteenth-century thoughts and values. This effect was experienced, first of all, on the level of curricular reform. As Christopher Stray and others have documented, the war resulted in Britain's reevaluation of an educational system that had focused on the principles of a humanistic education to the neglect, by and large, of the scientific and technological training that many believed had given Germany a tactical advantage.[1] Such beliefs prompted the prime minister to initiate, in 1916, formal inquiries into the balance of humanistic and scientific education throughout the country. One result of these inquiries was the abolition of compulsory Greek at Oxford and Cambridge, about which debates had arisen sporadically throughout the past fifty years. The removal of Greek to an optional course of study signified far more than changes in undergraduates' qualifying exams. It also marked a broad-based disillusionment with the peaceful, orderly ideal of the Greek golden age that had persisted throughout the Victorian era and signaled the collapse of the cultural hierarchies formed around and sustaining this ideal. As Paul Fussell has argued, the war destroyed a world where "values appeared stable and where the meanings of abstractions seemed permanent and reliable."[2] Having served as a symbolic marker of cultural stability throughout the preceding century, Greek, in its decline after the war, came to represent a privileged body of knowledge no longer consistent with the values of the age. In its place rose a reemphasis on Latin studies, which earned their reinstitution owing to the very reasons of greater practicality and accessibility that had put them behind Greek at the beginning of the nineteenth century. "This was by now the 'era of Latin,' of the self-disciplined citizen who could rise from a lower-class family background, through selective schooling, to the security and status of middle-class careers," writes Stray, commenting on the rise of "compulsory Latin" in the first half of the twentieth century. "Greek, which had been 'something special,' becomes, formally, just another specialism. . . . [W]hile support for Greek was thin and localized, Latin was seen as an important element in the curriculum by a wide range of interest groups. Newer subject associations, particularly those concerned with modern languages, saw Latin as the acceptable face of classics—an exemplar of the (grammatical) discipline their opponents claimed they lacked" (*Classics Transformed*, 277). Favored on one side by those who endorsed a modernized curriculum and on the other by those who were fighting to sustain a humanistic tradition, Latin reassumed its cultural dominance.

As a result of these curricular changes, when women were finally granted university degrees (at Oxford in 1920, at Cambridge in 1948), at least one set of values for which their Victorian predecessors had striven had shifted permanently out of reach. Although the decline of Hellenism and all that it represented to the Victorians may seem a slight loss, if not a gain, to a twentieth century that saw women's enfranchisement and growing authority in all aspects of culture and society, it also signified the death of an epoch to which some writers glanced with occasional nostalgia after the war. Virginia Woolf, hardly a proponent of nineteenth-century values, nevertheless equated the powerful immediacy of ancient Greek literature with a courageous, even heretical, prewar optimism: "In the vast catastrophe of the European war our emotions had to be broken up for us, and put at an angle from us, before we could allow ourselves to feel them in poetry or fiction," she wrote in her 1925 essay "On Not Knowing Greek." "There is a sadness at the back of life which they do not attempt to mitigate. Entirely aware of their own standing in the shadow, and yet alive to every tremor and gleam of existence, there they endure, and it is to the Greeks that we turn when we are sick of the vagueness, of the confusion, of the Christianity and its consolations, of our own age."[3] For Woolf, the ancient Greek world, by the war's end, represented not only a body of knowledge inaccessible to women who lacked a classical education but also a directness unsustainable in a new age that rejected emotion as sentimentality and honesty as naïveté. The parallels that Woolf implied between ancient Greek and prewar mentalities make it clear that although Victorian humanism and heresy worked as counterforces in the ways I attempt to illuminate in this book, both shared a straightforwardness and conviction that, for Woolf and other modernist writers, were as inaccessible as the Greeks themselves. Inherent in her expression of longing for the lost world of the Greeks is Woolf's intellectual sympathy with her direct forebears—writers similarly disenchanted with the confines of "Christianity and its consolations" and for whom Greek served as an instrument for accessing a vibrancy of existence and fullness of potential beyond the confines of their own age.

It is perhaps appropriate to conclude by returning to the figure with whom I began—whose concept of "heresy" has energized this work and whose abandonment of Greek studies toward the end of her life exemplifies the dual sense of loss expressed in Woolf's essay. The First World War severed Jane Harrison's lifelong love affair with Greek. In a 1917 contribution to the *Year's Work in Classical Studies,* she adopted an uncharacteristic tone of defeat, seeming deflated of all the fervor that she had put into her John the Baptist article only the year before: "[The scholar's] temple of learning the war lays [*sic*] in temporary ruins—ruins not only material, but spiritual," she wrote. "[H]is golden apple, plucked with such rapture from the Tree of Life and Knowledge, turns suddenly to ashes in his mouth. Who cares to-day whole-heartedly for Hittites or Minoans? Who raises to-day the question of the Origins of Tragedy or Comedy? . . . War upsets every value; the beam is suddenly kicked, and down falls the scale of learning."[4] Harrison refers here to a male scholar, forced to discard the hard-won fruit of his labors, but the disillusionment she expresses in her letters makes it obvious that the sense of devastation is her own. "Our work goes on, . . . though the number of classical entries goes down steadily," she wrote to Murray on November 19, 1916. "It is mainly scholarship we want—composition etc, I contribute the bright modernity—We have no one here who is good enough—plenty of second rate people—and as for the men—alas, alas! How futile it seems to be thinking of sound scholarship, but yet some time perhaps we shall feel again it is a good and pleasant thing to know Greek."[5] Harrison's serious concern here for a good "composition" man shows a remarkable shift in attitude toward "sound scholarship." The sudden absence of her customary formidable opponents—all first-rate men in their fields—brought home to Harrison as never before the crucial role of ideological conflict in sustaining the vitality of Greek knowledge. Without strong personalities against whom to stage her personal dramas, the theater of scholarship lost its allure for Harrison, and the hope that she held out at the end of 1916 quickly disintegrated. "I feel more and more that the only thing that keeps one's heart alive is the people," she wrote to Murray in the beginning of 1918, but the letter concluded with the despairing cry, "Lord, Lord will learning ever come to its own again?"[6] Harrison's sense of isolation, of being one of the last remaining worshippers in a crumbling temple, was the final proof of her scholarly legitimacy. Ironically, the realization that her very aloneness qualified her as a "sound scholar" also diminished that sense of "peril" that had drawn her to her field in the first place. "It looks as if this would be my last year in Cambridge (not public yet)," she wrote to Murray in December 1920. "I retire forceably the year after and I think it is better not to wait till one is hoofed out. Old Cambridge is gone—. . . Hope Mirrlees and I will probably take a flat in Paris."[7] Harrison and Mirrlees, a former student and Harrison's companion until the end of her life, did move to France after Harrison left Cambridge for good in the summer of 1922.

But Harrison had bidden farewell to Murray in spirit long before when, eight years earlier, he had decided to support the war. By nature and practice a pacifist,[8] Murray was completely swayed by Sir Edward Grey's justification of British policy against the Germans and fully endorsed the necessity of engagement.[9] In the first of his propagandistic essays, he had used his investment in the translation of Euripides' *Trojan Women* (*Troades*) to justify England's participation in the conflict. "Human nature is a mysterious thing, and man finds his weal and woe not in the obvious places," Murray wrote in "How Can War Ever Be Right?"

> To have something before you, clearly seen, which you know you must do, and can do, and will spend your utmost strength and perhaps your life doing, that is one form at least of very high happiness, and one that appeals—the facts prove it—not only to saints and heroes, but to average men. Doubtless the few who are wise enough and have enough imagination may find opportunity for that same happiness in everyday life, but in war ordinary men find it. This is the inward triumph which

> lies at the heart of the great tragedy. . . . I think again of the expressions on faces that I have seen or read about, something alert and glad and self-respecting in the eyes of those who are going to the front, and even of the wounded who are returning. . . . I do not forget the thousands left on the battlefield to die, or . . . the crashes of the guns. But there is a strange deep gladness as well. The wounded all want to get well and return to the fight. They fight with tears of joy in their eyes.[10]

In the final lines of his article, Murray suggests that the "beauty" of war brought out by its aesthetic representation might serve as an endorsement of the nobility and allure that lie at the heart of conflict. Going directly against an argument expressed by Murray some ten years earlier that tragedy, as an art form, must be seen as distinct from real suffering, this essay held the implication, disturbing to many, that Greek literature could be used as a justification for violence. For those who regarded Murray's exceptional brilliance as inseparable from his peace-loving nature,[11] the 1914 article implied a tenuous distinction between the visionary poet who devotes his life to cultivating his art and the "ordinary man" bent on his mission of destruction with "tears of joy in [his] eyes."[12]

Murray's article upset Harrison greatly. The division between art and reality that she had read into his 1904 comments about Euripides' play had formed the basis of an intellectual relationship that served as the catalyst for the high emotions and imaginative freedom that energized her professional work. Yet at the beginning of the war, she sensed that Murray's appreciation for the beauty of Euripides' tragedy had metamorphosed into enthusiasm for real suffering and conflict, and the fortifications of her own academic arena correspondingly began to crumble. Her letters to him in response to the article show the deep confusion that his attitude caused in her evaluation of him, in the assessment of her own values, in the nature of their friendship, and in the meaning of her scholarship. "There are two sentences I can't subscribe to in the Hibbert but I always turn out wrong so I want to be convinced," she wrote to him from Paris, where she was receiving shock treatments for her angina. "I feel war is, or ought to be the execution of a criminal—right awful and never making one 'glad'—and I can no more glory in a soldier's uniform than I can in a judge's black cap,—but you will put it all straight for me."[13] Here Harrison finds herself in the difficult position of contradicting the judgment of the wise man whom she had called in 1902 "so hypermoralized and super-spiritualized that you force me to think of 'righteousness—temperance and judgment-to-come.'"[14] To doubt his judgment was to erase the outlines that had defined her reality. His stability had provided the safe barriers within which to let loose her rebellious impulses.[15] It was to his authority that she had turned for a sense of moral rectitude. In the letter here, she is still turning toward him for assurance, willing to doubt her interpretation of his meaning rather than him. But Murray failed to supply her reassurance, and a month later, she commented again on the article, this time venturing to criticize his position more strongly.

> The last paragraph was beautiful. . . . [W]hy can't we care in that way for the things of peace? [W]hy can't we give our life in the same single glad way to finding out about the Pelasgians—I suppose that affects too small a group. . . . One thing still troubles me—you have brought me up (a man may bring up, tho' he may not marry his grandmother) to believe that it is never safe to trust emotion unless it is supported by reason—yet in a supreme case you turn on yr own position and say honour is unanalysed yet I trust my sense of it.[16]

In this letter, Harrison has moved from a willingness to submit to Murray's authority to a self-assertive disengagement from it. The letter is not clear on what her "sense" of Murray's meaning is; what is clear is that she is no longer hesitating to point out his hypocrisy, although she carefully pads the accusation with her customary self-deprecating humor. With her increasing reliance on her own judgment comes a role reversal: it is she who is thinking rationally, he who is contradicting himself by attaching honor—the ultimate good—to emotional impulse. The "grandmother" now assumes the sober reason of the "sound scholar," promoting the "gladness" to be gained from study, while Murray's (implicitly adolescent) "gladness" in the "crashes of guns" must be curbed. In a final refutation of his judgment, she concludes the letter with the remark that the injured soldiers she has met "don't all want to go back" to the war. The remark implicitly denies Murray's assertion that "the wounded all want to get well and return to the fight." Even Harrison's compliment on the beauty of Murray's last paragraph—on the joy of finding a passionate cause—is a deliberate misreading of Murray's endorsement of the war. Her rhetorical question acts as a not-too-subtle reminder that Murray ought to return to the "things of peace"—that is, his scholarship. The fact that Harrison felt she had to express this opinion indirectly through the indistinct "we" indicates her increasing hesitation in trusting Murray with her feelings. A self-defensiveness and caution has begun to creep into her letters to him, and they indicate her sense that their correspondence was no longer a safe place for intellectual play, as it had been for two decades. The disappearance of this crucial source of imaginative energy presaged Harrison's withdrawal from Greek scholarship.

Faced, for the first time, with a barrier in her friendship with Murray, Harrison used her professional writing to reflect on her relation with him and to communicate thoughts she felt she could no longer express directly in her letters to him. Her ultimately self-interested obsession with Murray's involvement in the war and her efforts to understand him distracted her from her work and involved her in political debates that she would have preferred to ignore. "[T]ill I knew you I never thought or wrote about anything except Pelasgians—and I suppose I ought to have gone on like that, but you came in and muddled me up and made me turn an over-focussed mind on practical things," she wrote in November 1914, while working on an essay about her response to the war. "I will try never to write anything else, except Pelasgians, when once I am rid of War and the Reaction. But the worst is that, worthless and childish though the stuff may be, it lies on my stomach and makes me sick till I get rid of it, so that I have literally no choice." Her essay on what she called "War and Reaction," eventually titled "Epilogue on the War: Peace with Patriotism," was as much a meditation on the change in Murray and on her subsequently altered view of scholarship as it was a reflection on the war.[17] What lay heavily on her was not so much the political situation as the sense that Murray had abandoned Greek and destroyed the entire foundation of the academic life that she had built for herself. While she could not express this sense of abandonment directly to Murray, dismissing her feelings as "childish," her essay shows that she was making a desperate attempt to understand Murray's point of view, perhaps for the first time, rather than seeing him as and transforming him into the person she wanted him to be. Her essay constructs a dialogue with his past articles, as if trying to reconstruct an image of Murray that might explain his current position—an image more stable and true than the amorphous roles she had assigned to him through the years. Some of the most poignant lines of her article come from her "dialogue" with quotations from Murray's *Euripides and His Age* (1913): "The plant of moral violence, and the instinctive faith in bloodshed and war, is curiously apt to spring up from the soil of academic life. . . . Long before the war broke out Professor Gilbert Murray with his accustomed insight into the human heart, touched this secret academic weakness. 'A man everlastingly wrapped round in good books and safe living cries out for something harsh and real—for blood and swear-words and crude, jagged sentences'" ("Epilogue," 230). Using Murray's insight into the human heart to reflect on his own soul, Harrison discovered a savage impulse far removed from the peaceful personality that she had attributed to him in the past. Whereas before the war, she had taken it for granted that Murray's passionate nature could be channeled into his academic work, her article suggests her realization that "crude, jagged sentences" are insufficient in curbing the desire "for something harsh and real." This sudden realization of the illusive insularity of "good books and safe living" caused Harrison to turn almost with horror against her own love of archaic religion. "[C]ldn't I have Paganism and Christ? It wld refresh me," she wrote to Murray in September 1914 shortly after returning to Cambridge from a trip to Norfolk. "This war is horribly exciting but I can't *live* on it—it is like being drunk all day and I want some hot milk—clean and feeding. I relieved my mind by writing on War and Reaction."[18] The same breaches in the barriers between scholarship and reality that had delivered dons to the battlefield allowed war's sordidness to seep into and corrupt Harrison's scholarly enthusiasm for paganism. The Dionysian drunkenness with which she had long identified the playful spirit of her scholarship became dangerously associated with a sobering reality that made any romanticizing metaphors of violence impossible. Though she might have been able to "live" on her work with archaic rituals before 1914, Harrison's realization of war's "horrible excitement" shows the unsustainability of such a life and the untenability of a friendship with one who seemed to have made the horror a part of his faith.[19]

Murray eventually became disillusioned with the war and abandoned his propagandist writings for a fervent endorsement of peace,[20] especially toward the war's end and beyond. But his initial enthusiasm for fighting had an irreversible effect on Harrison. Her break with her close friend represents both the nature of the heretical impulses that I discuss in this book and the reason why such heresy could not survive beyond the war. For although the heretical Hellenism I have been describing went against the humanistic traditions that dominated nineteenth-century culture, it nevertheless fed on the very forces against which it acted. This is certainly true for Jane Harrison, but it is also pertinent for the other writers

I have discussed. Would Charlotte Brontë have reached the conclusions she had about Greek tragedy and the nature of genius if M. Heger had not so vehemently advocated his Aristotelian principles? Certainly George Eliot could not have formulated so strong an argument for women's right to intellectual legacy had she not been conscious of a tradition that favored the opposite sex. In order for heresy to survive, there must be a tradition for it to oppose. And with the end of humanistic Hellenism came the inevitable death of the heresy to which it gave rise. However, if there is one thing that the writers I have been considering have proven, it is that Greek survives because of its malleability and its capacity for reinvention in the shape of individuals' passions and passionate conflicts. This characteristic, inherent to the legacy of the ancient Greek world and its mythology, is what sustains hope in the formation of new forms of heretical Hellenism.

Notes

Introduction

1. Membership in the society came to exceed two hundred four years later. Members eventually included Sir Francis Darwin, J. T. Sheppard (later provost of King's College), G. Lowes Dickinson, and J. M. Keynes. Through the years, notable speakers included Rebecca West (1918), Walter de la Mare and Lytton Strachey (1920), Edith Sitwell and Clive Bell (1921), and Roger Fry and Virginia Woolf (1923), who delivered her paper "Mr. Bennett and Mrs. Brown." For more on the Cambridge Society of Heretics, see P. Sargant Florence's "The Cambridge Heretics, 1909–1932," in *The Humanist Outlook,* ed. A. J. Ayer (London: Pemberton, 1968), 223–39.

2. Cambridge University was a center of the English Reformation, and after the 1662 Act of Uniformity, it became an exclusively Anglican school. Institutional ties to the Church of England were affirmed by such mandates as compulsory chapel attendance and assent to the Apostles' Creed. These were two of the requirements to which students began to object at the turn of the twentieth century. For more on relations between the church and the university, see Annabel Robinson, *The Life and Work of Jane Ellen Harrison* (Oxford: Oxford University Press, 2002); Michael Sanderson, *The Universities in the Nineteenth Century* (London: Routledge and Kegan Paul, 1975); and Christopher Stray, *Classics Transformed: Schools, Universities, and Society in England, 1830–1960* (Oxford: Clarendon, 1998).

3. Quoted in Florence, "Cambridge Heretics," 228.

4. Somerville and Lady Margaret colleges were founded at Oxford in 1879.

5. The Cambridge Tripos examinations were the tests that students needed to pass to receive an honors degree in their field. See chapter 4 for a more detailed discussion of the Classical Tripos.

6. The other keynote speaker was John Ellis McTaggart, a lecturer at Trinity College, whose paper was entitled "Dare to Be Wise."

7. Oxford historically allowed and encouraged more interpretive freedom in the study of ancient texts.

8. Jane Ellen Harrison, "Heresy and Humanity," in *Alpha and Omega* (London: Sidgwick and Jackson, 1915), 27–28.

9. For an extended discussion of the debates on compulsory Greek, see chapter 4.

10. Augusta Webster, *A Housewife's Opinions* (London: Macmillan, 1879), 101–2.

11. Finley Melville Kendall Foster, *English Translations from the Greek: A Bibliographical Survey* (New York: Columbia University Press, 1918), xv.

12. Bohn's was succeeded by the Loeb Classical Library in 1912. For more on these collections, see Foster, *English Translations,* and Isobel Hurst, *Victorian Women Writers and the Classics: The Feminine of Homer* (Oxford: Oxford University Press, 2006), 34.

13. *Gentleman's Magazine,* "Review of Valpy's Family Classical Library (1829)," University of Virginia Electronic Text Center, http://flowerdew.org/etcbin/eafbin2/toccereaf?id=eaf354&data=/texts/eaf&tag=public&part=back.

14. *Weekly Free Press,* "Review of Valpy's Family Classical Library (1829)," University of Virginia Electronic Text Center, http://flowerdew.org/etcbin/eafbin2/toccereaf?id=eaf354&data=/texts/eaf&tag=public&part=back.

15. For more on *Blackwood's* treatment of the *Odyssey,* see chapter 2.

16. "The Antiquity of the Homeric Poems," *Contemporary Review* 12 (September–December 1869): 53.

17. Charlotte Brontë, *Villette* (1853; New York: Penguin, 1979), 494.

18. Elizabeth Barrett Browning, *Aurora Leigh* (London: W.W. Norton, 1996), 41 (book 2, line 76). For the role of Greek in mediating the relationship between the poets, see Yopie Prins, "Elizabeth Barrett, Robert Browning and the *Différance* of Translation," *Victorian Poetry* 29 (1991): 435–51. See also Prins, "'Lady's Greek' (with the Accents): A Metrical Translation of Euripides by A. Mary F. Robinson," *Victorian Literature and Culture* 34 (2006): 591–618.

19. Ann Phillips, ed., *A Newnham Anthology* (Cambridge: Cambridge University Press, 1979), 9.

20. Frank M. Turner, *The Greek Heritage in Victorian Britain* (New Haven, CT: Yale University Press, 1981), 5, 10.

21. Florence Nightingale, *Cassandra* (written in 1852 but published posthumously in 1928; New York: City University of New York, Feminist Press, 1979), 25.

22. David Ferris, *Silent Urns: Romanticism, Hellenism, Modernity* (Stanford: Stanford University Press, 2000), 19.

23. For more about the political implications of Victorian Hellenism, see Turner, *Greek Heritage.*

24. See Paul Oskar Kristeller, *Renaissance Thought and Its Sources* (New York: Columbia University Press, 1979), 21–23.

25. John Henry Newman, *The Idea of a University* (New York: Longmans, Green, 1947), 102, 110.

26. W.Y. Sellar, *Roman Poets of the Augustan Age* (Oxford: Clarendon, 1877), 74.

27. Marianne Thormahlen, *The Brontës and Religion* (New York: Cambridge University Press, 1999), 24–25.

28. Quoted in Richard Jenkyns, *The Victorians and Ancient Greece* (Cambridge, MA: Harvard University Press, 1980), 70–71.

29. David DeLaura, *Hebrew and Hellene in Victorian England: Newman, Arnold, and Pater* (Austin: University of Texas Press, 1969), xiii.

30. Matthew Arnold, *Culture and Anarchy* (1869; New Haven, CT: Yale University Press, 1994), 26.

31. Reprinted in Matthew Arnold, *On the Classical Tradition* (Ann Arbor: University of Michigan Press, 1960), 20.

32. Quoted in Sanderson, *Universities,* 140.

33. Walter Pater, *The Renaissance: Studies in Art and Poetry* (Berkeley: University of California Press, 1980), 159.

34. Algernon Charles Swinburne, *Swinburne's Collected Poetical Works* (London: William Heinemann, 1924), 2:285.

35. Linda Dowling, *Hellenism and Homosexuality in Victorian Oxford* (Ithaca, NY: Cornell University Press, 1994), 93–94.

36. David G. Riede, "Swinburne and Romantic Authority," in *The Whole Music of Passion: New Essays on Swinburne,* ed. Rikky Rooksby and Nicholas Shrimpton (Brookfield, VT: Ashgate, 1993), 35.

37. Simon Goldhill, *Who Needs Greek? Contests in the Cultural History of Hellenism* (Cambridge: Cambridge University Press, 2002), 3.

38. Yopie Prins, *Victorian Sappho* (Princeton, NJ: Princeton University Press, 1999), 3.

39. I mean by "modern discipline" a classical field that includes multiple branches of study, including archaeology, art history, and religion, rather than the exclusive literary-linguistic study of the early nineteenth century.

40. See Phyllis Culham and Lowell Edmunds, eds., *Classics: A Discipline and Profession in Crisis?* (Lanham, MD: University Press of America, 1989).

Chapter 1: Victorian Medea

1. See Edith Hall, "Medea and British Legislation before the First World War," *Greece and Rome* 46, no. 1 (April 1999): 47.

 2. Ernest Legouvé, *Sixty Years of Recollections* (London: Eden, Remington, 1893), 1:190–91. Legouvé later sued Rachel for breaking her contract, forcing her to pay 6,000 francs, which Legouvé distributed between the Society of Dramatic Authors and the Society of Authors (1:201). Legouvé then published his piece and won himself a vacant chair at the academy, which he had always intended to gain through *Medea* (1:195).

3. *Times*, June 5, 1856, 12.

4. This number excludes ballets and operas. Information compiled from David Gowen, "*Medeas* on the Archive Database," in *Medea in Performance, 1500–2000*, ed. Edith Hall, Fiona Macintosh, and Oliver Taplin, (Oxford: European Humanities Research Center, 2000), 232–44.

5. See Hall, "Medea and British Legislation."

6. For more on the replacement of sensationalism by feminism in the 1880s, see Judith Knelman, *Twisting in the Wind: The Murderess and the English Press* (Toronto: University of Toronto Press, 1998).

7. Richard Altick notes a more general correspondence between popular plays that feature murder and real-life murder cases. Altick, *Victorian Studies in Scarlet* (New York: Norton, 1970), 88.

8. For sensationalism's reinforcement of the status quo, see Ann Cvetkovich, *Mixed Feelings: Feminism, Mass Culture and Victorian Sensationalism* (New Brunswick, NJ: Rutgers University Press, 1992).

9. Mary Poovey, *Uneven Developments: The Ideological Work of Gender in Mid-Victorian England* (Chicago: University of Chicago Press, 1988), 6.

10. *Illustrated London News*, October 27, 1849, 279.

11. *Times*, October 29, 1849, 5.

12. *Times*, November 14, 1849, 4.

13. I use the term *sensation*, or *sensationalist*, in reference to a genre of literature emerging in the early nineteenth century whose primary aim was provoke emotional excitement. For a more elaborate examination of this term, see Cvetkovich, *Mixed Feelings*.

14. The phrase is Richard Altick's. See his *Victorian Studies in Scarlet*, 10.

15. See Altick, *Victorian Studies in Scarlet*, 10, 17, 56.

16. The Manning trial reportedly yielded 2.5 million copies of the proceedings. Altick, *Victorian Studies in Scarlet*, 47.

17. Henry Mayhew, *London Labour and the London Poor* (New York: Dover, 1968), 1:302.

18. *Times*, November 14, 1849, 4.

19. The *Illustrated London News* reported 10,000 (November 17, 1849); the *Times*, 30,000 (November 14, 1849).

20. *Times*, November 14, 1849, 5.

21. See Cvetkovich, *Mixed Feelings*, 46–47.

22. *Morning Chronicle*, November 14, 1849, 3.

23. "The Mannings at Home," *Punch* 17 (July–December 1849): 213. According to Knelman, Maria Manning was the longest-standing murderer in the Chamber of Horrors (Knelman, 23).

24. Ellen Rosenman, "'Mimic Sorrows': Masochism and the Gendering of Pain in Victorian Melodrama," *Studies in the Novel* 35 (Spring 2003): 22. See also Peter Brooks, *The Melodramatic Imagination: Balzac, Henry James, Melodrama, and the Mode of Excess* (New York: Columbia University Press, 1985), which associates melodrama with a Manichean worldview.

25. *Spectator*, Saturday, June 7, 1856, 609.

26. *Times*, June 5, 1856, 12.

27. *Illustrated London News*, June 7, 1856, 622.

28. Henry Knepler, *The Gilded Stage: The Years of the Great International Actresses* (New York: William Morrow, 1968), 72.

29. William Winter, *Shadows of the Stage* (New York: Macmillan, 1893), 301–2.

30. Henry James, *The Scenic Art: Notes on Acting and the Drama, 1872–1901* (New Brunswick, NJ: Rutgers University Press, 1948), 29–30.

31. Adelaide Ristori, *Memoirs and Artistic Studies*, trans. G. Mantellini (New York: Doubleday, 1907), 187.

32. Michael R. Booth, *Theatre in the Victorian Age* (Cambridge: Cambridge University Press, 1991), 134.

33. Susan Bassnett, "Adelaide Ristori," in *Three Tragic Actresses: Siddons, Rachel, Ristori*, by Susan Bassnett, John Stokes, and Michael Booth (Cambridge: Cambridge University Press, 1996), 119.

34. Elaine Aston, "Ristori's Medea and Her Nineteenth-Century Successors," *Women and Theater: Occasional Papers* 1 (1992): 40.

35. Ernest Legouvé, *Théâtre complet: Pièces en vers* (Paris: Librairie Academique, 1873), preface.

36. Lynn Voskuil, *Acting Naturally: Victorian Theatricality and Authenticity* (Charlottesville: University of Virginia Press, 2004), 13.

37. George Henry Lewes, *On Actors and the Art of Acting* (New York: Greenwood, 1968), 148.

38. Barbara Godard, "Between Performative and Performance: Translation and Theater in the Canadian/Quebec Context," *Modern Drama* 43, no. 3 (Fall 2000): 331.

39. Patrice Pavis, *Theatre at the Crossroads of Culture*, trans. Loren Kruger (New York: Routledge, 1992), 26.

40. Legouvé, *Théâtre complet*, preface.

41. Ernest Legouvé, *Medea: A Tragedy in Three Acts*, trans. Thomas Williams (New York: John A. Gray and Green, 1867), 5.

 42. M. L. Clarke, *Greek Studies in England, 1700–1830* (Cambridge: Cambridge University Press, 1945), 153.

43. Ann Norris Michelini, *Euripides and the Tragic Tradition* (Madison: University of Wisconsin Press, 1987), 5.

44. H. D. F. Kitto, introduction to *Euripides and His Age,* by Gilbert Murray (London: Oxford University Press, 1965), vii.

45. See Fiona Macintosh's discussion of Grillparzer's play in the first chapter of Hall et al., *Medea in Performance.*

46. Robert Brough's *Medea; or, The Best of Mothers, with a Brute of a Husband* at the Olympic and Mark Lemon's *Medea; or, a Libel on the Lady of Colchis* at the Adelphi were both takeoffs on Ristori's performance.

47. James Robinson Planche, *The Golden Fleece,* in *Plays by James Robinson Planche,* ed. Donald Roy (Cambridge: Cambridge University Press, 1986), 10.

48. Legouvé, *Théâtre complet,* 5.

49. See George Behlmer, "Deadly Motherhood: Infanticide and Medical Opinion in Mid-Victorian England," *Journal of the History of Medicine and Allied Sciences* 34 (1979): 403–27.

50. Knelman, *Twisting in the Wind,* 50, 125.

51. Quoted in Ann R. Higginbotham, "'Sin of the Age': Infanticide and Illegitimacy in Victorian London," *Victorian Studies* 32 (Spring 1989): 319.

52. Higginbotham, "Sin of the Age," 319.

53. The moral ambivalence surrounding infanticide at this time is suggested by the extremely lenient punishment that women received for killing their children: very few women were sentenced to the capital punishment warranted by such a crime, and newspaper reports of trials often emphasized the pathetic nature of the distraught, victimized women. Another reason that women were often let off the hook was that women's bodies and minds were considered naturally more unstable than men's, and therefore infanticides could be blamed on temporary insanity. However, see Henry Humble's argument that women should be blamed for seducing men, in "Infanticide: Its Cause and Cure," in *The Church and the World: Essays on Questions of the Day, First Series,* ed. Rev. Orby Shipley (London: Longmans, Green, Reader, and Dyer, 1866), 51–69.

54. Medea's murder of her children is often referred to as infanticide, but in Victorian society, there was a legal distinction between infanticide (the killing of infants) and child murder. The "infanticide epidemic" provoked fear of both, but in Victorian courts, punishment for infanticide grew increasingly more lenient as sympathy for poor mothers increased. For a detailed discussion of infanticide and child murder in Victorian England, see Lionel Rose, *The Massacre of the Innocents: Infanticide in Britain, 1800–1939* (London: Routledge, 1986).

55. *Manchester Guardian,* April 11, 1856, 2.

56. *Spectator,* June 7, 1856, 609.

57. The famously debated lines 1025–80.

58. Rush Rehm, "*Medea* and the Logos of the Heroic," *Eranos* 87 (1989): 97–115.

59. Helene Foley, "Medea's Divided Self," *Classical Antiquity* 8 (1989): 83.

60. *Times,* July 2, 1857, 1.

61. Quoted in *Reynold's Newspaper,* July 2, 1857, 4.

62. *Reynold's Newspaper,* July 12, 1857, 4.

63. Quoted in *Reynold's Newspaper,* July 12, 1857, 4.

64. Euripides, *Medea,* trans. David Kovacs (Cambridge, MA: Harvard University Press, 1994): 629–30.

65. Robert Hariman, *Popular Trials: Rhetoric, Mass Media, and the Law* (Tuscaloosa: University of Alabama Press, 1990), 1.

66. John Heraud, *Medea in Corinth,* British Library Add. Ms. 52967(x), 21.

67. Matilda Heron, *Medea: A Tragedy in Three Acts; Translated from the French of Ernest Legouvé* (London: T. H. Lacy, 1861), 27.

68. See Knelman, *Twisting in the Wind,* 225, for expansion on this point.

69. Jennifer Jones, *Medea's Daughters: Forming and Performing the Woman Who Kills* (Columbus: Ohio State University Press, 2003), 36–37.

70. See Lorna Hardwick, "Theatres of the Mind: Greek Tragedy in Women's Writings in England in the Nineteenth Century," in *Theatre: Ancient and Modern,* ed. Lorna Hardwick et al. (Milton Keynes, UK: Open University, 2000), 71.

71. Catherine B. Burroughs, *Closet Stages: Joanna Baillie and the Theater Theory of British Romantic Women Writers* (Philadelphia: University of Pennsylvania Press, 1997), 8.

72. Susan Brown, "Determined Heroines: George Eliot, Augusta Webster, and Closet Drama by Victorian Women," *Victorian Poetry* 33 (Spring 1995): 105.

73. Angela Leighton, *Victorian Women Poets: Writing against the Heart* (Charlottesville: University Press of Virginia, 1992), 177.

74. *Contemporary Review* 8 (1868): 465–66.

75. *Westminster Review* 89 (April 1868): 290.

76. Lorna Hardwick has pointed out that Medea became part of a *rite de passage* for women's entry into the male territory of Greek translation. Hardwick, "Theatres of the Mind," 71.

77. Leighton argues that one reason for Webster's neglect as a poet has been the social consciousness that pervades her work. See *Victorian Women Poets,* 166–67.

78. Leighton, *Victorian Women Poets,* 173.

79. Robert Langbaum, *The Poetry of Experience: The Dramatic Monologue in Modern Literary Tradition* (New York: Norton, 1957), 96.

80. Augusta Webster, *A Housewife's Opinions* (London: Macmillan, 1879), 151.

81. Augusta Webster, *Portraits* (London: Macmillan, 1870), 1.

82. See Christine Sutphin, "The Representation of Women's Heterosexual Desire in Augusta Webster's 'Circe' and 'Medea in Athens,'" *Women's Writing* 5 (1998): 373–92.

83. Augusta Webster, *The Medea of Euripides* (London: Macmillan, 1868), 86.

84. Brown, "Determined Heroines," 104.

85. Ristori performed Medea in New York in 1866 and 1875. See David Gowen, "*Medeas* on the Archive Database," in *Medea in Performance.*

86. Amy Levy, *A Minor Poet and Other Verse* (New York: Frederic A. Stoker, 1891), 26.

87. Cynthia Scheinberg, "Canonizing the Jew: Amy Levy's Challenge to Victorian Poetic Identity," *Victorian Studies* 39 (Winter 1996): 174.

88. Levy, *Minor Poet,* 36.

89. See Linda Hunt Beckman, *Amy Levy: Her Life and Letters* (Athens: Ohio University Press, 2000), 113. Isobel Hurst, Lorna Hardwick, and Cynthia Scheinberg have also discussed the racial issues in Levy's poem. Levy wrote her play in Dresden and Lucerne, where she was traveling after leaving Newnham.

90. Beckman, *Amy Levy,* 113–14.

Chapter 2: Fragments of Genius

1. Juliet Barker, *The Brontës* (New York: St. Martin's, 1994), 147, 166. Barker notes that his sisters may have shared in some of Branwell's classics lessons, given by their father, Patrick Brontë. The girls also may have been exposed to some Greek and Latin through the Bible and prayer books that Patrick Brontë used for classical instruction. Finally, they would have encountered glosses of Greek words in the translations (for example, in Chapman's *Iliad*). I refer to Charlotte by her first name throughout the text to distinguish her from other members of her family, whom I also reference periodically.

2. Although *Blackwood's* contained by far the largest number of articles pertaining to ancient Greece, with topics ranging from Homer and the tragedians to transhistorical comparisons of authors ("Aeschylus, Shakespeare, Schiller" and "Homer, Dante, Michelangelo"), other journals such as the *Contemporary Review, Quarterly Review, Fraser's Magazine,* and *London Magazine* also frequently contained articles on Greek topics or reviews of books on ancient Greece.

3. The Reverend Patrick Brontë had attended St. John's College, Cambridge, in 1802 to obtain the degree necessary to become a clergyman. Accounts of Greek translations on the shelves of Ponden House include Chapman's and Pope's *Iliad* and *Lemprière's Classical Dictionary of Proper Names Mentioned in Ancient Authors,* which had been given as a gift to Patrick Brontë by one of the students whom he tutored at Cambridge. See Barker, *Brontës,* R. Willetts, editor of the 1984 edition of *Lemprière's* (London: Routledge and Kegan Paul, 1984), first published in 1788, notes that the dictionary "exercised a decisive impact on English literature" and that Keats consulted it for poetic inspiration (ix). For the Brontës' access to and likely use of nearby libraries, see Barker, *Brontës,* 147–48.

4. For brief comments on Charlotte's early interactions with the classics, see Barker, *Brontës,* 147; and Sue Lonoff, ed. and trans., *The Belgian Essays,* by Charlotte Brontë and Emily Brontë (New Haven, CT: Yale University Press, 1996), 354.

5. The *Quarterly Review* was founded in 1809 as a Tory reaction to the Whig *Edinburgh Review.* Both the *Quarterly Review* and the *Edinburgh Review* were of Scottish origin, and together they "introduced the concept of the review in the terms in which we understand them today." Ann Matheson, "Scottish Periodicals," in *Victorian Periodicals: A Guide to Research,* vol. 2, ed. J. Don Vann and Rosemary T. VanArsdel (New York: Modern Language Association, 1989), 99. One of the founders of the *Quarterly Review* was Sir Walter Scott, a hero to the Brontë children. Robert Southey, a literary hero and correspondent of Charlotte's, also became a frequent contributor to the *Quarterly Review.* While part of the "higher journalism" of the nineteenth century, these reviews attracted a wide range of readers, from the aristocracy to the educated working classes. For more on the readership of these journals, see Neil Berry, *Articles of Faith: The Story of British Intellectual Journalism* (London: Waywiser, 2002).

6. "Colonel Mure on the Literature of Ancient Greece: The Homeric Controversy," *Quarterly Review* 87 (September 1850): 437.

7. "Acland's Plains of Troy," *Quarterly Review* 66 (1840): 355–56.

8. Marjorie Levinson, *The Romantic Fragment Poem: A Critique of a Form* (Chapel Hill: University of North Carolina Press, 1986), 24–25.

9. The philosophy of fragmentation is perhaps best represented by the writing of Friedrich von Schlegel. Ginette Verstraete, *Fragments of the Feminine Sublime in Friedrich Schlegel and James Joyce* (New York: State University of New York Press, 1998).

10. "Athènes" was not Charlotte's first composition to deal with classical material. "The Violet," a poem written when Charlotte was fourteen, explicitly evokes Homer and the three Greek tragedians, whom Charlotte

 seems to have regarded with reverential awe as the founding geniuses of literary tradition.

11. Elizabeth Gaskell, *Life of Charlotte Brontë* (1857; New York: Penguin, 1975), 178.

12. Lonoff, *Belgian Essays,* xxxviii–xxxix.

13. "Surviving texts . . . indicate four practices of Heger's that Charlotte would have mocked or protested in anyone but her professor. He edited imperiously, not just student essays, but also the prose of authors; he reveled in sentiment; he based his teaching on sexist assumptions; and he weighted the readings toward Catholicism." Lonoff, *Belgian Essays,* lvi. For more on Heger as a teacher, see Frederika MacDonald, *The Secret of Charlotte Brontë Followed by Some Reminiscences of the Real Monsieur and Madame Heger* (London: T. C. and E. C. Jack, 1914).

14. Lonoff's translation, *Belgian Essays,* 240. I have used Sue Lonoff's translations throughout, by her kind permission. Except where noted, I have quoted only Charlotte's original words, minus her own and Heger's corrections and edits, which Lonoff includes in her text.

15. See especially Aristotle, *Poetics,* 8.30–35: "Just as, therefore, in the other mimetic arts a unitary mimesis has a unitary object, so too the plot, since it is mimesis of an action, should be of a unitary and indeed whole action; and the component events should be so structured that if any is displaced or removed, the sense of the whole is disturbed and dislocated: since that whose presence or absence has no clear significance is not an integral part of the whole." Translated by Stephen Halliwell (Cambridge, MA: Harvard University Press, 1995). See references to Heger's "synthetical teaching" in Lonoff's *Belgian Essays,* xxix, and in Gaskell's *Life of Charlotte Brontë,* 184.

16. Walter Graham, *English Literary Periodicals* (New York: Thomas Nelson and Sons, 1930), 284.

17. See Kenneth Curry, *"Blackwood's Edinburgh Magazine:* Background and Significance," in *An Index to the Critical Vocabulary of "Blackwood's Edinburgh Magazine," 1830–1840,* ed. J. Lasley Dameron and Pamela Palmer (West Cornwall, CT: Locust Hill, 1993), xiv.

18. Grevel Lindop, "De Quincey and the Edinburgh and Glasgow University Circles," in *Grub Street and the Ivory Tower: Literary Journalism and Literary Scholarship from Fielding to the Internet,* ed. Jeremy Treglown and Bridget Bennett (Oxford: Clarendon, 1998), 48.

19. Curry, *"Blackwood's Edinburgh Magazine,"* xi.

20. For the inconsistencies resulting from conflicting economic and philosophical interests in *Blackwood's Edinburgh Magazine,* see Robert Morrison, "William Blackwood and the Dynamics of Success," in *Print Culture and*

the Blackwood Tradition, 1805–1930, ed. David Finkelstein (Toronto: University of Toronto Press, 2006), 31. 209

21. Sales number is from David Finkelstein, *The House of Blackwood: Author-Publisher Relations in the Victorian Era* (University Park: Pennsylvania State University Press, 2002), 165.

22. Branwell once sent a translation of Horace's *Odes* to De Quincey, who was also one of the few to receive a personal gift copy of *Poems* by Currer, Ellis, and Acton Bell (pseudonyms for Charlotte, Emily, and Ann Brontë) when it was first published (Barker, *Brontës,* 332, 499).

23. For more on De Quincey's ambivalent relations with academia, see Lindop, "De Quincey."

24. Thomas De Quincey, "Homer and the Homeridae I," *Blackwood's Edinburgh Magazine* 50 (October 1841): 415. Hereafter cited as "Homer I."

25. Thomas De Quincey, "Homer and the Homeridae II," *Blackwood's Edinburgh Magazine* 50 (November 1841): 618. Hereafter cited as "Homer II."

26. Sue Lonoff points out that Charlotte, Branwell, Emily, and Anne referred to themselves as the four Genii of Glass Town, the children's first fantasy world. Several articles in *Blackwood's* referred to Homer and the Homeridae as the genii of ancient Greece. See, for instance, *Blackwood's Edinburgh Magazine* 29 (April 1831): 668.

27. Johann Herder, "Homer: A Favorite of Time," *Blackwood's Edinburgh Magazine* 42 (November 1837): 702–4. Emphasis in the original.

28. Herder also believed that language (if not writing) was essential to structuring thought, but this idea is not apparent in the excerpted article in *Blackwood's,* perhaps misleading Charlotte in her philosophies about the relation of thought to language.

29. Lonoff's translation, *Belgian Essays,* 248. Emphases in Lonoff's translation

30. It is interesting to note the interactions between English and French in the translation history of Plutarch. Plutarch was first translated into English by Sir Thomas North (1535–1601) in 1579. The translation was made from a French translation of the Greek by Jacques Amyot (1559). Shakespeare's Roman plays are largely indebted to North's translations, which inherited from and added to Amyot's considerable misunderstanding of the Greek. A five-volume translation "by several hands" was made from the Greek in 1683–86 under the general editorial guidance of John Dryden. This collection was re-edited after the French translation of the lives by Andre Dacier in 1694. Information compiled from *The Oxford Guide to Literature in English Translation* (Oxford: Oxford University Press 2001), 385–86. Both Enid Duthie and Sue Lonoff remark that Brontë and Heger may not have gone directly to Plutarch but to a retelling of the episode in

 an introduction of Casimir Delavigne's *Les Messeniennes* (1831) See Enid Duthie, *The Foreign Vision of Charlotte Brontë* (New York: Harper and Row, 1975), 217. The introduction was called "De lavie et des ouvrages de Callinus et de Tyrtee" and was written by M. Baron, one of Heger's colleagues at the Athenee Royal. Lonoff, *Belgian Essays*, 353, 450–55.

31. Euripides' life spanned 484–406 BC. The Peloponnesian War ended in 404 BC. Scholars date Euripides' *Electra* to the years 422–413 BC.

32. Plutarch, *Life of Lysander*, in *Plutarch's Lives*, trans. Bernadotte Perrin, vol. 4 (Cambridge, MA: Harvard University Press, 1968), 273. I have used the Loeb Classical Library series of translations, as this is the most widely used Greek-English parallel text.

33. Sue Lonoff notes in her commentary on "Athènes," "This episode may not seem to qualify as the 'trait' on which an essay would turn. But in French, 'trait' also connotes 'outline,' and Heger customarily dictated outlines that his students were expected to develop." Whether "Athènes" began as an outline dictated by Heger is unknown, but, as Lonoff continues, "the initiative to write a devoir so intricate could only have been Charlotte's" (*Belgian Essays*, 353).

34. The reference to myths as presented in Euripidean tragedy is itself a historical convention. Besides this reference in Plutarch, Thucydides also told of a similar episode during the Theban expedition. Also, *Lemprière's Classical Dictionary* includes the following account in the "Euripides" entry: "[Euripides'] writings became so much the admiration of his countrymen, that the unfortunate Greeks who had accompanied Nicias in his expedition against Syracuse were freed from slavery, only on repeating some verses from the pieces of Euripides."

35. "[History] relates actual events, [poetry] the kinds of things that might occur. Consequently, poetry is more philosophical and more elevated than history, since poetry relates more of the universal, while history relates particulars" (Aristotle *Poetics* 9.4–8).

36. Homer *Iliad*, trans. A. T. Murray (Cambridge, MA: Harvard University Press, 1925), 9.210–16.

37. Lonoff, *Belgian Essays*, 443. Lonoff notes that Brontë deleted the word from her revised version of the essay.

38. Homer *Iliad*, trans. Murray, 20.465–67, 20.502–3. Chapman's translation (1611; Princeton: Princeton University Press, 1984) of these same lines reads, "[Achilles] had no spirit to brooke that interim / In his hote furie, he was none of these remorsefull men, / Gentle and affable, but fierce at all times, and mad then[]" and "Thus to be magnified, / His most inaccessible hands in humane blood he died."

39. John Wilson, "Sotheby's Homer IV," *Blackwood's Edinburgh Magazine* 31 (December 1831): 848–49. Hereafter cited as "Sotheby's IV."

40. John Wilson, "Sotheby's Homer I," *Blackwood's Edinburgh Magazine* 29 (April 1831): 668. Hereafter cited as "Sotheby's I."

41. Wilson also shared De Quincey's anti-Aristotelian philosophy by emphasizing that the unity of the *Iliad* depends on the character of Achilles and, furthermore, on Achilles' opposing qualities. Aristotle stated, "A plot is not unified, as some think, if built around an individual. Any entity has innumberable [*sic*] features, not all of which cohere into a unity; likewise, an individual performs many actions which yield no unitary action. So all those poets are clearly at fault who have composed a Heracleid, a Theseid, and similar poems: they think that, since Heracles was an individual, the plot too must be unitary" (*Poetics* 8.16–21).

42. John Wilson, "Sotheby's Homer III," *Blackwood's Edinburgh Magazine* 30 (July 1831): 118, 120, 125. Hereafter cited as "Sotheby's III."

43. Aristotle *Poetics* 4.24–25.

44. For Heger's neoclassicism, see Lonoff, *Belgian Essays,* 356. Heger's high regard for epic as a form is evidenced also in his preference for French Romantic writers such as Chateaubriand who wrote epics to glorify Christianity, something that Heger, a devout Catholic, would have appreciated.

45. De Quincey, "Origin of the Homeric Poems," *Quarterly Review* 44 (January 1831): 149–50.

46. Aristotle *Poetics* 22.19–21.

47. During the Brontës' first year at the pensionnat, translation had been a regular exercise assigned by Heger for the perfection of Charlotte's and Emily's French, and it was not a strong point of Charlotte's. "I have written a translation which [M. Heger] chose to stigmatize as '*peu correct,*'" she wrote in an early letter of 1842. "He did not tell me so, but wrote the word on the margin of my book, and asked, in brief stern phrase, how it happened that my compositions were always better than my translations? adding that the thing seemed to him inexplicable. The fact is, some weeks ago, in a high-flown humour, he forbade me to use either dictionary or grammar in translating the most difficult English compositions into French. This makes the task rather arduous, and compels me every now and then to introduce an English word, which nearly plucks the eyes out of his head when he sees it." Gaskell, *Life of Charlotte Brontë,* 179.

48. George Chapman, preface to Homer *Iliad* (1611; Princeton: Princeton University Press, 1984), 15.

49. See Chapman's versified note "To the Reader," lines 164–75 (p. 11), and "Preface to the Reader," line 64 (p. 15). Chapman's "conversions" were more than "sleight." In the introduction to the Bollingen edition of Chapman's *Iliad,* Allardyce Nicoll writes that "[Chapman] understood Homer in his own way. . . . When he speaks of his 'English Homer' he does not mean simply 'Homer in English'; his words are to be interpreted

 literally and 'English Homer' is to be regarded as an independent exercise in the creative imagination. If on occasion he adds whole lines for which Homer gives him no authority, if continually provides his own qualifying epithets, . . . he is not to be blamed. This is merely part of his general endeavour, an integral and indeed necessary part of the work of art he has wrought" (xxi).

50. In her second year at the pensionnat, Brontë developed a renewed interest in translation. She had become much more proficient in French. She was also working on learning "as much German as [she thought] fit" (Gaskell, *Life of Charlotte Brontë*, 208) and voluntarily returned to translating "passages from Scott and Byron into French, poems by Belmontet and Barbier into English, and ballads by Schiller into French" (Lonoff, *Belgian Essays*, 254). This work as a translator undoubtedly gave her a more nuanced insight into the relationship between idea and form.

51. Charlotte had originally written "to" instead of "by," and Heger corrected her in his edits to the text.

52. < > indicates Heger's addition.

53. Phocis, along with all the republics of the Peloponnesus (except Argos and part of Achaia), was a Spartan ally.

54. There is a historical inaccuracy here. The Athenian singer could not have been a product of the academy, because Plato did not set up his school until 385 BC, nineteen years after the end of the Peloponnesian Wars and Athens' surrender in 404 BC. This anachronism seems to have escaped Heger's notice.

55. "Dicours prononcé par M. le professeur Constantin Heger, à la distribution des prix de l'Athénée Royal de Bruxelles, le 16 aout 1834," in Esther Alice Chadwick, "A Gift from M. Heger to C. Bronte," *Nineteenth Century* 81 (April 1917): 847–49. My translation.

56. Belgium won independence from France in 1830. In 1834, the year that Heger gave this speech, the Free University of Brussels was founded. One of the key elements of the Belgian Volksgeist was the establishment of a national literature in a country that saw French as the language of literature and culture yet was trying to separate itself from France as a nation. In "The Education of Charlotte Brontë: A Pedagogical Case Study," *Pedagogy* 1, no. 3 (2001): 457–77, Sue Lonoff notes that Heger's colleagues at the Athénée Royal were at this time publishing modern editions of the classics as part of their system of educating the new generation of Belgian leaders.

57. A letter to Ellen Nussey of April 1843 reads, "[I]f you were to pass a winter in Belgium, you would be ill. . . . There are privations and humiliations to submit to; there is monotony and uniformity of life; and,

above all, there is a constant sense of solitude in the midst of numbers. The Protestant, the foreigner, is a solitary being, whether as teacher or as pupil." Gaskell, *Life of Charlotte Brontë*, 200.

58. For more on the beginnings of this trend in the mid-eighteenth century, see Jenkyns, *Victorians and Ancient Greece.*

59. Most of the Elgin Marbles were remnants of the Parthenon, the temple of Athena that was commissioned by Pericles and designed by Pheidias in the fifth century BC.

60. Lord Elgin was forced to sell the marbles because of financial stress. By the time he sold the marbles to the British government, he had already spent over £70,000 in purchasing, shipping, and storing the artifacts. William St. Clair, *Lord Elgin and the Marbles* (London: Oxford University Press, 1967), 252.

61. Eric Gidal, *Poetic Exhibitions: Romantic Aesthetics and the Pleasures of the British Museum* (Lewisburg, PA: Bucknell University Press, 2001), 127.

62. The most vociferous critic of the Elgin Marbles was Richard Payne Knight, who argued that the damaged state of the statuary made it difficult to judge their quality and initially denied that the marbles dated back to the fifth century BC.

63. Quoted in *Report from the Select Committee of the House of Commons on the Earl of Elgin's Collection of Sculptured Marbles* (London: W. Bulmer and Co., 1816), 83.

64. Quoted in *Report from the Select Committee*, 90–91.

65. Quoted in Turner, *Greek Heritage*, 45.

66. The government purchased the marbles for £35,000, about half of the amount that Elgin had spent for their purchase, transportation, and maintenance.

67. Jenkyns points out that the appreciation for Greek tragedy that began at the end of the eighteenth century with the influence of the Schlegels developed through various comparisons of tragedy with ancient statuary: A.W. Schlegel likened Sophocles' works to the Niobe and Laocöon and Aeschylus to Pheidias, the chief sculptor of the Parthenon's statuary. See Jenkyns, *Victorians and Ancient Greece*, 88.

68. "Remarks on Greek Tragedy," *Blackwood's Edinburgh Magazine* 1 (April–September 1817): 39. Hereafter cited as "Remarks."

69. Jeannette King, *Tragedy in the Victorian Novel: Theory and Practice in the Novels of George Eliot, Thomas Hardy and Henry James* (Cambridge: Cambridge University Press, 1978), 2.

70. Gidal, *Poetic Exhibitions*, 119.

71. "On the Tragic Drama of Greece: Introductory to a Series of Scenes from the Greek Tragic Poets," *London Magazine* 7 (June 1823): 627.

 72. August Comte coined the term *sociology* in 1838, but the study of individuals as determined by their surrounding institutions and cultures began in the decades before sociology became a discrete discipline.

73. H. N. Coleridge, "Popular Specimens of the Greek Dramatic Poets," *Quarterly Review* 44 (January–February 1831): 394. H. N. Coleridge was a nephew of the poet.

74. Thomas De Quincey, "Theory of Greek Tragedy," *Blackwood's Edinburgh Magazine* 47 (February 1840): 149, 152. Hereafter cited as "Theory."

75. De Quincey, "Theory," 148. De Quincey's emphasis on the importance of "character" of course contrasts with Aristotle's emphasis on the primary importance of action in tragedy: "[T]ragedy is mimesis not of persons but of action and life. . . . [T]he goal is a certain kind of action, not a qualitative state. . . . So it is not in order to provide mimesis of character that the agents act; rather, their characters are included for the sake of their actions. Thus, the events and the plot are the goal of tragedy, and the goal is the most important thing of all" (*Poetics* 6.15–23).

76. See Lonoff, *Belgian Essays,* 254. Lonoff also notes that Brontë's later description of Cassandra at the end of "Athènes" borrows an image from Schiller's poem "The Veiled Image at Sais," which further suggests that Schiller was in Brontë's mind at the time she was writing this essay. As Frederic Ewen has noted, Schiller acquired tremendous popularity in the last decade of the eighteenth century and first half of the nineteenth century, directly influencing writers that Charlotte idolized as well as her own work. See Ewen, *The Prestige of Schiller in England, 1788–1859* (New York: Columbia University Press, 1932).

77. Friedrich Schiller, *Essays,* ed. Walter Hinderer and Daniel O. Dahlstrom (New York: Continuum, 1993), 12.

78. Schiller, "On the Pathetic," in *Essays,* 45.

79. Deborah Guth gives a lucid explanation of Schiller's idea of tragic sympathy in *George Eliot and Schiller: Intertextuality and Cross-Cultural Discourse* (Aldershot, UK: Ashgate, 2003), 145.

80. Schiller, "Art of Tragedy," in *Essays,* 20.

81. Schiller deems "circumstance" one of the essential features of "truthfulness" in tragedy (*Essays,* 14).

82. Euripides' Electra, for instance, recounts the wrongs done to her before the chorus and points to her filthy clothing and sordid hair as evidence of such injustice. She calls the gods, the chorus, and her husband as witnesses to her suffering and demands retribution (lines 175–90).

83. Vashti in *Villette* seems to be Charlotte's mature expression of the inexpressibility of suffering on stage. Her description of Vashti's performance is a confusion of sensual impressions that form no cohesive meaning.

84. Sophocles' tragedy is the only one featuring Electra that carries the harsh prohibition against mourning implied in Charlotte's essay. Electra's witnessing of Agamemnon's homecoming comes directly from Aeschylus's *Agamemnon.*

85. Aeschylus, *Agamemnon,* trans. Herbert Weir Smyth (Cambridge, MA: Harvard University Press, 1926), 1076–77, 1256–61.

86. Aeschylus, *Agamemnon,* 1063, 1061.

87. Charlotte had originally written "Lysander, his captains, and his helots slept, lying on their couches," but she crossed out "slept."

88. Charlotte Brontë, *Villette* (New York: Penguin, 1979), 494.

89. John Wilson, "Sotheby's Homer: The Odyssey I," *Blackwood's Edinburgh Magazine* 35 (January 1834): 13. Hereafter cited as "Sotheby's Odyssey I."

90. Karen Lawrence, *Penelope Voyages: Women and Travel in the British Literary Tradition* (Ithaca, NY: Cornell University Press, 1994), 2.

91. Wilson appears to have fully intended to treat the whole of the *Odyssey* four books at a time, for he ended the second article with a projection of his next. But this third installment was never published, and the series was discontinued after Wilson's treatment of the first eight books.

92. Charlotte Brontë, *Letters of Charlotte Brontë with a Selection of Letters by Family and Friends,* ed. Margaret Smith (Oxford: Clarendon, 1995–2004), 2:222.

93. Tony Tanner, introduction to *Villette,* by Charlotte Brontë (New York: Penguin, 1979), 12.

94. Eva Badowska, "Choseville: Brontë's *Villette* and the Art of Bourgeois Interiority," *PMLA* 120 (October 2005): 1519.

95. In book 9, Odysseus identifies himself as "Nobody" to the monster Cyclops to win his own and his men's release. As he is sailing away, he identifies himself as Odysseus, causing the Cyclops to ask his father, Poseidon, to put a curse on Odysseus, delaying his homecoming. On page 393 of *Villette,* Lucy resists being regarded as a "nobody" by Ginevra Fanshawe.

96. The sense of being a survivor also haunted Charlotte in the years leading to *Villette*'s conception. "They are both gone," she wrote to William Smith Williams shortly after Anne's death, "and so is poor Branwell—and Papa has now me only—the weakest—puniest—least promising of his six children—Consumption has taken the whole five" (*Letters,* 2:216). The desolation sent her on a wandering journey by the sea.

Chapter 3: Heretical Humanism

1. Marian Evans first visited Italy with Lewes from April to July 1860. Highlights included Rome, Naples, Florence, and Venice.

 2. George Eliot's first two novels were *Scenes of Clerical Life* (1858) and *Adam Bede* (1850). Eliot was identified as Marian Evans after the publication of the latter.

3. Letter to Sara Hennell, July 2, 1860, in George Eliot, *The George Eliot Letters*, ed. Gordon S. Haight (New Haven, CT: Yale University Press, 1954), 3:311.

4. J. W. Cross, *George Eliot's Life as Related in Her Life and Letters* (New York: Harper and Brothers, 1885), 2:127.

5. Margaret Harris and Judith Johnston, eds., *The Journals of George Eliot* (New York: Cambridge University Press, 1998), 334.

6. Marian Evans to John Blackwood, May 18, 1860, in Cross, *George Eliot's Life*, 2:166.

7. Letter to Major William Blackwood, May 27, 1860, in Eliot, *Letters*, 3:300.

8. For more on the origins of the *Cornhill Magazine*, see Graham, *English Literary Periodicals*, 302–5. For a thorough discussion of Frederic Leighton's illustrations of *Romola*, see Mark W. Turner, "George Eliot v. Frederic Leighton: Whose Text Is It Anyway?" in *From Author to Text: Re-reading George Eliot's Romola*, ed. Caroline Levine and Mark Turner (Brookfield, VT: Ashgate, 1998).

9. *Romola* was published in the *Cornhill Magazine* in fourteen monthly installments (1861–62). The publisher, George Smith, paid £7,000 for it, the largest sum ever paid for a novel at the time. See Rosemary Ashton, *George Eliot: A Life* (New York: Penguin, 1996), 257.

10. *Romola* did not boost *Cornhill* sales, and Smith lost money on its publication. When the three-volume edition came out a year later, it was a slow sell, with slightly more than 1,700 copies sold in the first year. Ashton, *George Eliot*, 269.

11. George Eliot, "R. W. Mackay's *The Progress of the Intellect*" (*Westminster Review*, January 1851), reprinted in *Selected Essays, Poems and Other Writings*, ed. A. S. Byatt (New York: Penguin, 1990), 269.

12. George Eliot, *The Mill on the Floss* (New York: Norton, 1994), 38 (book 1, chapter 6).

13. Eliot, *Selected Essays*, 270.

14. Like Charlotte Brontë, Eliot did not receive formal training in classics. However, she could read Greek, having learned the language in 1841 from the Reverend Thomas Sheepshanks, the headmaster of Coventry Grammar School. She was familiar with all the major Greek writers, and the references to the ancient world in her works recognize her belonging to a larger intellectual community, both national and international.

15. See Kristeller, *Renaissance Thought*, 22ff.

16. George Eliot, "Silly Novels by Lady Novelists" (*Westminster Review*, October 1856), in *Selected Essays*, 159.

17. Cross, *George Eliot's Life*, 2:255.

18. In Eliot, *Letters*, 3:473–74. Susan Greenstein, in "The Question of Vocation: From *Romola* to *Middlemarch*," *Nineteenth-Century Fiction* 35 (March 1981), sees Romola as "stillborn" and "merely encyclopedic." To Greenstein, *Romola* is a "true quarry for *Middlemarch*" (489), in which Eliot "ponders questions about the moral weight of learning and the self-serving uses to which scholarship attains" (498). While I agree with Greenstein's assessment of Eliot's ambivalence toward scholarship (see my discussion below), I think *Romola* makes very specific claims about the nature of historical legacy (and especially the moral legacy of archaic Greece) that makes it far more than a "warm-up" for *Middlemarch*.

19. Quoted in Gordon Haight, *George Eliot: A Biography* (New York: Oxford University Press, 1968), 468.

20. E. M. Butler famously discussed "the tyranny of Greece over Germany" in his book of that title in 1935.

21. George Grote, *A History of Greece from the Earliest Period to the Close of the Generation Contemporary with Alexander the Great* (Bristol: Thoemmes, 2000), 1:40.

22. Turner, *Greek Heritage*, 96. As Turner points out, the psychological and creative implications of Grote's work had an impact on writers such as John Ruskin, John Stuart Mill, and J. A. Symonds later in the century.

23. For Eliot's notes on Grote's work in her *Middlemarch* notebooks, see John Clark Pratt and Victor A. Neufeldt, eds., *George Eliot's Middlemarch Notebooks: A Transcription* (Berkeley: University of California Press, 1979). In their introduction, Pratt and Neufeldt discuss Eliot's application of Grote's theory of the poet/myth-maker as "'religious teacher, historian, and philosopher, all in one'" (xxxiv–xxxv) to her task as a novelist.

24. Eliot, *Selected Essays*, 278-79.

25. Cross, *George Eliot's Life*, 2:262.

26. George Eliot, *Romola* (New York: Penguin, 1996), 1.

27. Eliot disliked Pater's ideas and agreed with her friend and Cambridge classicist R. C. Jebb that Pater's *Renaissance* misrepresented the works of the age. See Haight, *George Eliot*, 464.

28. Bratti encounters Tito on the morning of April 9, 1492, but Tito arrived in Florence the night before, making his arrival simultaneous with the death of Lorenzo de Medici on April 8, 1492.

29. The fifteenth century was a particularly important moment in the revival of Greek learning in Italy. In *Scribes and Scholars: A Guide to the Transmission of Greek and Latin Literature* (Oxford: Oxford University Press, 1968),

 L. D. Reynolds and N. G. Wilson write, "During the fifteenth century the opportunities for an Italian to learn Greek were good. A number of Byzantines came to live in Italy, and after the defeat of their country in 1453 there was a stream of refugees, who generally reached Italy by way of Crete and Venice, and who were all anxious to earn a living by teaching their native language or copying texts. Fortunately for them the revival in knowledge of classical Latin caused a widespread desire to read the Greek authors so frequently quoted or mentioned in it. . . . A small minority of students had the energy or the means to seek instruction in Constantinople. . . . Another reason for travel to the East was the chance of bringing back manuscripts which might well include new texts. . . . From Florence Lorenzo de Medici dispatched Janus Lascaris, one of the scholar refugees, on a journey to various Byzantine provinces in 1492 in search of manuscripts" (123–24). As mentioned earlier in this chapter, Eliot spent a great deal of time researching the particulars of Greek learning in fifteenth-century Florence.

30. Kristeller, *Renaissance Thought,* 25.

31. Kristeller notes that knowledge of Greek was rare even in the Renaissance (*Renaissance Thought,* 27).

32. George Gordon Byron, "Childe Harold's Pilgrimage," in *The Collected Poems of Lord Byron* (Ware, UK: Wordsworth Editions, 1994), canto 2, line 9.

33. Quoted in Christopher Hitchens, *Imperial Spoils: The Curious Case of the Elgin Marbles* (New York: Hill and Wang, 1987), 64–65.

34. Quoted in St. Clair, *Lord Elgin,* 272.

35. Thomas Arnold, *History of the Peloponnesian War by Thucydides* (Oxford: John Henry and James Parker, 1857), 3:xiv.

36. Matthew Arnold, *On the Classical Tradition* (Ann Arbor: University of Michigan Press, 1960), 31.

37. The debate about material confiscation and destruction of Greek history also applied to the debate about the Elgin Marbles in Eliot's own time (and in ours). Did Lord Elgin rescue the marbles, or did he steal them from Greece? Should the marbles be returned to Greece?

38. The doxology was the utterance of praise to God, and the Roman Church believed the Holy Ghost to proceed from the Father and the Son, while the Greek Church believed the Holy Ghost to proceed from the Father alone. Eliot, *Romola,* 600.

39. For more on the concept of *sprezzatura,* see Peter Burke, *The Fortunes of the Courtier: The European Reception of Castiglione's Cortegiano* (University Park: Pennsylvania State University Press, 1995).

40. Eliot, "R. W. Mackay's *The Progress of the Intellect*" in *Selected Essays,* 270.

41. The Furies protected blood relations, guest-host relations, and other forms of mutual obligation. See David Konstan, *Friendship in the Classical World* (Cambridge: Cambridge University Press, 1997).

42. The maenads were women governed by a Dionysian frenzy. Maenads are often equated with the Furies (or Eumenides), who have a very specific duty of vengeance.

43. Nonnos was a Greek poet born in the fifth century. He wrote his sprawling, three-volume history of the god Dionysos (or Bacchos) sometime before AD 500. The work is a vast compilation of Greek myths about Dionysos, and much of its importance lies in the literary testimony it provides to the Orphic theology that arose in Athens in the sixth century BC. In his introduction to the Loeb edition of Nonnos's *Dionysiaca* (Cambridge, MA: Harvard University Press, 1940–42), H. J. Rose described the epic as "the longest and most elaborate example we have of Greek myths in their final stage of degeneracy" (x). He went on to observe that "for something like seven hundred years to the time when Nonnos wrote, mythology had been the raw material of realistic sketches, new and startling narratives, amatory and rhetorical descriptions. It had also had plenty of time to become stale and exhausted. . . . Now arose a writer who undertook to compose an epic on wholly mythological themes, the labours and ultimate triumph of Dionysos" (xii). Rose expressed scant appreciation for Nonnos's "sickly and unwholesome fancy" and stated that "for the student of religion or mythology, as opposed to the degenerescence of literature, Nonnos has here nothing to offer except the telling after his fashion of a few stories not to be found elsewhere" (xv). This less-than-glowing recommendation, however, is at odds both with Eliot's attention to the text and with the obvious respect in which Bardo holds it. "Stay, Romola; reach me my own copy of Nonnus," Bardo tells his daughter as she is about to read, "with a voice a little altered by some suppressed feeling," a quotation from the *Dionysiaca* out of a fellow Florentine's translation: "It is a more correct copy than any in Poliziano's hands, for I made emendations in it which have not yet been communicated to any man. I finished it in 1477, when my sight was fast failing me" (*Romola,* 49). Florence held the oldest and most authoritative manuscript of *Dionysiaca,* written in 1280, and Bardo's claim to having a superior interpretation indicates the contested state of Greek scholarship at the time.

44. Nonnos *Dionysiaca* 5.345–50. Eliot does not include the actual quotation: "Seating herself on a low stool, close to her father's knee, Romola took the book on her lap and read the four verses containing the exclamation of Actaeon" (*Romola,* 50).

45. For a discussion of the relationship between love and intellectual work in *Romola,* see Shona Simpson, "Mapping Romola: Physical Space, Woman's Place," in Levine and Turner, *From Author to Text.*

46. For a psychoanalytic reading of Romola's experience of loss, see Julian Corner, "Telling the Whole: Trauma, Drifting and Reconciliation in *Romola,*" in Levine and Turner, *From Author to Text.*

47. Dionysos is known as the "twice-born" god because he was first carried in his mother Semele's womb, but after Semele was killed, the unborn child was sown into his father Zeus's thigh, from which he was "born" once again.

48. Sappho, Fragment #105a, in *Greek Lyric: Sappho and Alcaeus,* trans. David A. Campbell (Cambridge, MA: Harvard University Press, 1982).

49. Eliot also associates Romola's images of Tito with that of "a sun god," suggesting that Tito is an embodiment of both Dionysos and his brother Apollo. Nietzsche saw these two gods as representing the opposing forces of rationality and irrationality, but by combining both gods in Romola's vision of Tito, Eliot suggested the coexistence of these forces within nature. For further discussion of the conjunction of Apollonian and Dionysian forces in Tito, see Lesley Gordon, "Tito, Dionysus, and Apollo: An Examination of Tito Melema in *Romola,*" *George Eliot Review* 25 (1994): 34–38.

50. Ovid, *Metamorphoses* (Cambridge, MA: Harvard University Press, 1984), book 3, lines 660–69.

51. See Felicia Bonaparte, *The Triptych and the Cross: The Central Myths of George Eliot's Poetic Imagination* (New York: New York University Press, 1979).

52. It is worth noting that Theseus is a figure of nobility and honor as the reigning king of Thebes in *Oedipus at Colonus.* He offers Oedipus (and Antigone) protection and punishes Oedipus's persecutors.

53. George Eliot, "The Antigone and Its Moral," *Leader* 7 (March 29, 1856), reprinted in *Selected Essays,* 363–66. Eliot's reaction to the production (at Drury Lane, May 1, 1850) was ambivalent, though she did not see the performance. Eliot's article was also written in reaction to Matthew Arnold's preface to the 1853 edition of his *Poems: Second Series,* in which he asserted that moderns can no longer sympathize with the actions of *Antigone.* Eliot wrote a review of Arnold's *Poems* in the *Westminster Review* (July 1855): 297–98. Her views were also undoubtedly influenced by Lewes's assessment of the play in his article "Sophocles' *Antigone* and Its Critics," published in the *Foreign Quarterly Review* in 1845. Lewes's article contributed to the debate among Victorian classicists about the moral implication of Sophocles' plays. For an account of the debate about *Antigone,* see Richard Dowgun, "Some Victorian Perceptions of Greek Tragedy," *Browning Institute Studies* 10, no. 1 (1982): 71–90. Dowgun suggests that Eliot's interpretation of the play was influenced by Lewes's Hegelianism. See Darell Mansell, "A Note on Hegel and George Eliot," *Victorian Newsletter* 27 (1965): 12–15, which is equally hypothetical and equally vigorous about Hegel's influence (in particular his *Aesthetik*) on Eliot's work. See also Sara Putzell-Korab, *The Evolving Consciousness: An Hegelian Reading of the Novels of George Eliot* (Klagenfurt, Austria: Institut für Anglistik und Amerikanistik, 1982).

54. Antigone's sense of duty to her brother falls into the same category of family honor as her devotion to her father, Oedipus. In the lament quoted above, when Antigone is calling out to her dead brother, father, and mother, she addresses each as *philei*, "dear."

55. Joseph Wiesenfarth, in *George Eliot's Mythmaking* (Heidelberg: Carl Winter Universitätsverlag, 1977), frames the opposition between Romola's identification with Antigone and Tito's identification with Bacchus as the contrast between the forces of civilization and those of chaos. For me, the opposition is not so clear, because Antigone's moral resolve (and Romola's) is as much a rebellion against the forces of outward law as an affirmation of sympathetic, interpersonal bonds.

56. In Eliot, *Letters*, 4:103–4. The critical tone of Sara's letter was muted by accompanying words of admiration, but Eliot's insecurities about her latest work would have made her particularly sensitive to the backhanded manner of her friend's compliment. Lewes was in the habit of screening Eliot's correspondence to make sure that she would not be exposed to criticism of her work. In an 1862 letter to Sara Hennell, he explained that he had "mislaid" one of her letters to Eliot citing an unfavorable review of *Romola*, and he went on to explain, "No one speaks about her books to her, but me; she sees no criticisms. The sum total of success is always ascertainable, and she is not asked to dwell on the details. Besides this general conviction, there is a special reason in her case—it is that excessive diffidence which prevented her writing at all, for so many years, and would prevent her now, if I were not beside her to encourage her. A thousand eulogies would not give her the slightest confidence, but one objection would increase her doubts. With regard to 'Romola' she has all along resisted writing it on the ground that no one would be interested in it; but a general sense of its not being possibly popular would not be half so dispiriting to her as the knowledge that any particular reader did not like it; and it is very desirable she should suffer no more pain in this life than can possibly be avoided" (quoted in Eliot, *Letters*, 4:58).

57. Here, Eliot's view of ancient versus modern does seem to coincide with that of Hegel, who saw in Greek tragedy, and in *Antigone* in particular, a unity of inward being and outward existence lacking in the modern world, calling the play the "supreme and absolute example of tragedy" (*Hegel on Tragedy*, ed. Anne and Henry Paolucci [Westport, CT: Greenwood Press, 1978], 325). The difference between Eliot and Hegel, however, lies in the fact that Eliot ascribed unity to the Greeks not as a fact of spiritual evolution but as an (imaginative) product of the modern sense of fragmentation.

58. The lines come from a chorus of Aeschylus's *Eumenides* (517–25) as the displaced Furies lament the passing of the old forms of justice. The last

 lines of the quoted antistrophe read, "But who that traineth not his heart in fear, be it State or be it man, is like in the future to reverence justice as heretofore?" Aeschylus, *Eumenides,* trans. Herbert Weir Smith (Cambridge, MA: Harvard University Press, 1999).

Chapter 4: The Daimon Archives

1. Jane Harrison, *Reminiscences of a Student's Life* (London: Hogarth, 1925), 45–46.

2. Girton College opened when Eliot was in the middle of writing *Middlemarch,* and she and George Lewes donated books to the college library. See Ashton, *George Eliot,* 309. Eliot also subscribed fifty pounds to Barbara Bodichon's and Emily Davies's school. See Haight, *George Eliot,* 397.

3. The early-nineteenth-century provincial life that Eliot wrote about helped Harrison understand an element of her nature that stood in ironic contrast to her pioneering achievements as a scholar. "Until I met Aunt Glegg in the Mill on the Floss, I never knew myself," Harrison wrote in her autobiography. "I am Aunt Glegg; with all reverence I say it. I wear before the world a mask of bland cosmopolitan courtesy and culture; I am advanced in my views, eager to be in touch with all modern movements, but beneath all that lies Aunt Glegg, rigidly, irrationally conservative, fibrous with prejudice, deep-rooted in her native soil" (*Reminiscences,* 12–13).

4. Harrison uses this term in her essay "Scientiae Sacra Fames," in *Alpha and Omega,* 137.

5. Most of her career was spent as a teacher and scholar at Newnham College, Cambridge. Cambridge did not officially grant membership to women, however, until 1948, although by 1926, women had become actively involved in teaching, examining, and research. For a full historical account of women students in late-nineteenth- and early-twentieth-century Cambridge, see Rita McWilliams-Tullberg, *Women at Cambridge* (Cambridge: Cambridge University Press, 1998).

6. Harrison first comprehensively defined the "sympathetic imagination" in her *Prolegomena to the Study of Greek Religion* (1903; New York: Meridian, 1955) as the critical faculty that allows moderns to "think back [to the] haze of the early morning [of mankind] . . . a protoplasmic fulness and forcefulness not yet articulate into the diverse forms of its ultimate births" (164).

7. "Cambridge presented an obvious contrast to Oxford, where a very different style of classical scholarship prevailed in the 1860s [that is, before reforms to the classical curricula of both schools were proposed in earnest]. . . . The Oxford style . . . constituted a high-profile public discourse

which encouraged the conscious creation of Platonic guardians for Britain and its empire. . . . Cambridge . . . focused much more on the close linguistic analysis of texts, and made no large claims to a wider cultural resonance." Stray, *Classics Transformed*, 121–22.

8. For the autobiographical unreliability of Harrison's *Reminiscences*, see Mary Beard, *The Invention of Jane Harrison* (Cambridge, MA: Harvard University Press, 2000).

9. This was in reference to her stepmother's doctrine that "God would have our whole hearts or nothing" (Harrison, *Reminiscences*, 19).

10. Harrison, "Scientiae Sacra Fames," in *Alpha and Omega*, 117.

11. Jane Harrison to Gilbert G. Murray (JEH to GGM), November 24, 1901, Jane Harrison Archives, Box 1, Newnham College, Cambridge. Hereafter cited as Jane Harrison Archives.

12. Girton was founded in 1869 by Emily Davies but under quite a different philosophy from Newnham. McWilliams-Tullberg, *Women at Cambridge*, 44. Harrison entered Newnham in 1874 after taking the Cambridge University Examination for Women and winning a scholarship awarded to the best candidate.

13. The "gates of learning" were opening up for women at this time. When Harrison attended Cheltenham's Ladies' College in 1867, the School Inspection Commission (known as the Taunton Commission) publicly recognized the deplorable condition of girls' public schools and two years later prompted the Endowed Schools Act, which allotted money to girls' schools for their improvement. Although Cheltenham was a devout evangelical institution guided by the same religious strictures as Harrison's childhood home, it was also committed to providing its students with a grammar school education equal to that of boys and was known as a model girls' grammar school by a public increasingly attentive to the state of girls' education. Its principal, Dorothea Beale, was one of the women who helped Emily Davies launch Girton, the first university-level women's college, which, by its opening in 1869, provided an answer to the nagging five-year-old question, to what end were girls being admitted to Local University Examinations?

14. Because women were not members of the university and could not receive degrees, many did not even consider taking the Tripos exams when they went up to Cambridge; those who did sit them before 1881 did so informally, before private examiners. When Harrison sat her Classical Tripos in 1879, the examination consisted of 14 three-hour "papers" (that is, tests) scattered over eight days in a week-and-a-half period. In 1880, the year after Harrison sat her Tripos, the Classical Tripos was divided into two parts. Part II was optional but could only be taken after satisfactory completion

 of Part I. Part I still focused on translation and composition. Part II still required translation and composition (A) but then allowed students to choose one or two special areas of focus: ancient philosophy (B), history (C), archaeology (D), or language (E). *Cambridge University Reporter,* March 11, 1879, 435. Taking the undivided Tripos, Harrison was top of the second but as Annabel Robinson states, "it was a bitter, bitter disappointment" to her. Robinson, *Life and Work,* 53.

15. In a discussion of the Tripos division in the Arts School on March 27, 1879, Verrall vehemently argued that "the present system was insufficient." As recounted by the *Cambridge University Reporter* (April 1, 1879), Verrall also objected to "adding together marks obtained in so many different subjects [in Part II of the Tripos] . . . the joint mark [has] no meaning."

16. Testimonials from S. H. Butcher and A.W. Verrall, Jane Harrison Archives, Box 18.

17. While at Newnham, Harrison supplemented her Greek study with readings of poets such as Byron, Shelley, and Swinburne, who re-created ancient Greece for their contemporary audience. Robinson, *Life and Work,* 50–51. Reading these works as well as helping to stage the first Greek play at Newnham, Euripides' *Electra* in 1877, Harrison had plenty of time to indulge her propensity to reimagine the historical past.

18. During the twenty years away from Newnham, Harrison studied archaeology at the British Museum; traveled to Germany, Italy, and Greece for her research; lectured on Greek art and archaeology; and published numerous articles and three books. She supported herself through her teaching, but she also received an annuity left to her by her mother's will. Her friends and acquaintances during this time included Mary Kingsley, Robert Browning, Walter Pater and his sisters, Henry James, Herbert Spencer, Walter Raleigh, Eleanor Tennyson (who took Harrison to see her father-in-law, Alfred Lord Tennyson), Mabel Malleson (close friend and neighbor of George Eliot's and George Lewes's), and Virginia and Leonard Woolf. For more on these years, see Robinson, *Life and Work,* 58–73. Harrison spoke of her "hurt pride" over her dismissal from Newnham in the obituary that she wrote for her dear friend Margaret Merrifield (Verrall), published in the *Newnham College Roll Letter* (1916), 53.

19. JEH to Lady Mary Murray, April 14, 1902 (Jane Harrison Archives, Box 1). "I never had a peaceful moment till I got [to school]—at the mature age of 17! . . . I sometimes have a Platonic fit and foresee that we make all live in institutions renouncing the rank egotism of Home Life!"

20. "A Woman's View of the Greek Question," *Pall Mall Gazette,* November 4, 1891, 1.

21. *Cambridge Review*, October 22, 1891, 18. The importance of Greek as a marker of university intellectual traditions is set out in the compulsory Greek debates, which began in 1870 at Cambridge. Briefly, the debates had to do with whether Greek should be a required subject in the Previous Examinations, or "Little-Go," which undergraduate men had to pass to take either the Tripos Examination (for an honors degree) or a Poll Examination (for an ordinary degree). Debates about compulsory Greek continued until after the First World War. See Judith Raphaely, "Nothing but Gibberish and Shibboleths? The Compulsory Greek Debates, 1870–1919," in *Classics in 19th and 20th Century Cambridge: Curriculum, Culture and Community* (Cambridge: Cambridge Philological Society, 1999), 71–94.

22. At the time of this interview, there was increasing pressure at Cambridge to encourage students to take Part II, which was not mandatory for an honors degree. In 1892, a third paper was added to the questions in Part I "so that Candidates for Part I may be further encouraged to study the elements of subjects included in Part II" (*Cambridge University Reporter*, October 11, 1892, 52). In 1898, a proposal was made to make Part II mandatory for an honors degree, but this was rejected by the senate (*Cambridge University Reporter*, November 29, 1898, and February 21, 1899). In 1900, a proposal was passed to add three papers (in philosophy, literature, and sculpture and architecture) to Part I to make it sufficient for an honors degree (*Cambridge University Reporter*, November 12, 1900).

23. "A Woman's View," 1.

24. Harrison took the London matriculation examination in 1870, during her last year at Cheltenham (1).

25. *Cambridge University Reporter*, June 9, 1891, 953.

26. Arguments for and against the Tripos division in 1879 help to define terminology that was used in arguments for and against compulsory Greek—namely, "pure scholarship" and "culture." "In most of the other subjects of university study, the element of learning had a much larger place and culture of mind a somewhat smaller," the *Cambridge University Reporter* wrote of one argument for the importance of classical study in the 1879 discussion; "for men not very highly distinguished in them, the proportion of culture to learning was less than in classics and mathematics. It was exceedingly important for these men to get more culture than from their own study, and they should be encouraged to study one of the two old subjects." The same *Reporter* article summarized Mr. Jackson's argument for the Tripos division with the following description of what "pure scholarship" meant, in reference to the period before 1870, which was defined as "[t]he golden age . . . the age of 'pure scholarship.' What their 'pure scholarship' meant was this. They read Thucydides, but not Grote; they studied the

construction of the speeches, but did not confuse themselves by trying to study their drift. They read the Phaedrus, but had no Theory of Ideas. . . . They got a great deal of good, no doubt, but no thanks to the University or to the Tripos" (*Cambridge University Reporter,* April 1, 1879, 493–98). Jackson and his colleagues were responding particularly to a letter in the *London Times* written by T. E. Page, a Cambridge-trained schoolmaster, in 1879, objecting vehemently to the splitting of the Tripos. This letter began a debate in the pages of the *Times* in 1879 over "general" versus "specialized" knowledge in classics.

27. *Cambridge University Reporter,* June 9, 1891, 954.

28. *Cambridge University Reporter,* June 9, 1891, 955. Jebb was a friend of George Eliot's, Cambridge professor of Greek, and one of the key figures behind the founding of the Society for the Promotion of Hellenic Studies in 1879, which was aimed to sustain the high-culture status of Greek scholarship and research. See Stray, *Classics Transformed,* 138. Stray notes that Jebb "combined the conventional gentlemanly skills of versifying elegance with a concern for scientific scholarship and a willingness to support archaeology. . . . As perhaps the most celebrated Hellenist of the later Victorian period, Jebb was the leading exemplar of the classical scholar as culture hero" (139). Despite his support of the scientific man and his popular reputation, Jebb clearly also held a high-culture bias in matters of university tradition.

29. Harrison had immense respect for Dörpfeld, who in 1888 was excavating the Acropolis for the German Archaeological Institute, and they remained correspondents and friends throughout Harrison's life.

30. This book was recommended reading for Part II, Section D, paper 2 of the Classical Tripos in 1900. *Cambridge University Reporter,* March 15, 1898.

31. In an interview with the *Women's Penny Paper* in 1889, after her second failed candidacy, Harrison clearly identified herself with the scientific man. When asked whether she felt that her sex was a disadvantage to her, she replied, "Not at all. A woman was a novelty in this field, and my being one was in my favour with regard to professional popularity." *Women's Penny Paper,* August 24, 1889, 1.

32. Jane Harrison, "Hellas at Cambridge," *Magazine of Art* 7 (1884): 510.

33. Harrison was offered a research fellowship at Newnham in 1898. This allowed her plenty of time for her own writing and research and did not require her to take on the teaching and tutorial obligations that other staff had, largely because of the considerable reputation she had already built. See Robinson, *Life and Work,* 122ff.

34. The 1879 division of the Classical Tripos had placed religion in Group D of Part II, with art and archaeology. See Mary Beard, "The Inven-

tion (and Re-invention) of 'Group D': An Archaeology of the Classical Tripos, 1879–1984," in Stray, *Classics in 19th and 20th Century*, 95–134. 227

35. The speaker was E. S. Thompson, classicist and fellow of Christ's College. *Cambridge University Reporter*, November 8, 1892, 161–64.

36. Mary Beard has pointed this out in "Invention (and Re-invention)." A glance at the papers set out for Section D in 1892 emphasizes the anomaly: Paper 1—History of sculpture and sculptors of Greece and Rome; Paper 2—History of architecture and monuments; Paper 3—Mythology, religious rites and ceremonies and domestic antiquities; Paper 4—Painting, minor arts, inscriptions. The list of papers was followed by the comment, "In all of the above papers the questions shall be so framed as to test the knowledge possessed by the Candidates both of ancient authorities and of extant monuments." *Cambridge University Reporter*, October 11, 1892, 47–52.

37. Jane Harrison, "Greek Myths in Greek Art VI," *Magazine of Art* 7 (1884): 317–23.

38. W. H. D. Rouse, "Review of Jane Harrison's *Prolegomena to the Study of Greek Religion*," *Classical Review* 18 (1904): 465–70.

39. In 1903, five questions in the Classical Tripos exam were taken directly from Harrison's *Prolegomena*.

40. Liddell and Scott's *Greek-English Lexicon* gives the definition of *enagizein* as "to offer sacrifice to the dead." Henry George Liddell and Robert Scott, *A Greek-English Lexicon* (New York: Oxford University Press, 1968).

41. Martha Carpentier, *Ritual, Myth and the Modernist Text: The Influence of Jane Ellen Harrison on Joyce, Eliot, and Woolf* (Amsterdam: Gordon and Breach, 1998), 6.

42. The development of classical journals in the mid-nineteenth century marked the consolidation of a professional field of advanced, university-based research distinct from the "gentlemanly knowledge" of amateur historians and schoolmasters. For a history of the development of classical journals in England, see Stray, *Classics Transformed*.

43. JEH to GGM, June 1907, Jane Harrison Archives, Box 2.

44. Jane Harrison, "Review of Lewis Farnell's *Cults of the Greek States*," *Cambridge Review*, May 30, 1907, 440–41.

45. Percy Gardner, "Response to Jane Harrison's Review of Lewis Farnell's *Cults of the Greek States*," *Cambridge Review*, June 13, 1907, 482.

46. *Cambridge Review*, June 13, 1907, 483.

47. Lewis Farnell, *The Cults of the Greek States*, vol. 1 (Oxford: Oxford University Press, 1869), ix–x.

48. The *Classical Review* was founded in 1887 with the expansion of the Cambridge classical curriculum (for example, into specialties of art and archaeology). In *Classics Transformed*, Christopher Stray gives an idea of the

 journal's broad range of audience: "Among the benefits [that the *Classical Review*'s] editors envisaged . . . were: that scholars would no longer work in the dark; that schoolmasters would learn what to recommend to their pupils [that is, through the journal's book reviews]; unproductive scholars would be encouraged to write; the antagonists of classics would see that the subject meant more than writing verses in a dead language . . . ; that an organ of international communication between scholars would be provided" (135).

49. Quotations are from Jane Harrison, "The Head of John Baptist," *Classical Review* 30, no. 8 (1916): 216–19.

50. Euripides *Bacchae* 1.1169ff. See Euripides, *Bacchae*, trans. David Kovacs (Cambridge, MA: Harvard University Press, 2003).

51. Jane Harrison, *Themis: A Study of the Social Origins of Greek Religion* (New York: University Books, 1962), xvii.

52. Turner, *Greek Heritage*, 80. For additional details about eighteenth-century relations between mythographers and Christianity, see Robert Ackerman, *The Cambridge Group and the Origins of Myth Criticism* (Ann Arbor, MI: UMI, 1980) and *The Myth and Ritual School: J. G. Frazer and the Cambridge Ritualists* (New York: Garland, 1991).

53. F. M. Müller was a Sanskrit professor at Oxford who famously theorized that myths derived from words whose original meanings had been forgotten or changed and that the central concept upon which all myths built was the sun. Müller believed that uncovering the source of these myths in "the disease of language" would help scholars understand the innate religious instinct in mankind. J. G. Frazer, author of *The Golden Bough* (1870), examined the common elements of religious beliefs, including Christianity, and focused particularly on the recurring theme of the death and resurrection of a king-god figure.

54. The mutually reinforcing relationship between Britain's two oldest universities and the Anglican church was foremost among the values underpinning the ideal of classical scholarship throughout most of the nineteenth century. As Christopher Stray remarks in his introduction to *Classics in 19th and 20th Century Cambridge*, "Oxford and Cambridge were the educational wings of the Established Church" (3). Michael Sanderson notes that 62 percent of Cambridge students and 64.2 percent of Oxford students went into the church between 1752 and 1886. Not until the 1871 University Tests Act could dons at Oxford and Cambridge be excused from taking holy orders, and dissenters were permitted to take degrees and fellowships. Sanderson, *Universities*, 142. By the end of the nineteenth century, the bond between the church and the university had weakened because of the increasing availability of secular professions and the subsequent expansion of

the university curriculum. However, the fact that knowing Greek provided direct access to the word of God in the New Testament ensured a lasting bond between Greek scholarship and the Anglican church.

55. M. R. James, "Some Remarks on 'The Head of John Baptist,'" *Classical Review* 31, no. 1 (1917): 1–4.

56. M. R. James, "Vice-Chancellor's Speech," *Cambridge Review*, October 14, 1914, 5.

57. MRJ to Gordon Carey, January 28, 1917, King's College Archives, Cambridge.

58. One letter from a professor (Austin H. Johnson) to the *Cambridge Review* in 1915 reads, "If [a university] remain true to herself, she must keep outside the battle of the nations; upon her strife will always inflict a loss, which nothing can repay. . . . [I]f we are members of a University we must see to it that what is left in our guardianship is fully and lovingly cared for, so that it may maintain its place in the world." *Cambridge Review*, June 9, 1915, 381.

59. James, "Vice-Chancellor's Speech." By the end of 1916, the number of undergraduates at Cambridge had fallen from 3,263 in 1913 to 575. One-tenth of 12,500 enlisted Cambridge men were dead, and 1,700 were wounded. Information compiled from the *Cambridge Review* 38 (1916–17). It is telling that by 1915, Newnham—one of the two (unofficial) women's colleges at Cambridge—had become the largest college in the university. *Newnham College Roll Letter*, 1914–15.

60. University sermon delivered by Reverend F. J. Foakes-Jackson, dean and assistant tutor of Jesus College, printed in *Cambridge Review* 36 (1914–15): 16. Foakes-Jackson was later a candidate for the Regius Professor of Divinity position.

61. Remarking on Harrison's analysis of the devil's discussion with Christ, James noted in his *Classical Review* article that "[t]he devil's statement gains in precision (unlike Miss Harrison's)."

62. T. R. Glover, "Jesus as a Historic Personality," *Cambridge Review* 38 (1916): 98. Glover was a lecturer of ancient history at Cambridge and was a Fellow of St. John's College at the time. In June 1917, Glover was appointed Wilde Lecturer in Natural and Comparative Religion at Oxford.

63. See J. H. Holden, *The World and the Gospel* (London: United Council for Missionary Education, 1916). This was reviewed in the *Cambridge Review*, December 6, 1916: "[The book paints the] now familiar picture of the war as a judgment of a diseased society . . . a reminder that a society based on selfishness must in the end destroy itself" (132).

64. MRJ to GVC, April 19, 1917, King's College Archives, Cambridge. James also mentioned rereading the *Bacchae* in a letter to his friend Gwen

 McBryde, stating, "My mind has been improved since I left you by the reading of 3 Greek plays in the train." April 23, 1917, *Letters to a Friend,* King's College Archives, Cambridge.

65. James would almost definitely have been reading the plays in the original Greek.

66. In her preface to the second edition (1927) of *Themis,* Harrison admitted to being a "disciple of Nietzsche" but qualified that by stating, "I ought never to have forgotten that humanity needs not only the intoxication of Dionysos the daimon (who is the escape into the suffering will behind phenomena), but also, and perhaps even more, that 'appeasement in form' which is Apollo the Olympian" (viii).

67. Walter Pater, "A Study of Dionysus: The Spiritual Form of Fire and Dew," in *Greek Studies: A Series of Essays* (London: Macmillan, 1910), 11. Harrison had met Pater during her years in London and wrote, "I always think of him as a soft, kind cat; he purred so persuasively that I lost the sense of what he was saying" (*Reminiscences,* 46).

68. Leighton and Alma-Tadema are two of the most famous painters of late-nineteenth-century classicism. See Leighton's *Bacchante* (1895) and Alma-Tadema's *Dedication to Bacchus* (1889) and *Autumn* (1877). Other Dionysian painters of the classicist school include Simeon Solomon (*Bacchus,* 1867, 1868), John Collier (*The Priestess of Bacchus,* 1885–89), John Godward (*A Priestess of Bacchus,* 1890), and Arthur Wardle (*A Bacchante,* 1909). For a history of late-nineteenth-century classicism and its relation to aestheticism and the Pre-Raphaelite movement, see Christopher Wood, *Victorian Painting* (New York: Bullfinch, 1999).

69. Frazer also discusses the Dionysian ritual of rending an animal to pieces in a reenactment of the myth of Dionysos's murder in the shape of a bull by his enemies the Titans. See chapter 43, "Dionysus," in *The Golden Bough* (1890). This myth has been the foundation of later (post-Harrison) criticism linking Dionysos's death to the sacrament of Christ. See Arthur Evans, *The God of Ecstasy: Sex-Roles and the Madness of Dionysos* (New York: St. Martin's, 1988); Jan Kott, *The Eating of the Gods: An Interpretation of Greek Tragedy,* trans. Boleslaw Taborski and Edward J. Czerwinski (New York: Random House, 1970); and Park McGinty, *Interpretation and Dionysos: Method in the Study of a God* (New York: Mouton, 1978).

70. Gilbert Murray, *A History of Ancient Greek Literature* (London: W. Heinemann, 1897), 272.

71. JEH to GGM, April/May 1902, Jane Harrison Archives, Box 1.

72. For a discussion of Pater's influence on Harrison, see Yopie Prins, "Greek Maenads, Victorian Spinsters," in *Victorian Sexual Dissidence,* ed. Richard Dellamora (Chicago: University of Chicago Press, 1999), 43–81.

73. JEH to GGM, May 14, 1907, Jane Harrison Archives, Box 2.

74. Dionysos was ripped to pieces by the Titans and resurrected by Rhea.

75. Orpheus, like Dionysos, was killed and, to some extent, resurrected. After he was torn apart by maenads, Orpheus's severed head floated to Lesbos, where it was honored as an oracle.

76. See Euripides *Bacchae* lines 231ff. James's sympathies would have been contrary to popular interpretations of the play at the time, which saw Pentheus as rightly punished for his resistance to Dionysian forces.

77. James's sense of purposelessness and despair surfaces in letters of 1916–17 to Gordon Carey (King's College Archives, Cambridge). A subtle but poignant passage refers to his digging trenches for potatoes: "I have dug trenches in the ground, in which potatoes were placed. Much depends upon the way in which this is done, as you hardly need to be told, & I think I have the right to say that—well, I don't want to claim more than I ought" (April 19, 1917).

78. M. R. James, "Sermon on the Anniversary of Sts. Simon and Jude," *Cambridge Review*, November 29, 1917, 163–65.

79. Jane Harrison, "The Influence of Darwinism on the Study of Religions" (1914), in *Alpha and Omega*, 143–78.

80. James, "Sermon on the Anniversary," 163–65.

81. MRJ to GVC, July 31, 1917, King's College Archives, Cambridge.

82. For more on James's scholarly work during this period, see Richard William Pfaff, *Montague Rhodes James* (London: Scholar, 1980), 252ff.

83. JEH to FMC, November 24, 1918, Jane Harrison Archives, Box 20b.

84. The quotation is from Harrison's essay "Alpha and Omega," in *Alpha and Omega*, 179–208, which compares and contrasts the magic of archaic religion with modern theology.

85. Harrison, "Alpha and Omega," 197.

86. Review of the *Annual of the British School of Athens*, no. 19 (1912–13), *Cambridge Review*, November 11, 1914, 81.

87. Jane Harrison, "Epilogue on the War: Peace with Patriotism," in *Alpha and Omega*, 228.

88. JEH to GGM, August 27, 1914, Jane Harrison Archives, Box 4.

89. JEH to GGM, January 1914, Jane Harrison Archives, Box 4: "I am working hard in the light part of my favorite saint—John Baptist."

90. The debate about whether John the Baptist ought to be regarded as a prophet of the Old Testament or as an initiator of the new order is an old one and was being carried on at that time in Cambridge. T. R. Glover's lectures had forceably argued Jesus's uniqueness as the hero of the New Testament, claiming that "whatever may be the historical connexion between [John Baptist and Jesus], it is important for us . . . to realize the

 broad gulf that separates them." T. R. Glover, *The Jesus of History* (London: Student Christian Movement, 1917), 149. The *Cambridge Review* indicates that the discussion of John the Baptist versus Jesus was discussed in the Cambridge lectures.

91. "I have been in the depth of depression—no one seemed to feel the Horned Horror [her Minotaur article] had any significance," she wrote. "[William] Ridgeway openly insulting. ABC [Arthur Bernard Cook] afraid for The Most High and FMC [Cornford] not knowing enough of the Leaf-Arnold business to catch on. I was so disheartened I felt like John Baptist." JEH to GGM, March 1914, Jane Harrison Archives, Box 4.

92. JEH to GGM, September 1912, Jane Harrison Archives, Box 4.

93. It is worth noting that Jesus states in Luke that John "had a devil" (Luke 7:33).

94. *Cambridge Review*, February 21, 1917, 233.

95. Published in the next number of the same volume of the *Classical Review*.

96. JEH to GGM, February 1917, Jane Harrison Archives, Box 4.

97. In a letter to Murray, Harrison stated her regret and also stuck to her guns—as she had done after her Farnell review. "I do wish I wasn't so careless. I'll try not to be tho' I am safe to forget. . . . They wldn't stop me anyhow if I get an idea into my head." JEH to GGM, February 1917, Jane Harrison Archives, Box 4.

98. In the same letter to Murray (as above), Harrison wrote, "I do wish *you* wld write and tell him how silly he is about Comparative Mythology being dangerous for the young." JEH to GGM, February 1917, Jane Harrison Archives, Box 4.

99. JEH to GGM, February 1917, Jane Harrison Archives, Box 4.

100. JEH to GGM, February 1917, Jane Harrison Archives, Box 4.

101. "If I write [a response to James] I am sure to be rude and ineffectual," Harrison wrote to Murray. Then, after reading Murray's letter, she wrote, "Yr screed leaves me free just to write a polite formal acknowledgment of my errors and to thank him for pointing them out. . . . [I]f there wasn't you to defend me I should get enraged and scarified, and now I feel as full of Christian love and charity as a lamb unborn." JEH to GGM, February 1917, Jane Harrison Archives, Box 4.

102. M. R. James was, of course, better known as a ghost-story writer than as a medievalist, a cataloguer of library and museum collections, a provost, a vice-chancellor, or any of his other numerous titles. His first volume of stories—*Ghost Stories of an Antiquary*—was published in the same year (1903) as Harrison's first edition of the *Prolegomena*. The two publications—both dealing with ghosts, spirits, and fear—reveal a curious compatibility

between Harrison's and James's superstitious natures, despite their apparently opposing religious views.

103. Harrison, "Scientiae Sacra Fames," in *Alpha and Omega,* 136.

104. JEH to GGM, February 1912, Jane Harrison Archives, Box 3.

105. The group consisted of Harrison, Murray, Francis MacDonald Cornford, and Arthur Bernard Cook. Cornford was formerly Harrison's student. He became a fellow of Trinity College, Cambridge, upon graduation and came to specialize in Greek philosophy. Murray by this time had become Regius Professor of Greek at Oxford and was the most popular translator of Euripides. Cook was a Cambridge archaeologist only marginally connected with the "group." Robinson notes that a large part of this marginality owed to the fact that he was a devout Christian and that his "evangelical convictions unnerved [Harrison]" (*Life and Work,* 272). As Mary Beard (*Inventor of Jane Harrison,* 109) and Christopher Stray (*Classics Transformed,* 161) have pointed out, the phrase "Cambridge Ritualists" is a back-formation, a shorthand term used by contemporary critics to refer to the common focus on ritual theory developed by Harrison in *Themis.* Jessie Stewart has described it as a "complete Free Trade of ideas" (draft of "Jane Harrison in the Light of Her Letters," Jane Harrison Archives, Box 20a). And Gilbert Murray, after Harrison's death, reflected that "it was . . . a remarkable group. We somehow had the same general aim or outlook or something and the work of each contributed to the work of the others." GGM to Jessie Stewart, undated letter, Jane Harrison Archives, Box20a. Her letters illustrate that Harrison was the central touch-point in the three-person idea trade, often orchestrating meetings and communications between Murray and Cornford. The group would not have existed without her.

106. Stanley Edgar Hyman, "Leaping for Goodly Themis," *New Leader,* October 29, 1962, 24–25 (Jane Harrison Archives, Box 20a).

107. J. A. K. Thomson was a rising Greek scholar at Oxford who worked with Murray and admired Harrison.

108. *Classical Review* 27 (1913): 132–34.

109. Lewis Farnell, "Review of *Themis,*" *Hibbert Journal: A Quarterly Review of Religion, Theology and Philosophy* 11, no. 2 (January 1913): 453–58.

Afterword

1. Stray, *Classics Transformed,* 264.

2. Paul Fussell, *The Great War and Modern Memory* (New York: Oxford University Press, 1975), 21.

3. Virginia Woolf, "On Not Knowing Greek" in *The Common Reader,* ed. Andrew McNeillie (New York: Harcourt, Brace, 1925), 34, 38.

 4. Jane Harrison, "Greek Religion and Mythology," *The Year's Work in Classical Studies* 12 (1917): 79.

5. JEH to GGM, November 19, 1916, Jane Harrison Archives, Box 5.

6. JEH to GGM, February 7, 1918, Jane Harrison Archives, Box 5.

7. JEH to GGM, December 1920, Jane Harrison Archives, Box 5.

8. Murray had been a staunch opponent of the Boer War at the beginning of the century.

9. Murray had originally signed a protest to the war but changed his mind after hearing Grey's speech to the House of Commons on August 3, 1914.

10. Gilbert Murray, "How Can War Ever Be Right?" reprinted in *Faith, War, and Policy: Lectures and Essays* (Boston: Houghton Mifflin, 1918), 45.

11. According to Murray's biographer Francis West, Murray's close friends Bertrand Russell and Noel Brailsford "were shocked by Murray's strong support for the war." West, *Gilbert Murray: A Life* (London: Croom Helm, 1984), 145. West goes on to argue, somewhat dubiously given the evidence of Murray's writings and his friends' attitudes, that Murray "was never a pacifist, and he always regretted the association of radical causes with pacifism because the latter damaged the former in public opinion" (145).

12. Murray later softened his militaristic stance as the war progressed. Even at the height of his prowar propaganda, he still felt the pull of his innate pacifism. In a letter to Mary dated September 7, 1914, Murray expressed the conflict between his sense of duty and his pacifism: "I have hours in which I feel . . . utterly abased and crushed by the misery of the war. . . . But mostly I feel strung up and exalted by a feeling of the tremendous issue and the absolute duty that lies upon us to save Europe and humanity." Quoted in Duncan Wilson, *Gilbert Murray OM, 1866–1957* (Oxford: Clarendon, 1987), 218.

13. JEH to GGM, October 1914, Jane Harrison Archives, Box 4. The *Hibbert Journal* first published Murray's article.

14. JEH to GGM, January 1902, Jane Harrison Archives, Box 1.

15. One need only look at the chaos caused by her 1907 review of Farnell's *Cults of the Greek States*, when Murray was away in America, for proof of the sanitizing and protective force that Murray exerted against Harrison's (at times) career- and self-destructive intensity.

16. JEH to GGM, November 1914, Jane Harrison Archives, Box 4.

17. "What I am in search of is a certain inward war in our members [soldiers and scholars alike] which makes perpetually for international conflict," Harrison wrote in the first pages of her essay. Harrison, "Epilogue on the War," in *Alpha and Omega*, 225.

18. JEH to GGM, September 17, 1914, Jane Harrison Archives, Box 4.

19. It is interesting to note the contrast between Harrison's endless enthusiasm for Murray's translations of Euripides before the war and her support for his translations of Aeschylus after the war. "Oh do make your HUM book centre around the Supplices, it is so beautiful," she wrote to him on May 20, 1919. She meant HUL (the Home University Library of Modern Knowledge), a series launched in 1911 by publishers Williams and Norgate, who asked Murray to become the series' general editor. Murray was responsible for finding appropriate authors to write short (50,000 words), simply styled books on various scholarly subjects. The series appealed to those who "had passed through newly established secondary schools, had acquired a taste for knowledge and had no chance of going to a university." Wilson, *Gilbert Murray,* 187–88. Harrison contributed *Ancient Art and Ritual* (London: Williams and Norgate, 1913) to the series in 1913. Harrison's encouragement of his focus on *Supplices* is significant. *Supplices,* the oldest extant Aeschylus play, tells how the fifty daughters of Danaus fled from forced marriage with the fifty sons of Aegyptus. They sought asylum with the king of Argos, Pelasgus. Pelasgus was finally convinced by the vote of his people to offer them shelter, but the brothers eventually appeared to reclaim the maidens. The play centers on ideas of justice, mercy, and the quest for asylum, in contradistinction to Euripides' emphasis on violence and the powers of irrationality. "[A]dd Moira [fate or due reverence, consideration] and Dike [justice] to your Aidos [shame]," continued Harrison in the same letter. "I begin to think that Aeschylus was a more amazing sheer genius than Euripides—is this rank blasphemy? You must (here the inkpot upset from emotion) translate him. . . . How he hated that *brotoloiois ares* [war, the bane of men] should be husband of Aphrodite." JEH to GGM, May 20, 1919, Jane Harrison Archives, Box 5. In encouraging Murray to translate Aeschylus, Harrison was, I think, trying to draw out the pacifist, gentle nature she had known for fourteen years before the war. The emphasis on Aeschylean themes of *moira* and *dike* contrasts with her support of Euripidean values in her earlier letters. If translating Euripides had somehow nurtured Murray's turn to real violence, perhaps she believed that translating Aeschylus could bring him back to thoughts of peace and justice. Whatever the reasons for Harrison's shift in attitude, Murray did indeed begin to translate Aeschylus after the war. However, he did not translate *Supplices* until 1930, two years after Harrison's death.

20. The change in Murray's stance is best exemplified by his essay "Herd Instinct and the War," which was delivered as a lecture at Bedford College in February 1915 and published in the *Atlantic Monthly* in June of that year. While acknowledging the war's positive effects on the national

236 character (for example, "a greater seriousness of life, less complaining, less obvious selfishness, and more hardihood" [830]), the article emphasized the far less encouraging notion that the driving impulse of the war lay in "the immense stimulation of the herd or group instincts" (831). "[H]erd union," wrote Murray, "actually deadens and shuts down those [emotions] which are felt only by the individual. The herd is . . . habitually callous toward the sufferings of its individual members, and it infects each member with its own callousness. . . . Herd union deadens thought. Collective anger, collective punishment, is always opposed to justice, bcause justice applies only to individuals" (835–36). Murray, "Herd Instinct and the War," *Atlantic Monthly* 115, no. 6 (1915): 830–39. After reading this article, Harrison wrote a letter to Murray subtly welcoming the return of his pacifist stance. Murray later became one of the founders of the League of Nations Union for disarmament, serving as the chair of its executive council from 1923 to 1938. The union helped to develop and explain the rationale behind the formation of the League of Nations, whose covenant was drawn up in 1919. The goal of the League of Nations was "to bring about such a world organization as will guarantee the freedom of nations, and as trustee and guardian of backward races, maintain international order and finally liberate mankind from war and its effects." Wilson, *Gilbert Murray,* 60. Murray was also the driving force behind the Council for Education in World Citizenship, an offshoot of the League of Nations Union, as well as the president of the Committee for Intellectual Cooperation.

Bibliography

Ackerman, Robert. *The Cambridge Group and the Origins of Myth Criticism.* Ann Arbor, MI: UMI, 1980.

———. *The Myth and Ritual School: J. G. Frazer and the Cambridge Ritualists.* New York: Garland, 1991.

Adams, Robert M. *Proteus, His Lies, His Truth: Discussions of Literary Translation.* New York: Norton, 1973.

Aeschylus. *Agamemnon.* Translated by Herbert Weir Smyth. Cambridge, MA: Harvard University Press, 1926.

———. *Eumenides.* Translated by Herbert Weir Smyth. Cambridge, MA: Harvard University Press, 1999.

Altick, Richard D. *Victorian Studies in Scarlet.* New York: Norton, 1970.

Anderson, Warren. *Matthew Arnold and the Classical Tradition.* Ann Arbor: University of Michigan Press, 1965.

Appleton, William W. *Madame Vestris and the London Stage.* New York: Columbia University Press, 1974.

Aristotle. *Poetics.* Translated by Stephen Halliwell. Cambridge, MA: Harvard University Press, 1995.

Arlen, Shelley. *The Cambridge Ritualists: An Annotated Bibliography of the Works by and about Jane Ellen Harrison, Gilbert Murray, Francis M. Cornford, and Arthur Bernard Cook.* Metuchen, NJ: Scarecrow, 1990.

Armstrong, Isobel. *Victorian Poetry: Poetry, Poetics and Politics.* New York: Routledge, 1993.

Arnold, Matthew. *Culture and Anarchy.* 1869. New Haven, CT: Yale University Press, 1994.

———. *On the Classical Tradition.* Edited by R. H. Super. Ann Arbor: University of Michigan Press, 1960.

———. *Poems: Second Series.* London: Longman, Brown, Green and Longmans, 1855.

Arnold, Thomas. *History of the Peloponnesian Wars by Thucydides.* 3 vols. Oxford, UK: John Henry and James Parker, 1857.

Arnot, Margaret. "Infant Death, Child Care and the State: The Baby-Farming Scandal and the First Infant Life Protection Legislation of 1872." *Continuity and Change* 9, no. 2 (1994): 271–312.

Ashton, Rosemary. *George Eliot: A Life.* New York: Penguin, 1996.

Aston, Elaine. "Ristori's Medea and Her Nineteenth-Century Successors." *Women and Theatre: Occasional Papers* 1 (1992): 38–47.

Auerbach, Nina. *Private Theatricals: The Lives of the Victorians.* Cambridge, MA: Harvard University Press, 1990.

———. *Romantic Imprisonment: Women and Other Glorified Outcasts.* New York: Columbia University Press, 1985.

———. *Woman and the Demon: The Life of a Victorian Myth.* Cambridge, MA: Harvard University Press, 1982.

Badowska, Eva. "Choseville: Brontë's *Villette* and the Art of Bourgeois Interiority." *PMLA* 120, no. 5 (October 2005): 1509–23.

Barker, Juliet. *The Brontës.* New York: St. Martin's, 1994.

———. *The Brontës: A Life in Letters.* New York: Overlook, 1998.

Bassnett, Susan. "Adelaide Ristori." In *Three Tragic Actresses: Siddons, Rachel, Ristori,* by Susan Bassnett, John Stokes, and Michael Booth, 117–69. Cambridge: Cambridge University Press, 1996.

———. *Translation Studies.* New York: Routledge, 1980.

———. "Still Trapped in the Labyrinth: Further Reflections on Translation and Theatre." In *Constructing Cultures: Essays on Literary Translation,* edited by Susan Bassnett and Andre Lefevere, 90–108. Philadelphia: Multilingual Matters, 1998.

Bateson, F.W. *Cambridge Bibliography of English Literature.* Vol. 3, *1800–1900.* Cambridge: Cambridge University Press, 1940.

Beard, Mary. *The Invention of Jane Harrison.* Cambridge, MA: Harvard University Press, 2000.

———. "The Invention (and Re-invention) of 'Group D': An Archaeology of the Classical Tripos, 1879–1984." In Stray, *Classics in 19th and 20th Century,* 95–134.

———. "'While Ridgeway lives, research can ne'er be dull': Professor Ridgeway, Aeschylus, Supplices 304ff." Unpublished manuscript. Published as "While RIDGEWAY lives, research can ne'er be dull" in *The Owl of Minerva: The Cambridge Praelections of 1906. Reassessments of Richard Jebb, James Adam, Walter Headlam, Henry Jackson, William Ridgeway, and Arthur Verrall,* edited by Christopher Stray. Cambridge: PCPS Supplementary Volume no. 28 (2005): 111–41.

Beckman, Linda Hunt. *Amy Levy: Her Life and Letters.* Athens: Ohio University Press, 2000.

Behlmer, George. *Child Abuse and Moral Reform in England, 1870–1908.* Stanford: Stanford University Press, 1982.

———. "Deadly Motherhood: Infanticide and Medical Opinion in Mid-Victorian England." *Journal of the History of Medicine and Allied Sciences* 34 (1979): 403–27.

Bellamy, Joan, Anne Laurence, and Gill Perry, eds. *Women, Scholarship and Criticism: Gender and Knowledge, c. 1790–1900.* New York: Manchester University Press, 2000.

Bergren, Ann. "Odyssean Temporality: Many (Re)Turns." In *Approaches to Homer,* edited by Cynthia Shelmerdine and Carl Rutherford, 38–73. Austin: University of Texas Press, 1983.

Berry, Neil. *Articles of Faith: The Story of British Intellectual Journalism.* London: Waywiser, 2002.

Blackwood's Edinburgh Magazine. "Remarks on Greek Tragedy I." 1 (April 1817): 39–42.

———. "Remarks on Greek Tragedy II." 1 (May 1817): 147–51.

———. "Remarks on Greek Tragedy III." 1 (July 1817): 352–57.

———. "Remarks on Greek Tragedy IV." 1 (September 1817): 593–96.

Bonaparte, Felicia. *The Triptych and the Cross: The Central Myths of George Eliot's Poetic Imagination.* New York: New York University Press, 1979.

Booth, Michael R. *Theatre in the Victorian Age.* Cambridge: Cambridge University Press, 1991.

———. *Victorian Spectacular Theatre, 1850–1910.* Boston: Routledge and Kegan Paul, 1981.

Borowitz, Albert. *The Woman Who Murdered Black Satin: The Bermondsey Horror.* Columbus: Ohio State University Press, 1981.

Brake, Laurel, Aled Jones, and Lionel Madden, eds. *Investigating Victorian Journalism.* New York: St. Martin's, 1990.

Breay, Claire. "Women and the Classical Tripos, 1869–1914." In Stray, *Classics in 19th and 20th Century,* 49–70.

Brecht, Bertold. *Brecht on Theatre: The Development of an Aesthetic.* Edited and translated by John Willett. New York: Hill and Wang, 1964.

Briggs, Ward W., and William Calder III, eds. *Classical Scholarship: A Biographical Encyclopedia.* New York: Garland, 1990.

Brink, C. O. *English Classical Scholarship: Historical Reflections on Bentley, Porson, and Housman.* Cambridge: James Clarke and Co., 1985.

Brontë, Charlotte. *Letters of Charlotte Brontë with a Selection of Letters by Family and Friends.* 3 vols. Edited by Margaret Smith. Oxford: Clarendon, 1995–2004.

———. *Villette.* 1853. Edited by Tony Tanner. New York: Penguin, 1979.

Brontë, Charlotte, and Emily Brontë. *The Belgian Essays: A Critical Edition.* Edited and translated by Sue Lonoff. New Haven, CT: Yale University Press, 1996.

Brooks, Peter. *The Melodramatic Imagination: Balzac, Henry James, Melodrama, and the Mode of Excess.* New York: Columbia University Press, 1985.

240 Brown, Susan. "Determined Heroines: George Eliot, Augusta Webster, and Closet Drama by Victorian Women." *Victorian Poetry* 33 (Spring 1995): 89–109.

Browning, Elizabeth Barrett. *Aurora Leigh*. London: W. W. Norton, 1996.

Brummett, Barry. "Mediating the Laws: Popular Trials and the Mass Media." In *Popular Trials: Rhetoric, Mass Media, and the Law*, edited by Robert Hariman, 179–93. Tuscaloosa: University of Alabama Press, 1990.

Burke, Peter. *The Fortunes of the Courtier: The European Reception of Castiglione's Cortegiano*. University Park: Pennsylvania State University Press, 1995.

Burnett, Anne. "Medea and the Tragedy of Revenge." *Classical Philology* 68 (1973): 1–24.

Burroughs, Catherine B. *Closet Stages: Joanna Baillie and the Theater Theory of British Romantic Women Writers*. Philadelphia: University of Pennsylvania Press, 1997.

Burrows, Montagu. "Female Education." *Quarterly Review* 126, no. 252 (April 1869): 448–79.

Burstyn, Joan N. *Victorian Education and the Ideal of Womanhood*. London: Croom Helm, 1980.

Butler, E. M. *The Tyranny of Greece over Germany*. Cambridge, UK: Cambridge University Press, 1935.

Byron, George Gordon, 6th Baron. *The Collected Poems of Lord Byron*. Ware, UK: Wordsworth Editions, 1994.

Calder, William M., ed. *The Cambridge Ritualists Reconsidered*. Atlanta: Scholars, 1991.

Carlson, Marvin. *The Italian Stage: From Goldoni to D'Annunzio*. Jefferson, NC: McFarland, 1981.

Carpentier, Martha. *Ritual, Myth and the Modernist Text: The Influence of Jane Ellen Harrison on Joyce, Eliot, and Woolf*. Amsterdam: Gordon and Breach, 1998.

Carroll, David, ed. *George Eliot: The Critical Heritage*. New York: Barnes and Noble, 1971.

Chadwick, Esther Alice. "A Gift from M. Heger to C. Bronte." *Nineteenth Century* 81 (April 1917): 846–61.

Chapman, George. "Preface to the Reader." In Homer, *Iliad*, translated by George Chapman, 14–18. 1611. Princeton, NJ: Princeton University Press, 1984.

———. "To the Reader." In Homer, *Iliad*, translated by George Chapman, 7–13. 1611. Princeton: Princeton University Press, 1984.

Clarke, G. W., ed. *Rediscovering Hellenism: The Hellenic Inheritance and the English Imagination*. New York: Cambridge University Press, 1989.

Clarke, M. L. *Greek Studies in England, 1700–1830.* Cambridge: Cambridge University Press, 1945.

Clauss, James, and Sarah Iles Johnston, eds. *Medea: Essays on Medea in Myth, Literature, Philosophy and Art.* Princeton: Princeton University Press, 1997.

Connell, W. F. *The Educational Thought and Influence of Matthew Arnold.* London: Routledge and Kegan Paul, 1950.

Conolly, L. W. *The Censorship of English Drama, 1737–1824.* San Marino, CA: Huntington Library, 1976.

Contemporary Review. "The Antiquity of the Homeric Poems." 12 (September–December 1869): 50–78.

———. "*The Medea of Euripides*" (book review). 8 (1868): 465–567.

Cooke, William. *The Elements of Dramatic Criticism.* 1775. New York: Georg Olms, 1976.

Corner, Julian. "Telling the Whole: Trauma, Drifting and Reconciliation in *Romola.*" In Levine and Turner, *From Author to Text,* 67–88.

Cross, J. W. *George Eliot's Life as Related in Her Life and Letters.* 3 vols. New York: Harper and Brothers, 1885.

Culham, Phyllis, and Lowell Edmunds, eds. *Classics: A Discipline and Profession in Crisis?* Lanham, MD: University Press of America, 1989.

Curry, Kenneth. "*Blackwood's Edinburgh Magazine:* Background and Significance." In Dameron and Palmer, *An Index to the Critical Vocabulary,* xi–xv.

Cvetkovich, Ann. *Mixed Feelings: Feminism, Mass Culture and Victorian Sensationalism.* New Brunswick, NJ: Rutgers University Press, 1992.

Dameron, J. Lasley, and Pamela Palmer. *An Index to the Critical Vocabulary of "Blackwood's Edinburgh Magazine," 1830–1840.* West Cornwall, CT: Locust Hill, 1993.

Davis, Tracy. *Actresses as Working Women: Their Social Identity in Victorian Culture.* New York: Routledge, 1991.

DeLaura, David. *Hebrew and Hellene in Victorian England: Newman, Arnold, and Pater.* Austin: University of Texas Press, 1969.

De Quincey, Thomas. "Homer and the Homeridae I." *Blackwood's Edinburgh Magazine* 50 (October 1841): 411–27.

———. "Homer and the Homeridae II." *Blackwood's Edinburgh Magazine* 50 (November 1841): 618–31.

———. "Theory of Greek Tragedy." *Blackwood's Edinburgh Magazine* 47 (February 1840): 145–53.

Detienne, Marcel. *The Creation of Mythology.* 1981. Translated by Margaret Cook. Chicago: University of Chicago Press, 1986.

Detienne, Marcel, and Jean-Pierre Vernant. *Cunning Intelligence in Greek Culture and Society.* Translated by Janet Lloyd. Sussex: Harvester, 1978.

Diamond, Michael. *Victorian Sensation: Or, the Spectacular, the Shocking and the Scandalous in Nineteenth-Century Britain.* London: Anthem, 2003.

Donohue, Joseph. "Women in the Victorian Theatre: Images, Illusions, Realities." In *Gender in Performance: The Presentation of Difference in the Performing Arts,* edited by Laurence Senelick, 117–40. Lebanon, NH: University Press of New England, 1992.

Dowgun, Richard. "Some Victorian Perceptions of Greek Tragedy." *Browning Institute Studies* 10, no. 1 (1982): 71–90.

Dowling, Linda. *Hellenism and Homosexuality in Victorian Oxford.* Ithaca, NY: Cornell University Press, 1994.

Dubois, Page. *Trojan Horses: Saving the Classics from Conservatives.* New York: New York University Press, 2001.

Duthie, Enid L. *The Foreign Vision of Charlotte Brontë.* New York: Harper and Row, 1975.

Eliot, George. *Essays of George Eliot.* Edited by Thomas Pinney. New York: Columbia University Press, 1963.

———. *The George Eliot Letters.* 7 vols. Edited by Gordon S. Haight. New Haven, CT: Yale University Press, 1954.

———. *The Mill on the Floss.* New York: Norton, 1994.

———. *Romola.* 1862. New York: Penguin, 1996.

———. *Selected Essays, Poems and Other Writings.* Edited by A. S. Byatt. New York: Penguin, 1990.

Emsley, Clive. *Crime and Society in England, 1750–1900.* London: Longman, 1987.

Euripides. *Bacchae.* Translated by David Kovacs. Cambridge, MA: Harvard University Press, 2003.

———. *Medea.* Translated by David Kovacs. Cambridge, MA: Harvard University Press, 1994.

Evans, Arthur. *The God of Ecstasy: Sex-Roles and the Madness of Dionysos.* New York: St. Martin's, 1988.

Ewen, Frederic. *The Prestige of Schiller in England, 1788–1859.* New York: Columbia University Press, 1932.

Farnell, Lewis. *The Cults of the Greek States.* 5 vols. Oxford: Oxford University Press, 1869.

———. "Review of *Themis.*" *Hibbert Journal: A Quarterly Review of Religion, Theology and Philosophy.* 11, no. 2 (January 1913): 453.

Ferris, David. *Silent Urns: Romanticism, Hellenism, Modernity.* Stanford: Stanford University Press, 2000.

Findlater, Richard. *Banned! A Review of Theatrical Censorship in Britain.* London: MacGibbon and Kee, 1967.

Finkelstein, David. *The House of Blackwood: Author-Publisher Relations in the Victorian Era.* University Park: Pennsylvania State University Press, 2002.

———, ed. *Print Culture and the Blackwood Tradition, 1805–1930*. Toronto: University of Toronto Press, 2006.

Florence, P. Sargant. "The Cambridge Heretics, 1909–1932." In *The Humanist Outlook*, edited by A. J. Ayer, 223–39. London: Pemberton, 1968.

Foley, Helene. "Medea's Divided Self." *Classical Antiquity* 8 (1989): 61–85.

Foster, Finley Melville Kendall. *English Translation from the Greeks: A Bibliographical Survey*. New York: Columbia University Press, 1918.

Fowell, Frank, and Frank Palmer. *Censorship in England*. London: Benjamin Blom, 1913.

Fowler, R. "'On Not Knowing Greek': The Classics and the Woman of Letters." *Classics Journal* 78, no. 4 (April–May 1983): 337–49.

Fraser, Hilary, Stephanie Green, and Judith Johnston. *Gender and the Victorian Periodical*. Cambridge: Cambridge University Press, 2003.

Fraser, Robert, ed. *Sir James Frazer and the Literary Imagination: Essays in Affinity and Influence*. London: Macmillan, 1990.

Frazer, J. G. *The Golden Bough: A Study in Magic and Religion*. 2 vols. London: Macmillan, 1890.

Fussell, Paul. *The Great War and Modern Memory*. New York: Oxford University Press, 1975.

Gardner, Percy. "Response to Jane Harrison's Review of Lewis Farnell's *Cults of the Greek States*." *Cambridge Review*, June 13, 1907, 482.

———. "Women at Oxford and Cambridge." *Quarterly Review* 186, no. 372 (October 1897): 529–51.

Gardner, Vivien, and Susan Rutherford, eds. *The New Woman and Her Sisters: Feminism and Theatre, 1850–1914*. Ann Arbor: University of Michigan Press, 1992.

Gaskell, Elizabeth. *Life of Charlotte Brontë*. 1857. New York: Penguin, 1975.

Genette, Gerard. *Narrative Discourse*. Translated by Jane E. Lewin. Oxford, UK: Blackwell, 1980.

Gerin, Winifred. *Charlotte Brontë: The Evolution of Genius*. London: Oxford University Press, 1967.

Gidal, Eric. *Poetic Exhibitions: Romantic Aesthetics and the Pleasures of the British Museum*. Lewisburg, PA: Bucknell University Press, 2001.

Glasstone, Victor. *Victorian and Edwardian Theatres: An Architectural and Social Survey*. Cambridge, MA: Harvard University Press, 1975.

Glover, T. R. *The Influence of Christ in the Ancient World*. Cambridge: Cambridge University Press, 1929.

———. "Jesus as a Historic Personality." *Cambridge Review* 38 (1916): 98.

———. *The Jesus of History*. London: Student Christian Movement, 1917.

———. *The World of the New Testament*. Cambridge: Cambridge University Press, 1931.

Godard, Barbara. "Between Performative and Performance: Translation and Theatre in the Canadian/Quebec Context." *Modern Drama* 43, no. 3 (Fall 2000): 327–58.

Goldhill, Simon. *The Poet's Voice: Essays on Poetics and Greek Literature.* Cambridge: Cambridge University Press, 1991.

———. *Reading Greek Tragedy.* Cambridge: Cambridge University Press, 1986.

———. *Who Needs Greek? Contests in the Cultural History of Hellenism.* Cambridge: Cambridge University Press, 2002.

———, and Robin Osborne, eds. *Performance Culture and Athenian Democracy.* Cambridge University Press, 1999.

Gordon, Lesley. "Greek Scholarship and Renaissance Florence in George Eliot's *Romola.*" In Rignall, *George Eliot,* 178–89.

———. "Tito, Dionysus, and Apollo: An Examination of Tito Melema in *Romola.*" *George Eliot Review* 25 (1994): 34–38.

Gowen, David. "*Medeas* on the Archive Database." In *Medea in Performance, 1500–2000,* edited by Edith Hall, Fiona Macintosh, and Oliver Taplin, 232–74. Oxford: European Humanities Research Center, 2000.

Graham, Joseph F., ed. *Difference in Translation.* Ithaca, NY: Cornell University Press, 1985.

Graham, Walter. *English Literary Periodicals.* New York: Thomas Nelson and Sons, 1930.

Greenstein, Susan M. "The Question of Vocation: From *Romola* to *Middlemarch.*" *Nineteenth Century Fiction* 35, no. 4 (March 1981): 487–505.

Grote, George. *A History of Greece from the Earliest Period to the Close of the Generation Contemporary with Alexander the Great.* 10 vols. Bristol, UK: Thoemmes, 2000.

Guth, Deborah. *George Eliot and Schiller: Intertextuality and Cross-Cultural Discourse.* Aldershot, UK: Ashgate, 2003.

Guthrie, W. K. C. *Orpheus and Greek Religion: A Study of the Orphic Movement.* London: Methuen, 1935.

Haight, Gordon. *George Eliot: A Biography.* New York: Oxford University Press, 1968.

Hall, Edith. "Medea and British Legislation before the First World War." *Greece and Rome* 46, no. 1 (April 1999): 42–77.

———. "Talfourd's Ancient Greeks in the Theatre of Reform." *International Journal of the Classical Tradition* 3, no. 3 (Winter 1997): 283–308.

Hall, Edith, Fiona Macintosh, and Oliver Taplin, eds. *Medea in Performance, 1500–2000.* Oxford: European Humanities Research Center, 2000.

Hall, Edith, Fiona Macintosh, and Amanda Wrigley, eds. *Dionysus since 69: Greek Tragedy at the Dawn of the Third Millenium.* Oxford: Oxford University Press, 2004.

Hardwick, Lorna. "Theatres of the Mind: Greek Tragedy in Women's Writings in England in the Nineteenth Century." In *Theatre: Ancient and Modern*, edited by Lorna Hardwick, Pat Easterling, Stanley Ireland, Nick Lowe, and Fiona Macintosh. Milton Keynes, UK: Open University, 2000.

———. *Translating Words, Translating Cultures*. London: Gerald Duckworth, 2000.

———. "Women, Translation, and Empowerment." In Bellamy, Laurence, and Perry, *Women, Scholarship and Criticism*, 180–203.

Hariman, Robert. "Performing the Law: Popular Trials and Social Knowledge." In *Popular Trials: Rhetoric, Mass Media, and the Law*, edited by Robert Hariman, 17–30. Tuscaloosa: University of Alabama Press, 1990.

Harris, Margaret, and Judith Johnston, eds. *The Journals of George Eliot*. New York: Cambridge University Press, 1998.

Harrison, Jane Ellen. *Alpha and Omega*. London: Sidgwick and Jackson, 1915.

———. *Ancient Art and Ritual*. London: Williams and Norgate 1913.

———. "The Dawn of Greece." *Quarterly Review* 194, no. 387 (1901): 218–43.

———. "Delphika." *Journal of Hellenic Studies* 19 (1899): 205–51.

———. "Durkheim's *Elementary Forms of Religious Life*." *New Statesman* 6, no. 133 (October 23, 1915): 62–64.

———. "Greek Myths in Greek Art VI: Theseus and Ariadne." *Magazine of Art* 7 (1884): 317–23.

———. "Greek Religion and Mythology." *The Year's Work in Classical Studies* 12 (1917): 79–101.

———. "The Head of John Baptist." *Classical Review* 30, no. 8 (1916): 216–19.

———. "Hellas at Cambridge." *Magazine of Art* 7 (1884): 510–15.

———. "The Kouretes and Zeus Kouros: A Study in Pre-Historic Sociology." *Annual of the British School at Athens* 15 (1908–9): 309–38.

———. "Pandora's Box." *Journal of Hellenic Studies* 20 (1900): 99–115.

———. *Prolegomena to the Study of Greek Religion*. New York: Meridian, 1955.

———. *Reminiscences of a Student's Life*. London: Hogarth, 1925.

———. "Review of Lewis Farnell's *Cults of the Greek States*." *Cambridge Review* 28 (May 30, 1907): 440–41.

———. "Rohde's *Psyche*." *Classical Review* 4, no. 8 (1890): 376–77.

———. "Rohde's *Psyche* pt. II." *Classical Review* 8, no.4 (1894): 165–66.

———."The Sculptured Tombs of Hellas." *Edinburgh Review* 185 (April 1897): 441–64.

———. *Themis: A Study of the Social Origins of Greek Religion*. New York: University Books, 1962.

Harter, Deborah. *Bodies in Pieces: Fantastic Narrative and the Poetics of the Fragment.* Stanford: Stanford University Press, 1996.

Hartman, Mary S. *Victorian Murderesses: A True History of Thirteen Respectable French and English Women Accused of Unspeakable Crimes.* New York: Schocken Books, 1977.

Hazlitt, William. *Hazlitt on Theatre.* Edited by William Archer and Robert Lowe. New York: Hill and Wang, 1895.

Hegel, G. W. F. *Hegel on Tragedy.* Edited by Anne and Henry Paolucci. Westport, CT: Greenwood Press, 1978.

Heraud, Edith. *Memoirs of John Heraud.* London: George Redway, 1898.

Heraud, John. *Medea in Corinth.* 1857. British Library Add. Ms. 52967.

Herder, Johann. "Homer: A Favorite of Time." *Blackwood's Edinburgh Magazine* 42 (November 1837): 702–14.

Heron, Matilda. *Medea: A Tragedy in Three Acts; Translated from the French of Ernest Legouvé.* London: T. H. Lacy, 1861.

Higginbotham, Ann R. "'Sin of the Age': Infanticide and Illegitimacy in Victorian London." *Victorian Studies* 32 (Spring 1989): 319–37.

Hitchens, Christopher. *Imperial Spoils: The Curious Case of the Elgin Marbles.* New York: Hill and Wang, 1987.

Hoffer, Peter C., and N. E. H. Hull. *Murdering Mothers: Infanticide in England and New England, 1558–1803.* New York: New York University Press, 1981.

Holden, J. H. *The World and the Gospel.* London: United Council for Missionary Education, 1916.

Holmstrom, John, ed. *George Eliot and Her Readers: A Selection of Contemporary Reviews.* New York: Barnes and Noble, 1966.

Homer. *Iliad.* 1925. Translated by A. T. Murray. Cambridge, MA: Harvard University Press, 1999.

———. *Odyssey.* 1919. Translated by A. T. Murray. Cambridge, MA: Harvard University Press, 1995.

Honan, Park. *Matthew Arnold: A Life.* Cambridge, MA: Harvard University Press, 1983.

Howe, Elisabeth. *The Dramatic Monologue.* New York: Twayne, 1996.

Huet, Marie-Hélène. *Monstrous Imagination.* Cambridge, MA: Harvard University Press, 1993.

Humble, Henry. "Infanticide: Its Cause and Cure." In *The Church and the World: Essays on Questions of the Day, First Series,* edited by Rev. Orby Shipley, 51–69. London: Longmans, Green, Reader, and Dyer, 1866.

Hunt, Peter. *The Madeleine Smith Affair.* London: Carroll and Nicholson, 1950.

Hurst, Isobel. *Victorian Women Writers and the Classics: The Feminine of Homer.* Oxford: Oxford University Press, 2006.

Hutton, R. H. "Review of *Romola*." *The Spectator*, July 18, 1863. Reprinted in *George Eliot and Her Readers*, edited by John Holmstrom. New York: Barnes and Noble, 1966.

Huxley, Michael, and Noel Watts. *The Twentieth-Century Performance Reader*. New York: Routledge, 1996.

Hyman, Stanley Edgar. "Leaping for Goodly Themis." *New Leader*, October 29, 1962, 24–25.

James, Henry. *The Scenic Art: Notes on Acting and the Drama, 1872–1901*. Edited by Allan Wade. New Brunswick, NJ: Rutgers University Press, 1948.

James, M. R. *Casting the Runes and Other Ghost Stories*. New York: Oxford University Press, 1998.

———. *Ghost Stories of an Antiquary*. New York: Dover, 1971.

———. *Letters to a Friend*. Edited by Gwendolyn McBryde. London: Camelot, 1956.

———. "Sermon on the Anniversary of Sts. Simon and Jude." *Cambridge Review*, November 29, 1917, 163–65.

———. "Some Remarks on 'The Head of John Baptist.'" *Classical Review* 31, no. 1 (1917): 1–4.

———. "Vice-Chancellor's Speech." *Cambridge Review*, October 14, 1914, 5.

Jenkyns, Richard. *The Victorians and Ancient Greece*. Cambridge, MA: Harvard University Press, 1980.

Jesse, F. Tennyson, ed. *Trial of Madeleine Smith*. Edinburgh: William Hodge, 1905.

Johnson, Gordon. *University Politics: F. M. Cornford's Cambridge and His Advice to the Young Academic Politician*. Cambridge: Cambridge University Press, 1994.

Johnson, Patricia. "'This Heretic Narrative': The Strategy of the Split Narrative in Charlotte Brontë's *Villette*." *Studies in English Literature, 1500–1900* 30 (1990): 617–31.

Johnstone, Peggy Fitzhugh. *The Transformation of Rage: Mourning and Creativity in George Eliot's Fiction*. New York: New York University Press, 1994.

Jones, Jennifer. *Medea's Daughters: Forming and Performing the Woman Who Kills*. Columbus: Ohio State University Press, 2003.

Kaminsky, Alice, ed. *The Literary Criticism of George Henry Lewes*. Lincoln: University of Nebraska Press, 1964.

Kazan, Francesca. "Heresy, the Image, and Description; or, Picturing the Invisible: Charlotte Brontë's *Villette*." *Texas Studies in Literature and Language* 32 (1990): 543–66.

Keegan, John. *The First World War*. New York: Knopf, 1999.

Kelly, L. G. *The True Interpreter: A History of Translation Theory and Practice in the West*. New York: St. Martin's, 1979.

Kelman, John. *Prophets of Yesterday and Their Message for Today.* New York: Books for Libraries Press, 1924.

Kent, Christopher A. "Victorian Periodicals and the Constructing of Victorian Reality." In *Victorian Periodicals: A Guide to Research,* vol. 2, edited by J. Don Vann and Rosemary T. VanArsdel, 1–12. New York: Modern Language Association, 1989.

Kestner, Joseph. *Mythology and Misogyny: The Social Discourse of Nineteenth-Century British Classical-Subject Painting.* Madison: University of Wisconsin Press, 1989.

King, Jeannette. *Tragedy in the Victorian Novel: Theory and Practice in the Novels of George Eliot, Thomas Hardy and Henry James.* Cambridge: Cambridge University Press, 1978.

Kitto, H. D. F. Introduction to *Euripides and His Age,* by Gilbert Murray. London: Oxford University Press, 1965.

Knelman, Judith. *Twisting in the Wind: The Murderess and the English Press.* Toronto: University of Toronto Press, 1998.

Knepler, Henry. *The Gilded Stage: The Years of the Great International Actresses.* New York: William Morrow, 1968.

Knight, Joseph. *A History of the Stage during the Victorian Era.* New York: Garland, 1986.

Konstan, David. *Friendship in the Classical World.* Cambridge: Cambridge University Press, 1997.

Kott, Jan. *The Eating of the Gods: An Interpretation of Greek Tragedy.* Translated by Boleslaw Taborski and Edward J. Czerwinski. New York: Random House, 1970.

Kowzan, Tadeusz. *Littérature et spectacle.* Paris: Mouton, 1975.

Kristeller, Paul Oskar. *Renaissance Thought and Its Sources.* New York: Columbia University Press, 1979.

Langbaum, Robert. *The Poetry of Experience: The Dramatic Monologue in Modern Literary Tradition.* New York: Norton, 1957.

Lawrence, Karen. *Penelope Voyages: Women and Travel in the British Literary Tradition.* Ithaca, NY: Cornell University Press, 1994.

Leckie, Barbara. *Culture and Adultery: The Novel, the Newspaper, and the Law, 1857–1914.* Philadelphia: University of Pennsylvania Press, 1999.

Legouvé, Ernest. *Medea: A Tragedy in Three Acts.* Translated from the Italian version of Joseph Montanelli by Thomas Williams (as represented by Madame Ristori). New York: John A. Gray and Green, 1867.

———. *Sixty Years of Recollections.* 2 vols. Translated by Albert D. Vandam. London: Eden, Remington, 1893.

———. *Théâtre complet: Pièces en vers.* Paris: Librairie Academique, 1873.

Leighton, Angela. *Victorian Women Poets: Writing against the Heart.* Charlottesville: University Press of Virginia, 1992.

Lemprière, John. *Lemprière's Classical Dictionary of Proper Names Mentioned in Ancient Authors Writ Large.* 1788. London: Routledge and Kegan Paul, 1984.

Levine, Caroline, and Mark Turner, eds. *From Author to Text: Re-reading George Eliot's Romola.* Brookfield, VT: Ashgate, 1998.

Levinson, Marjorie. *The Romantic Fragment Poem: A Critique of a Form.* Chapel Hill: University of North Carolina Press, 1986.

Levy, Amy. *A Minor Poet and Other Verse.* New York: Frederic A. Stoker, 1891.

Lewes, George Henry. *On Actors and the Art of Acting.* New York: Greenwood, 1968.

Liddell, Henry George, and Robert Scott. *A Greek-English Lexicon.* New York: Oxford University Press, 1968.

Lindop, Grevel. "De Quincey and the Edinburgh and Glasgow University Circles." In *Grub Street and the Ivory Tower: Literary Journalism and Literary Scholarship from Fielding to the Internet,* edited by Jeremy Treglown and Bridget Bennett, 41–57. Oxford: Clarendon, 1998.

Litvak, Joseph. "Charlotte Bronte and the Scene of Instruction: Authority and Subversion in *Villette.*" *Nineteenth-Century Literature* 42 (1988): 467–89.

London Magazine. "On the Tragic Drama of Greece: Introductory to a Series of Scenes from the Greek Tragic Poets." 7 (June 1823): 625–33.

Lonoff, Sue, ed. and trans. *The Belgian Essays,* by Charlotte Brontë and Emily Brontë. New Haven, CT: Yale University Press, 1996.

———. "Charlotte Brontë's Belgian Essays: The Discourse of Empowerment." *Victorian Studies* 32 (1989): 387–409.

———. "The Education of Charlotte Brontë: A Pedagogical Case Study." *Pedagogy* 1, no. 3 (2001): 457–77.

Louis, Margot. *Swinburne and His Gods: The Roots and Growth of an Agnostic Poetry.* Montreal: McGill-Queen's University Press, 1990.

Lucas, F. L. *Euripides and His Influence.* New York: Cooper Square, 1963.

MacDonald, Frederika. *The Secret of Charlotte Brontë Followed by Some Reminiscences of the Real Monsieur and Madame Heger.* London: T. C. and E. C. Jack, 1914.

MacGowan, Douglas. *Murder in Victorian Scotland: The Trial of Madeleine Smith.* Westport, CT: Prager, 1999.

Mansell, Darell. "A Note on Hegel and George Eliot." *Victorian Newsletter* 27 (1965): 12–15.

Marshall, Gail. *Actresses on the Victorian Stage: Feminine Performance and the Galatea Myth.* Cambridge: Cambridge University Press, 1998.

Matheson, Ann. "Scottish Periodicals." In *Victorian Periodicals: A Guide to Research,* vol. 2, edited by J. Don Vann and Rosemary T. VanArsdel, 99–109. New York: Modern Language Association, 1989.

Mayhew, Edward. *Stage Effect, or the Principles Which Command Dramatic Success in the Theatre.* London: C. Mitchell, 1840.

Mayhew, Henry. *London Labour and the London Poor,* 1861. vol. 1. Reprint New York: Dover, 1968.

McDonagh, Josephine. *Child Murder and British Culture, 1720–1900.* Cambridge: Cambridge University Press, 2003.

———. "Infanticide and the Boundaries of Culture from Hume to Arnold." In *Inventing Maternity: Politics, Science, and Literature, 1650–1865,* edited by Susan C. Greenfield and Carol Barash. Lexington: University Press of Kentucky, 1999.

McGinty, Park. *Interpretation and Dionysos: Method in the Study of a God.* New York: Mouton, 1978.

McManus, Barbara F. *Classics and Feminism: Gendering the Classics.* New York: Twayne, 1997.

McWilliams-Tullberg, Rita. *Women at Cambridge.* Cambridge: Cambridge University Press, 1998.

Meisel, Martin. *Realizations: Narrative, Pictorial, and Theatrical Arts in Nineteenth-Century England.* Princeton: Princeton University Press, 1983.

Michelini, Ann Norris. *Euripides and the Tragic Tradition.* Madison: University of Wisconsin Press, 1987.

Mileur, Jean-Pierre. *The Critical Romance: The Critic as Reader, Writer, Hero.* Madison: University of Wisconsin Press, 1990.

Monfasani, John. *Greeks and Latins in Renaissance Italy.* Brookfield, VT: Ashgate, 2004.

Morley, Henry. *The Journal of a London Playgoer.* Leicester: Leicester University Press, 1974.

Morrison, Robert. "William Blackwood and the Dynamics of Success." In Finkelstein, *Print Culture,* 21–41.

Mullin, Donald, comp. *Victorian Actors and Actresses in Review: A Dictionary of Contemporary Views of Representative British and American Actors and Actresses, 1837–1901.* Westport, CT: Greenwood, 1983.

———. *Victorian Plays: A Record of Significant Productions on the London Stage, 1837–1901.* New York: Greenwood, 1987.

Murphy, Paul Thomas. *Toward a Working-Class Canon: Literary Criticism in British Working-Class Periodicals, 1816–1858.* Columbus: Ohio State University Press, 1994.

Murray, Gilbert. "The Conception of Another Life." *Edinburgh Review* 221, no. 451 (1915): 122–40.

———. *Euripides and His Age.* London: Oxford University Press, 1965.

———. *Faith, War, and Policy: Lectures and Essays.* Boston: Houghton Mifflin, 1918.

———. *The Five Stages of Greek Religion.* 3rd ed. Boston: Beacon, 1951.

———. "Herd Instinct and the War." *Atlantic Monthly* 115, no. 6 (February 1915): 830–39.

———. *A History of Ancient Greek Literature*. London: W. Heinemann, 1897.

———. "How Can War Ever Be Right?" *Oxford Pamphlet No. 18* (September 1914). Reprinted in *Faith, War, and Policy*.

Neufeldt, Victor A. *The Poems of Charlotte Brontë: A New Text and Commentary*. New York: Garland, 1985.

Newey, Katherine. *Women's Theatre Writing in Victorian Britain*. New York: Palgrave Macmillan, 2005.

Newman, John Henry. *The Idea of a University*. New York: Longmans, Green, 1947.

Nicoll, Allardyce. Introduction to *Chapman's Homer: The Iliad*. Princeton, NJ: Princeton University Press, 1984.

Nightingale, Florence. *Cassandra*. New York: City University of New York, Feminist Press, 1979.

Nonnos. *Dionysiaca*. Translated by W. H. D. Rouse. Cambridge, MA: Harvard University Press, 1940–42.

O'Day, Rosemary. "Women and Education in Nineteenth-Century England." In Bellamy et al., *Women, Scholarship and Criticism*, 91–109.

O'Hara, Daniel T. *The Romance of Interpretation: Visionary Criticism from Pater to deMan*. New York: Columbia University Press, 1985.

Ovid. *Metamorphoses*. Translated by Frank J. Miller. Cambridge, MA: Harvard University Press, 1984.

Pall Mall Gazette. "A Woman's View of the Greek Question" (interview with Jane Harrison), November 4, 1891, 1–2.

Parker, Mark. *Literary Magazines and British Romanticism*. Cambridge: Cambridge University Press, 2000.

Pater, Walter. *Greek Studies: A Series of Essays*. London: Macmillan, 1910.

———. *The Renaissance: Studies in Art and Poetry*. Berkeley: University of California Press, 1980.

Pavis, Patrice. *Theatre at the Crossroads of Culture*. Translated by Loren Kruger. New York: Routledge, 1992.

Peacock, Sandra. *Jane Ellen Harrison: The Mask and the Self*. New Haven, CT: Yale University Press, 1988.

Pellegrini, P. Galli. "Lettere inedite di Ernest Legouve ad Adelaide Ristori." *Teatro Archivio* 1 (1979): 4–23.

Pfaff, Richard William. *Montague Rhodes James*. London: Scholar, 1980.

Phillips, Ann, ed. *A Newnham Anthology*. Cambridge: Cambridge University Press, 1979.

Planche, James Robinson. *The Golden Fleece; or, Jason in Colchis, and Medea in Corinth*. In *Plays by James Robinson Planche*, edited by Donald Roy, 145–71. Cambridge: Cambridge University Press, 1986.

———. *Recollections and Reflections: A Professional Autobiography.* New York: Da Capo, 1978.

Plutarch. *Life of Lysander,* in *Plutarch's Lives,* vol. 4, 233–321. Translated by Bernadotte Perrin. Cambridge, MA: Harvard University Press, 1968.

Poovey, Mary. *Uneven Developments: The Ideological Work of Gender in Mid-Victorian England.* Chicago: University of Chicago Press, 1988.

Powell, Kerry. *Women and Victorian Theatre.* Cambridge: Cambridge University Press, 1997.

Pratt, John Clark, and Victor A. Neufeldt, eds. *George Eliot's Middlemarch Notebooks: A Transcription.* Berkeley: University of California Press, 1979.

Prins, Yopie. "Elizabeth Barrett, Robert Browning, and the *Différance* of Translation." *Victorian Poetry* 29 (1991): 435–51.

———. "Greek Maenads, Victorian Spinsters." In *Victorian Sexual Dissidence,* edited by Richard Dellamora, 43–81. Chicago: University of Chicago Press, 1999.

———. "'Lady's Greek' (with the Accents): A Metrical Translation of Euripides by A. Mary F. Robinson." *Victorian Literature and Culture* 34 (2006): 591–618.

———. *Victorian Sappho.* Princeton, NJ: Princeton University Press, 1999.

Pucci, Pietro. *Odysseus Polutropos: Intertextual Readings in the Odyssey and the Iliad.* Ithaca, NY: Cornell University Press, 1987.

———. *The Violence of Pity in Euripides's Medea.* Ithaca, NY: Cornell University Press, 1980.

Punch. "The Mannings at Home." 17 (July–December 1849): 213.

Putzell-Korab, Sara. *The Evolving Consciousness: An Hegelian Reading of the Novels of George Eliot.* Klagenfurt, Austria: Institut für Anglistik und Amerikanistik, 1982.

Pykett, Lyn. "Reading the Periodical Press: Text and Context." In *Investigating Victorian Journalism,* edited by Laurel Brake, Aled Jones, and Lionel Madden, 2–18. New York: St. Martin's, 1990.

Quarterly Review. "Acland's Plains of Troy." 66 (1840): 355–74.

———. "Colonel Mure on The Literature of Ancient Greece: The Homeric Controversy." 87 (September 1850): 435–68.

———. "Lord Elgin's Collection of Sculptured Marbles." 14 (January 1816): 513–47.

———. "Origin of the Homeric Poems." 44 (January 1831): 121–67.

———. "Popular Specimens of the Greek Dramatic Poets." *Quarterly Review* 44 (January–February 1831): 389–414.

Raphaely, Judith. "Nothing but Gibberish and Shibboleths? The Compulsory Greek Debates, 1870–1919." In Stray, *Classics in 19th and 20th Century Cambridge,* 71–94.

Rehm, Rush. "*Medea* and the Logos of the Heroic." *Eranos* 87 (1989): 97–115.

Renoir, Alain. "Fragment: An Oral-Formulaic Nondefinition." In *Fragments: Incompletion and Discontinuity*, edited by Lawrence Kritzman, 39–50. New York: New York Literary Forum 8 9, 1981.

Reynolds, L. D., and N. G. Wilson. *Scribes and Scholars: A Guide to the Transmission of Greek and Latin Literature*. Oxford: Oxford University Press, 1968.

Riede, David G. "Swinburne and Romantic Authority." In *The Whole Music of Passion: New Essays on Swinburne*, edited by Rikky Rooksby and Nicholas Shrimpton, 22–39. Brookfield, VT: Ashgate, 1993.

Rignall, John, ed. *George Eliot and Europe*. Brookfield, VT: Ashgate, 1997.

Ristori, Adelaide. *Memoirs and Artistic Studies*. Translated by G. Mantellini. New York: Doubleday, 1907.

Roach, John. *Public Examinations in England, 1850–1900*. Cambridge: Cambridge University Press, 1971.

Robertson, Linda K. "From Reality to Fiction: Benefits and Hazards in Continental Education." In *George Eliot and Europe*, edited by John Rignall, 156–65. Brookfield, VT: Ashgate, 1997.

———. *The Power of Knowledge: George Eliot and Education*. New York: Peter Lang, 1997.

Robinson, Annabel. *The Life and Work of Jane Ellen Harrison*. Oxford: Oxford University Press, 2002.

Rohde, Erwin. *Psyche: The Cult of Souls and Belief in Immortality among the Greeks*. Translated by W. B. Hillis. New York: Harper and Row, 1966.

Rooksby, Rikky, and Nicholas Shrimpton, eds. *The Whole Music of Passion: New Essays on Swinburne*. Brookfield, VT: Ashgate, 1993.

Rose, H. J. Introduction to *Dionysiaca* by Nonnos, translated by W. H. D. Rouse, x–xv. Cambridge, MA: Harvard University Press, 1940–42.

Rose, Lionel. *The Massacre of the Innocents: Infanticide in Britain, 1800–1939*. London: Routledge, 1986.

Rosenberg, Brian. "George Eliot and the Victorian 'Historic Imagination.'" *Victorian Newsletter* 61 (Spring 1982): 1–5.

Rosenman, Ellen. "'Mimic Sorrows': Masochism and the Gendering of Pain in Victorian Melodrama." *Studies in the Novel* 35 (Spring 2003): 22–43.

Rothblatt, Sheldon. *The Revolution of the Dons: Cambridge and Society in Victorian England*. London: Faber and Faber, 1968.

Rouse, W. H. D. "Review of Jane Harrison's *Prolegomena to the Study of Greek Religion*." *Classical Review* 18 (1904): 465–70.

Rowbotham, Judith, and Kim Stevenson, eds. *Criminal Conversations: Victorian Crimes, Social Panic, and Moral Outrage*. Columbus: Ohio State University Press, 2005.

254 Rowell, George. *The Victorian Theatre, 1792–1914: A Survey.* Cambridge: Cambridge University Press, 1978.

Rutland, William R. *Swinburne: A Nineteenth Century Hellene.* Oxford, UK: Basil Blackwell, 1931.

Sanderson, Michael. *The Universities in the Nineteenth Century.* London: Routledge and Kegan Paul, 1975.

Sappho. *Greek Lyric: Sappho and Alcaeus.* Translated by David A. Campbell. Cambridge, MA: Harvard University Press, 1982.

Schechner, Richard. *Performance Studies: An Introduction.* New York: Routledge, 2002.

Scheinberg, Cynthia. "Canonizing the Jew: Amy Levy's Challenge to Victorian Poetic Identity." *Victorian Studies* 39 (Winter 1996): 173–200.

Schiller, Friedrich. *Essays.* Edited by Walter Hinderer and Daniel O. Dahlstrom. New York: Continuum, 1993.

Schino, Mirella. "La Duse e la Ristori." *Teatro Archivio* 8 (1984): 123–81.

Schlegel, Augustus William. *A Course of Lectures on Dramatic Art and Literature.* Translated by John Black. London: Henry G. Bohn, 1846.

Schlegel, Friedrich. *Lectures on the History of Literature Ancient and Modern.* London: William Blackwood and Sons, 1841.

———. *On the Study of Greek Poetry.* Translated by Stuart Barnett. New York: State University of New York Press, 2001.

———. *The Philosophy of Life and Philosophy of Language.* New York: AMS Press, 1973.

Schoch, Richard W. *Not Shakespeare: Bardolatry and Burlesque in the Nineteenth Century.* Cambridge: Cambridge University Press, 2002.

Schulte, Rainer, and John Biguenet, eds. *Theories of Translation: An Anthology of Essays from Dryden to Derrida.* Chicago: University of Chicago Press, 1992.

Scott, Clement. *The Drama of Yesterday and Today,* vol. 2. New York: Garland, 1986.

Select Committee. *Report from the Select Committee of the House of Commons on the Earl of Elgin's Collection of Sculptured Marbles, etc.* London: W. Bulmer, 1816.

Sellar, W. Y. *Roman Poets of the Augustan Age.* Oxford: Clarendon, 1877.

Seneca. *Medea.* Translated by David R. Slavitt in *Seneca: The Tragedies,* vol. 1. Baltimore, MD: Johns Hopkins University Press, 1992.

Silk, M. S., ed. *Tragedy and the Tragic: Greek Theatre and Beyond.* Oxford: Clarendon, 1996.

Simon, Sherry. *Gender in Translation: Cultural Identity and the Politics of Transmission.* New York: Routledge, 1996.

Simpson, Shona. "Mapping Romola: Physical Space, Woman's Place." In Levine and Turner, *From Author to Text,* 53–66.

Smith, Margaret, ed. *The Letters of Charlotte Brontë.* 3 vols. Oxford: Clarendon, 2000.

Smith, Peter, ed. *Matthew Arnold and the Education of the New Order: A Selection of Arnold's Writings on Education.* Cambridge: Cambridge University Press, 1969.

Snow, Thomas Collins. "Imagination in Utopia." *Hibbert Journal: A Quarterly Review of Religion, Theology, and Philosophy* 9, no. 4 (July 1913): 751–65.

Spielmann, Marin. "The Inner History of the Bronte-Heger Letters." *Fortnightly Review* 111 (1919): 599–605.

Spivak, Gayatri Chakravorty. "The Politics of Translation." In *Destabilizing Theory: Contemporary Feminist Debates,* edited by Michèle Barrett and Anne Phillips. Stanford, CA: Stanford University Press, 1992.

Stanton, Graham H. *The Gospels and Jesus.* Oxford: Oxford University Press, 1989.

St. Clair, William. *Lord Elgin and the Marbles.* London: Oxford University Press, 1967.

Steiner, George. *After Babel: Aspects of Language and Translation.* New York: Oxford University Press, 1992.

Steiner, T. R. *English Translation Theory, 1650–1800.* Amsterdam: Van Gorcum, Assen, 1975.

Stewart, Jessie. *Jane Ellen Harrison: A Portrait in Letters.* London: Merlin, 1959.

Stocking, George. *Race, Culture, and Evolution: Essays in the History of Anthropology.* New York: Free Press, 1968.

———. *Victorian Anthropology.* New York: Free Press, 1987.

Strathman, Christopher A. *Romantic Poetry and the Fragmentary Imperative: Schlegel, Byron, Joyce, and Blanchot.* New York: State University of New York Press, 2006.

Stray, Christopher, ed. *Classics in 19th and 20th Century Cambridge: Curriculum, Culture and Community.* Cambridge, UK: Cambridge Philological Society, 1999.

———. *Classics Transformed: Schools, Universities, and Society in England, 1830–1960.* Oxford: Clarendon, 1998.

Sutphin, Christine. "The Representation of Women's Heterosexual Desire in Augusta Webster's 'Circe' and 'Medea in Athens.'" *Women's Writing* 5 (1998): 373–92.

Swinburne, Algernon Charles. *Swinburne's Collected Poetical Works.* 2 vols. London: William Heinemann, 1924.

Tanner, Tony. Introduction to *Villette,* by Charlotte Brontë, 7–51. New York: Penguin, 1979.

Thompson, Andrew. *George Eliot and Italy: Literary, Cultural and Political Influences from Dante to the Risorgimento.* New York: St. Martin's, 1998.

Thomson, Peter, and Glendyr Sacks. *The Cambridge Companion to Brecht.* Cambridge: Cambridge University Press, 1994.

Thormahlen, Marianne. *The Brontës and Religion.* New York: Cambridge University Press, 1999.

Tillyard, A. I. *A History of University Reform from 1800 A.D. to the Present Time with Suggestions towards a Complete Scheme for the University of Cambridge.* Cambridge, UK: W. Heffer and Sons, 1913.

Turner, Frank M. *The Greek Heritage in Victorian Britain.* New Haven, CT: Yale University Press, 1981.

Turner, Mark W. "George Eliot v. Frederic Leighton: Whose Text Is It Anyway?" In Levine and Turner, *From Author to Text,* 17–36.

Ubersfeld, Anne. *Lire le théâtre.* Paris: Éditions Sociales, 1978.

Van Riper, A. Bowdoin. *Men among the Mammoths: Victorian Science and the Discovery of Human Prehistory.* Chicago: University of Chicago Press, 1993.

Venuti, Lawrence. *The Scandals of Translation: Towards an Ethics of Difference.* New York: Routledge, 1998.

———. *The Translator's Invisibility: A History of Translation.* New York: Routledge, 1995.

Vernant, Jean-Pierre, and Pierre Vidal-Naquet. *Myth and Tragedy in Ancient Greece.* Translated by Janet Lloyd. New York: Zone Books, 1990.

Verstraete, Ginette. *Fragments of the Feminine Sublime in Friedrich Schlegel and James Joyce.* New York: State University of New York Press, 1998.

Vlock, Deborah. *Dickens, Novel Reading, and the Victorian Popular Theatre.* Cambridge: Cambridge University Press, 1998.

Von Flotow, Luise. *Translation and Gender: Translating in the "Era of Feminism."* Ottawa: University of Ottawa Press, 1997.

Voskuil, Lynn M. *Acting Naturally: Victorian Theatricality and Authenticity.* Charlottesville: University of Virginia Press, 2004.

Vrettos, Theodore. *The Elgin Affair: The Abduction of Antiquity's Greatest Treasures and the Passions It Aroused.* New York: Arcade, 1997.

Walkowitz, Judith. *City of Dreadful Delight: Narratives of Sexual Danger in Late-Victorian London.* Chicago: University of Chicago Press, 1992.

Wallace, Jennifer. *Shelley and Greece: Rethinking Romantic Hellenism.* New York: St. Martin's, 1997.

Webb, Timothy. "Appropriating the Stones: The 'Elgin Marbles' and English National Taste." In *Claiming the Stones, Naming the Bones: Cultural Property and the Negotiation of National and Ethnic Identity,* edited by Elazar Barkan and Ronald Bush, 51–96. Los Angeles: Getty Research Institute, 2002.

———. *English Romantic Hellenism, 1700–1824.* London: Manchester University Press, 1982.

———. *The Violet in the Crucible: Shelley and Translation.* Oxford: Clarendon, 1976.

Webster, Augusta. *A Housewife's Opinions*. London: Macmillan, 1879.

———. *The Medea of Euripides*. London: Macmillan, 1868.

———. *Portraits*. London: Macmillan, 1870.

West, Francis. *Gilbert Murray: A Life*. London: Croom Helm, 1984.

Westminster Review. "*The Medea of Euripides*" (book review). 89 (1868): 290.

Wiener, Martin J. "Judges v. Jurors: Courtroom Tensions in Murder Trials and the Law of Criminal Responsibility in Nineteenth-Century England." *Law and History Review* 17, no. 3 (Fall 1999): 467–506.

———. *Reconstructing the Criminal: Culture, Law, and Policy in England, 1830–1914*. Cambridge: Cambridge University Press, 1990.

Wiesenfarth, Joseph. *George Eliot's Mythmaking*. Heidelberg: Carl Winter Universitätsverlag, 1977.

William, Carolyn D. *Pope, Homer, and Manliness: Some Aspects of Eighteenth-Century Classical Learning*. New York: Routledge, 1993.

Williams, Clifford John. *Madame Vestris: A Theatrical Biography*. London: Sidgwick and Jackson, 1973.

Williams, Raymond. *Drama in Performance*. London: Dufour Editions, 1954.

Wilson, Duncan. *Gilbert Murray OM, 1866–1957*. Oxford, UK: Clarendon, 1987.

Wilson, John. "Sotheby's Homer I." *Blackwood's Edinburgh Magazine* 29 (April 1831): 668–87.

———. "Sotheby's Homer II." *Blackwood's Edinburgh Magazine* 29 (May 1831): 829–66.

———. "Sotheby's Homer III." *Blackwood's Edinburgh Magazine* 30 (July 1831): 93–125.

———. "Sotheby's Homer IV." *Blackwood's Edinburgh Magazine* 31 (December 1831): 847–89.

———. "Sotheby's Homer V." *Blackwood's Edinburgh Magazine* 31 (February 1832): 145–80.

———. "Sotheby's Homer: The Odyssey I." *Blackwood's Edinburgh Magazine* 35 (January 1834): 1–26.

———. "Sotheby's Homer: The Odyssey II." *Blackwood's Edinburgh Magazine* 35 (February 1834): 153–82.

Winstanley, D. A. *Later Victorian Cambridge*. Cambridge: Cambridge University Press, 1947.

Winter, William. *Shadows of the Stage*. New York: Macmillan, 1893.

Wolf, F. A. *Prolegomena to Homer*. Translated by Anthony Grafton, Glenn W. Most, and James E. G. Zetzel. Princeton, NJ: Princeton University Press, 1985.

Wood, Christopher. *Victorian Painting*. New York: Bullfinch, 1999.

Woolf, Virginia. "On Not Knowing Greek." In *The Common Reader*, edited by Andrew McNeillie, 23–38. New York: Harcourt, Brace, 1925.

Index